EXTREME TOYOTA

EXTREME TOYOTA

Radical Contradictions That Drive Success at the World's Best Manufacturer

EMI OSONO | **NORIHIKO SHIMIZU** | **HIROTAKA TAKEUCHI**

with JOHN KYLE DORTON

SUSAN J. BIGELOW, Manuscript Editor

WILEY

John Wiley & Sons, Inc.

Published by John Wiley & Sons, Inc., Hoboken, New Jersey.
Published simultaneously in Canada.

For general information on our other products and services or for technical support, please
contact our Customer Care Department within the United States at (800) 762-2974, outside
the United States at (317) 572-3993 or fax (317) 572-4002.

Wiley also publishes its books in a variety of electronic formats. Some content that appears
in print may not be available in electronic books. For more information about Wiley products, visit our web site at www.wiley.com.

Library of Congress Cataloging-in-Publication Data:

Osono, Emi, 1965–
    Extreme Toyota : radical contradictions that drive success at the world's best
manufacturer/Emi Osono, Norihiko Shimizu, Hirotaka Takeuchi; with John Kyle Dorton.
      p. cm.
    Includes index.
    ISBN 978-0-470-26762-2 (cloth)
      1. Toyota Jidosha Kabushiki Kaisha—Management. 2. Automobile industry and
    trade—Japan—Management 3. Total Takeuchi, 1946– II. Takeuchi, Hirotaka. III. Title
HD9710.J34087 2008
629.2068—dc22

                                        2008001404

Printed in the United States of America.

10 9 8 7 6 5 4 3 2 1

*To Ikujiro Nonaka,
our colleague, mentor,
and spiritual leader.*

To a casual observer, Toyota's ascent in the global auto industry reads like a rags-to-riches story. In 1950, a crippling labor dispute forced its factories to close for two months, and it almost went bankrupt. As a condition for refinancing its loans, Toyota had to lay off one-fourth of its work force, and president and auto company founder, Kiichiro Toyoda, resigned. In 1957, Toyota's first export to the United States, the *Toyopet Crown*, was poorly received, and the unsold inventory was withdrawn. Fifty years later, however, the *Corolla*, the *Camry*, the *Lexus*, the *Prius*, the *Scion*, and the *Tundra* have become household names, and today Toyota rivals General Motors as the world's largest automaker. Toyota is now recognized as a paradigm of superior performance among the world's best-run, most successful manufacturing companies.

To an industry observer, however, Toyota's success is hard to understand. The company moves gradually with bursts of advancement in big leaps. It is frugal with resources yet spends extravagantly on people and projects. It is operationally efficient—thanks to cost-effective production practices such as the Toyota Production System—but redundant in human resource management. It cultivates an environment of stability and paranoia at the same time. It is hierarchical and bureaucratic, but encourages dissent. It demands simplified communication while building complex, multilayered communication networks.

Moreover, to a professional manager or MBA, Toyota's success is an outright mystery. While it appears successful based on conventional measures like profit, revenue growth, and cost leadership, it lacks many of the characteristics typical of a large, globally successful company. If anything, Toyota resembles a failing or stagnant company. It has no clear business strategy; it tries anything and everything. It pays low dividends and hoards idle cash. Its management is homogeneous in contrast to other global companies that encourage diversity. It has an *up-and-in* culture, as opposed to the up-or-out culture where employees either rise through the ranks or are pushed out. The founding Toyoda family owns just 2 percent of the company, yet wields strong influence over important decisions.

So what explains Toyota's phenomenal success? This book is our attempt to answer this question. It is the culmination of six years of research, including over 220 interviews with Toyota executives from President Katsuaki Watanabe down to shop floor employees, as well as distributors and dealers in 11 countries. We were also given unprecedented access to Toyota's facilities, internal documents, and activities, including the Toyota World Conventions and Lexus Dealer Meetings.

During the course of our research, we discovered that unearthing Toyota's inner workings was like peeling an onion and never reaching the center. After peeling many layers and making seemingly conflicting observations, we realized the company actively embraces and cultivates contradictions instead of passively coping with them. Toyota actually thrives on paradoxes; it harnesses opposing propositions to energize itself.

The breakthrough occurred when we realized that these contradictions, opposing propositions, and paradoxes were central to our investigation. While other companies still function according to the logic of the industrial age and stamp out such differences, at Toyota they are a way of life. As a car manufacturer, Toyota is the quintessential industrial firm, but it is also staging a successful transition to the postindustrial, knowledge age.

In the industrial age, contradictions, opposites, and paradoxes were commonly viewed as characteristics to be avoided or eliminated. In the knowledge age however, new knowledge is created by reconciling our unique perspective with those of others who disagree with us. Recognizing opposing insights is essential to understand the organic whole.

What differentiates Toyota from its rivals is its view of the factory worker as more than a pair of hands on the assembly line. Each is a *knowledge worker* who accumulates new knowledge through direct experience and interaction with others. What Toyota is postulating is a new management model fit for industrial production in the knowledge age, where growth depends not only on operational efficiency but also on people and organizational capability. Toyota's model represents a more human approach to industrial production because it positions humans, not machines, at the center of all things.

After six years of peeling the onion, we identified six contradictory forces keeping Toyota on the move. It relentlessly pits these forces against each other to realize continuous innovation and constant renewal. This is a mirror of human creativity— always growing and always incomplete. Toyota tries to remain a "green tomato," in which the potential to develop still lies ahead.

The six contradictory forces are self-generated and deliberately imposed. They drive Toyota to the "extreme," a state of disequilibrium where radical contradictions coexist, propelling it away from its comfort zone and creating healthy tension and instability within the organization. This tension becomes the catalyst for movement forward, to find new solutions beyond contradiction. Not in compromise or balance, but in higher levels of performance. The bulk of the book is devoted to explaining the six forces.

The three authors are professors at a business school in Tokyo that is still a "green tomato." Although Hitotsubashi University is more than 130 years old, the Graduate School of International Corporate Strategy (ICS) was established in 2000 in downtown Tokyo. The spiritual leader at Hitotsubashi University ICS is Ikujiro Nonaka, who teaches the signature courses on Knowledge Management in the MBA program. All classes in this program are taught in English, which is partly why seventy percent of our MBA students are non-Japanese. One of them, John Kyle Dorton received an MBA from ICS in 2006 (he also has a graduate degree in Mechanical Engineering) and is now in our doctoral program.

This research would not have been possible without the assistance of Yoshio Ishizaka, Senior Advisor of Toyota Motor Corporation. He was the champion of a joint research project that started in 2001 between Hitotsubashi University ICS and the Global Marketing Division of Toyota Motor Corporation. This joint research project, headed by Emi Osono and Norihiko Shimizu, produced six case studies—on Lexus (2001), Asia after the financial crisis (2002), the turnaround in Europe (2003), Scion (2004), the Global Knowledge Center (2005), and the Innovative International Multipurpose Vehicle (IMV) project (2006). When the IMV case was taught at ICS recently, the students were surprised to find Executive Vice President Akio Toyoda had been sitting quietly in the back of the room during the case discussion before carrying out an open dialogue with the entire class. We are indebted to executives like Akio Toyoda, as well as the hundreds of other executives and associates at Toyota with whom we have interfaced with over the years, for their part in making our research a reality.

We are very grateful to Alberto Moel and Yasuki Sato of Monitor Group for their constructive comments and for conducting the literature review, which is included in Appendix B. Susan J. Bigelow acted as our original manuscript editor and added immeasurably to the book. Thanks are due to Richard Narramore of John Wiley & Sons for his skillful editing. In the end, all interpretations presented here, including any errors, are our own.

CHAPTER I

Extreme Toyota: An Organization Powered by Creative Contradictions

An Amazing Track Record

Fifty years ago, Toyota Motor Corporation dipped its toe into the big pond of the U.S. automobile market with a tiny car that could only have been viewed with derision. It was 1957—an era of huge front-end Buicks and tail-fin Cadillacs. As one of the company founders Shoichiro Toyoda recently described it, the *Toyopet Crown* couldn't make it onto the highway unless the on-ramp was downhill. But true to its practice of continuous improvement (*kaizen*), Toyota kept on trying to get it right. It went on to produce the more sensible *Corona* in 1965, followed by the *Corolla*, the *Camry*, the *Lexus*, the *Prius*, the *Tundra*, and you know the rest.

Toyota is now a top dog and has become, by all conventional measures, an amazing company. In 2007, it sold 9.37 million cars and trucks, to rival General Motors as the world's biggest auto producer. In *profitability*, Toyota's net income has consistently surpassed the other auto companies by a factor of over two to one for the past several years. And thanks to a high rate of growth (averaging 11 percent in recent years) and profitability, Toyota's stock (*market capitalization*) at the end of 2007 was worth two times that of the next contender (the then) DaimlerChrysler, and almost 14 times that of General Motors, its largest rival.[1]

The Toyota brand has also become synonymous with strong engineering, durability, and dependability. Surveys on vehicle quality by the marketing information firm J.D. Power and Associates consistently rated Toyota highest among the volume brands, while Toyota's Lexus brand claimed the top position in vehicle dependability for the thirteenth year in a row—above Mercedes, BMW, and the rest.[2] This reputation ensures that the vehicles hold their resale value well into automobile old age. With the Prius, Toyota became the first carmaker to successfully market a hybrid alternative to the conventional internal combustion engine, addressing the public's concern about the effects of fossil fuel consumption on the environment.

By all these measures, Toyota is a paradigm of superior performance among the best and most successful manufacturing companies in the world. What explains this phenomenal success? In our attempt to answer that question, we have based this book on six years of research and unprecedented access to Toyota's facilities (regional headquarters, production sites, training centers, distributors, and dealers) in 11 countries, internal documents (Green Book, Silver Book, Best Practice Bulletins, among others), and activities (Toyota World Conventions, Toyota Way in Sales and Marketing Champions Meetings, Lexus Dealer Meetings, and internal training sessions), including hundreds of interviews from President Katsuaki Watanabe down to shop floor employees.

The results of our research were unexpected and offer important lessons that may help your organization learn from Toyota. Our key discovery was that Toyota's success can be found not just in its famous manufacturing process, the "Toyota Production System," but also in its unique management practice of creating and promoting a fascinating set of contradictions, opposites, and paradoxes within the organization. These paradoxes can be implemented by managers in any organization, with powerful results, as discussed in Chapter 11.

Before identifying Toyota's management paradoxes, let's take a brief look at the systems innovations—the *hard* side of the company—that have contributed to its success.

The Hard Side of Toyota

Toyota's best-known secret weapon is its brilliant and unorthodox system of manufacturing, which it pioneered during the mid-twentieth century as an alternative to traditional mass production. The Toyota Production System (TPS) has enabled the manufacture of high-quality, reliable cars at a lower production cost. This system also has made Toyota nimble in response to fluctuating market demand and able to produce cars fast to match the orders coming in from dealers. Toyota's renowned logistics management system has also been a significant operational advantage for the company, enabling it to monitor inventory levels for parts and raw materials as well as finished products, and keep those levels low.

This optimization of resources in the production of cars allows Toyota to maintain a strong cash-flow position. In combination, these systems keep Toyota competitive in their operational costs. Its short cycle for product development has also been the focus of frequent study. Because Toyota takes substantially less time to introduce a new car compared with many of its global competitors, it can respond more effectively to changes in customer needs.

Both for-profit and nonprofit organizations are now trying to learn and adapt Toyota's methods and processes. Chrysler recently hired two senior Toyota executives to help revive its struggling auto business, and the Japan Post Service recently appointed a former chief of Toyota Motor Italy as its first CEO. In the auto industry, every carmaker has tried to learn from and adapt the Toyota Production System. The quality gap between the manufacturers has been diminishing with each passing year as they successfully emulate Toyota's hard systems innovations.

The Powerful and Mysterious Soft Side

But how about Toyota's *soft* side of management—its practices related to human resources, dealer management, and corporate culture? These practices are as important as the Toyota Production System—and far less understood. The same holds true for Toyota's

underlying management philosophy that binds together employees, dealers, and suppliers as well as its intricate, multilayered
face-to-face communication infrastructure that enables the organization to function like a small-town company where everybody
knows everyone else's business. This book offers a peek at the
secrets to the powerful and mysterious soft side of Toyota.

The soft side of management has gained relevance because
a once-in-a-century shift from the industrial society to the
knowledge society has taken place. These two ages are set
apart by their means of production. In the industrial society,
the means of production focused on assembly lines, machinery,
robotics, and automation. In the knowledge society, the means
of production shifted to the "deep smarts" embodied in the head
and hand of every employee, dealer, and business partner.[3]

Toyota has developed a new management model fit for industrial production in the knowledge age by viewing the auto industry
as a knowledge-driven industry, where growth depends not only
on operational efficiency, but also on people and organizational
capability. Toyota's model represents a more human approach to
industrial production because it positions humans, rather than
machines, at the center of all things.

What differentiates Toyota from its rivals is its view of
the factory worker as a knowledge worker who accumulates the
wisdom of experience from the production lines. It recognizes
that cultivating ideas from anywhere—not just the factory floor,
but from the office, the field, and the outside world—is critical in the knowledge-driven industry. This is why Toyota goes
to great lengths to train, develop, and retain employees and to
build better dealers, suppliers, and business partners. Toyota
takes a long-term view and invests resources to cultivate people
and capability inside and outside the organization.

How Toyota Is Like a Failed, Stagnant Company

While Toyota appears to have succeeded in developing a management model fit for industrial production in the knowledge
age, at the same time it lacks many characteristics typical of

other large, globally successful companies. The following Toyota policies and organizational patterns resemble those associated with failing or stagnant companies:

- While Toyota is innovative, its management remains homogeneous, in contrast to the more typical innovative organizations that encourage diversity. Toyota management, particularly in Japan, is predominantly male and Japanese. They are proud to be a company from the rural backwater Mikawa region, a suburb of the major commercial city of Nagoya. Regional pride is strong in Japan and the company's rural origin accounts for its male-dominant culture, as well as its simplicity and humility. They have no plans to relocate their headquarters to central Tokyo as Honda, Hitachi, and many other large Japanese companies have done.

- While Toyota is famous for its efficiency, its allocation of human resources seems inefficient. Every company has meetings, but it is amazing to see how many people attend a Toyota business meeting. Many of the employees who attend do not participate in the discussion. There are also excessive numbers of employees working at the management level whose responsibilities bear no relation to operational or financial performance. In its sales organization, Toyota deliberately assigns more employees to regional offices than other auto companies do.

- The formal structure of Toyota is hierarchical and bureaucratic. Many of the top executives are inaccessible to middle managers, and there are clear indications of subtle differences in status at each level of management in the organization, reflecting the rigid social hierarchies in Japanese culture. Visitors to the company get a very different reception when they are meeting a middle manager than when they are meeting an executive vice president. In the former instance, they will be asked to wear a visitor badge and the receptionist will see them off with a 35-degree bow. In the latter case, they will be treated as a trusted guest;

they won't have to wear a visitor badge, and the receptionist will give them a 90-degree bow.

- As opposed to the "up-or-out" culture at companies where employees either rise through the ranks or are pushed out, Toyota practices an "up-and-in" culture that seems counterintuitive in a company where employees must work very hard and compete with each other. When the Japanese economic bubble burst in the 1990s and many companies shed personnel, Toyota did not. By comparison, General Electric's personnel system under Jack Welch systematically weeded out the bottom 10 percent of performers in the organization.

- Toyota does not have a clear strategic focus. Rather, the company seems to try anything and everything to stay ahead of all the others in the auto industry, and it tries to be good at all of it.

Furthermore, we have observed practices that are unusual for a well-run company and that do not make sense from a financial perspective. Toyota's ratio of dividend payouts is very low, averaging just 20 percent of their earnings over the past 10 years. While it has substantially increased its dividend per share, Toyota's payout ratio in 2006 of 21.3 percent was only on par with that of its smaller rivals Nissan and Hyundai-Kia (with 22.9 percent and 17.4 percent, respectively), and far behind its peer DaimlerChrysler (with 47.5 percent).[4] As a result, the company has accumulated substantial idle cash, which in 2007 amounted to $20 billion, earning the company the moniker, "Toyota Bank."

Toyota's performance, as measured by return on invested capital (ROIC),[5] suggests that the company is a mediocre player, even though it has been improving in recent years. Toyota has not utilized its invested capital as productively as other measures of its success, such as revenues, operating margin, and net income, might imply. This combination of paying low dividends, hoarding idle cash, and overinvesting in a mature industry is unique to Toyota and is considered to be a wasteful and ineffective financial practice. What's more, it is prevalent in its employment of human capital as well. As shown in upcoming chapters, Toyota deploys more people in the field than its competitors, retains poor performers, and rejects downsizing its workforce. Instead, it invests in people, hiring large numbers of employees and training them with a view to developing their potential over the long term. Toyota's tendency to accumulate excessive capital and human resources is completely opposite to the actions of most well-managed, profitable, and investor-oriented companies.

Furthermore, employee compensation levels at Toyota are not what one would expect from a successful, established company. The average annual compensation for Toyota's top 33 executives is one-tenth that of Ford's, and much lower relative to their counterparts at the other auto companies, with the exception of Honda.[6] Many Toyota top executives have been celebrated in U.S. magazines like *Fortune* and *BusinessWeek*, as well as in leading Japanese magazines including the *Nikkei Business* and *Toyo Keizai*, yet their compensation levels remain substantially lower than the industry average. In addition, the speed of promotion inside Toyota is very slow. As of 2007, the youngest executive on the board (which consists of internal executives) was 51 years old, while the average age was 61.[7] What motivates these people to work so hard for Toyota?

Another oddity at Toyota is the continuing strong influence of members of the founding Toyoda family, even though their ownership is just 2 percent. Compare this with the share of family ownership at Ford—40 percent; and at BMW—50 percent. For many years, Toyota's CEOs came directly from the Toyoda family. Although nonfamily members have occupied the CEO position from time to time, there is increasing speculation that the next company president will be a Toyoda. Thus, the family retains great influence over many important decisions, although its style of soliciting agreement is different from that of other companies. Governance is not open and transparent, and it is unclear to outsiders exactly how the family wields its power. Many see the family as playing a symbolic role in the company, but they also have a substantial impact on decision making that has been effective for the company so far. This is also at odds with common practice and contributes to the mystery of why Toyota might be considered a model of contemporary business practice.

Management Orchestrated Contradictions, Opposites, and Paradoxes

From the perspective of conventional business practice, Toyota may simply be successful despite itself. Its success contradicts established, successful practice, but in fact, this seeming paradox is key to its success. It is an organization steeped in contradictions, opposites, and paradoxes. Such contradictions are not necessarily seen as bad things at Toyota. In fact, the company actively embraces and cultivates contradictions instead of passively coping with them. It thrives on paradoxes, harnessing opposing propositions to energize itself.

As Akio Matsubara, Senior Managing Director in charge of Human Resource Management, described it, Toyota intentionally builds a positive level of tension within the organization:

> We are constantly confronted with two opposing propositions, sometimes three opposing propositions, sometimes even as many as four opposing propositions. It is a way of deliberately introducing a positive level of tension into the workplace on a regular basis. Each organizational unit avoids making any kind of compromise and we argue it out till the end across the units. This process ensures that we come up with the best solution.[8]

Toyota is hard to understand because contradictions, opposing propositions, and paradoxes are a way of life within the company, whereas other companies are still functioning according to the logic of the industrial era and try to stamp out such differences. As an automotive manufacturer, Toyota is the quintessential industrial firm, but it has survived by staging a successful transition to the postindustrial, knowledge age. The "Toyota Way" is about finding a better way . . . for realizing continuous innovation and constant renewal. We have identified six contradictory tendencies at Toyota that help to unravel the mystery and peculiarity of its success:

1. Moving gradually and also taking big leaps
2. Cultivating frugality while spending huge sums
3. Operating efficiently as well as redundantly
4. Cultivating stability and a paranoid mindset
5. Respecting bureaucratic hierarchy and allowing freedom to dissent
6. Maintaining simplified and complex communication[9]

Moving Gradually and Taking Big Leaps

Seen from the outside, Toyota progresses more like a tortoise than a rabbit in day-to-day operations. It moves step-by-step, experiments, deliberates, and takes time to get things done. The Lexus *LS400* underwent eight design reviews and 50 wind tunnel tests before the first model was approved. In fact, it took six years of development to get the first Lexus out of the factory. When *Scion* (a new brand targeting the American youth market) was launched in the United States, Toyota rolled it out gradually, starting in California in June 2003. It took eight months—until February 2004—to achieve the second launch, in the South and on the East Coast of the United States. The third launch, in the Midwest, was not until June 2004. In between, Toyota conducted experiments and made adjustments to improve each subsequent launch.

In a similar vein, Toyota saved information and anecdotes to include in a booklet on the company's unique culture and methods for more than 70 years. Called *The Toyota Way 2001* and known inside the company as the "Green Book," it includes stories from the company's founder Sakichi Toyoda, who first built the Toyoda Automatic Loom Works, and his son Kiichiro, who established the Toyota Motor Corporation in 1937. The Green Book was finally published in 2001 as a 13-page pamphlet, in Japanese and English, filled with historical information and words of wisdom from the company founders and other senior managers, whose combined reign spanned almost eight decades.

The Lexus was developed gradually. The Scion was launched gradually. And content for *The Toyota Way 2001* was accumulated gradually, over many years. However, all three projects enabled Toyota to make big leaps forward. The leap for Lexus was the creation of a brand-new dealer organization in the United States that the company, in the "Lexus Covenant," describes as the "finest dealer network in the industry" because it treats each customer "as though they were a guest in our home."[10] Scion's big jump, in addition to opening the youth market for Toyota, was setting up a "pure pricing" scheme that let customers know the retail price in advance and eliminated price negotiation. Although first introduced by Saturn, this was an innovative practice for the company and was well received by young customers. *The Toyota Way 2001* resulted in the creation in 2002 of the Toyota Institute in Japan and the Global Knowledge Center in the United States, a big leap toward disseminating the philosophy, beliefs, and values of the company on a global scale.

The 1997 launch of the Prius, an energy-saving hybrid car that combined the high-speed power of an internal combustion engine with the clean efficiency and low-speed torque of an electric motor, was a technological leap in a company better known for its culture of continuous improvement, or kaizen. The practice of kaizen typifies Toyota's gradualism, whereas Prius is the symbol of its ability to leap forward.

A Frugal Big Spender

Toyota is known for its frugality, although for the past two decades, it has held an average of over $15 billion in assets in cash and short-term investments. At the same time, and despite holding such a high level of liquid assets, the company has maintained a very low dividend payout of under $3 billion per year.

For a company most often referred to as the Toyota Bank, its reputation for penny-pinching is matched only by Wal-Mart in the United States. This behavior is evident in the company's humble-looking headquarters in Toyota City and its custom of turning all lights off during lunchtime. Office staff work in crowded conditions, usually all together in one large room (known as *obeya*) with no partitions between desks. "Let's say a piece of equipment broke down," said Masaharu Yamamoto, a retired factory worker. "At Toyota, we do not send it out for repairs or buy a new one. Workers at the factory fix it by themselves and try to reuse it. . . . The thinking goes like this: 'Fix it yourself. Make the best use of what we already have. Let's endure with what we already have.'"[11]

Toyota's frugality is practiced in the United States as well. As the head of United Auto Workers local recalled, when Toyota started running its joint-venture plant with General Motors in Fremont, California, back in 1984, company executives and plant bosses began eating in the same cafeteria as the rank and file. "That never happened when GM was running the factory," he said.[12]

As mentioned, Toyota is also frugal when it comes to executive compensation. Top executives at the company are at the low end of the pay scale, especially compared with smaller rivals like Nissan, Hyundai-Kia, or Renault, where senior managers are paid more than double that of Toyota.

However, Toyota is not timid about investing huge sums of money in research and development, manufacturing facilities, brand equity, dealer networks, and human resources development. It spent $1 billion developing the first Lexus (the LS400). It spent more than 20 billion yen ($170 million) a year competing in Formula One races since its entry in 2002,[13] for a cumulative total of over $1 billion in 2007.

In addition, Toyota would not think twice about spending millions of dollars to bring in distributors from around the world to attend its worldwide distributor conference or bring dealers from all over the United States to the dealers' convention. The weeklong distributors' conference takes place in Japan once every four years. To conduct research for this book, we attended part of the 2003 and 2007 Toyota World Conventions for distributors, which brought together 800 people including spouses from 160 countries, as well as guests from within Japan involved in Toyota's global business, and the company's top 100 executives. The entire program required a year and a half of preparation and consisted of a general meeting, a dinner reception, regional break-out sessions, entertainment programs, a farewell party, and a visit to the Tokyo Motor Show, among numerous other visits and events.

We also attended the Lexus Dealer Meeting in San Francisco in October 2002. A total of 1,000 individuals attended this two-day conference, including 200 Lexus dealers and their spouses from the United States as well as top Toyota executives from Japan, including Dr. and Mrs. Shoichiro Toyoda. What impressed us even more was that the Toyota executives from Japan spent two extra days visiting Lexus dealers and participating in the "New Luxury Tour" training session on how to implement the Lexus customer relations philosophy at every touch point with the customer.

Finally, the company has made huge investments building the University of Toyota and the Global Knowledge Center in Torrance, California, as well as the Toyota Institute in Japan. The University of Toyota was established in April 1998 to continuously improve associate and dealer training at Toyota's U.S. operations through lifelong learning. The Global Knowledge Center, which is housed in the same building as the University of Toyota, was established in July 2002 as a center and unifier of the knowledge and expertise of Toyota distributors from around the world. The Toyota Institute was established at Toyota's headquarters in January 2002 and conducts training at an eye-catching Global Learning Center located near the scenic lakeside town of Mikkabi, a one-hour drive from Toyota City and close to Sakichi Toyoda's birthplace. Its purpose is to develop global leaders and global middle managers by sharing the philosophies and values expounded in *The Toyota Way 2001*.

Operational Efficiency and Redundance

Probably no one would deny that Toyota is the epitome of operational efficiency as an automaker. The famous Toyota Production System turns out high-quality, reliable cars at lower production cost, and makes Toyota nimble in response to changes in market demand. The car that best represents these qualities is the Corolla, which went on sale in Japan for the reasonable price of 432,000 yen in 1966. Forty years later, in 2006, the tenth generation Corolla was priced at 1,400,000 yen (just over $12,000[14]). It is by far the best-selling car for Toyota, with cumulative sales exceeding 32 million units in 144 countries for the past 40 years.[15]

The company also has a proven track record with its short cycle of product development, supply chain management, just-in-time inventory control, and the use of *andon* monitoring boards to immediately locate any problem in the production line so it can stop production and fix it. These well-known strengths, now emulated by other manufacturers, are all part of the hard side that makes Toyota operationally efficient. Contrasted with some of the soft side practices, Toyota starts to look downright redundant. As noted, Toyota holds a lot of meetings attended by a lot of people, many of whom do not participate in the discussion. When we interviewed an executive from Toyota at the Tokyo office in 2006, the meeting was also attended by five other Toyota employees, observing and listening intently, and taking copious notes, but rarely saying anything. Toyota employs numerous "coordinators": multilingual employees who help break down cultural and language barriers between its Japan-based headquarters and its international operations. This liaison-functional role was abolished at Nissan under Carlos Ghosn.

During the Toyota World Conventions in 2003 and 2007, we were astonished to find hundreds of Toyota employees serving as attendants to guests and their spouses, including Toyota's executive hosts for a whole week. In fact, there were as many Toyota staff members as there were guests. We concluded, half jokingly, that so many employees were there to ensure that the meetings took place "just in time" and to serve as a buffer "just in case" something happened. This employee presence had also been evident at the 2002 Lexus Dealer Meeting.

In addition, Toyota assigns more employees to regional sales offices in the United States relative to other carmakers, to build deeper communication links with dealers. "I think the most important thing that differentiates Toyota from other companies is the zone manager concept, and the way it treats its dealers in its business operations," said Yoshimi Inaba, Executive Vice President and former President of Toyota Motor Sales, U.S.A. "Toyota is different from other manufacturers in its philosophy toward dealers. Simply said, we treat our dealers as partners. We truly listen to their opinions and incorporate them as an integral part of our entire business formula. We pursue growth with our dealers based on the same Toyota principles while helping to make them profitable."[16]

Redundancy is also apparent among the ranks of senior executives, who spend an inordinate amount of time visiting dealers. Toyota executives constantly mine their dealers for insights about the car market, while executives at other car companies tend to view the dealers as unmanageable obstacles separating the factory from the customers.[17] A living legend within Toyota when it comes to dealer visits is Jim Press, former President of Toyota Motor North America. He would frequent the dealer's showroom, talking to everyone from technicians in charge of parts, service, and car washing to receptionists. His detailed notes were passed on to corresponding divisions and area offices for action to be taken up later.

Stability and Paranoia

By most measures, Toyota is a stable company. Except for a short period leading up to 1950, when the company faced near bankruptcy and over 1,500 employees were laid off, the company has recorded stable sales and net income growth. With high growth, excellent profitability, and earnings stability, the company has attained a consistently higher valuation in the capital markets during the past 10 years relative to its competitors.

The number of employees has grown steadily over the years, reaching close to 300,000 in 2007, partly as a result of Toyota's "up-and-in" personnel policy. As noted, Toyota did not shed personnel, even after the Japanese economic bubble burst in the 1990s, choosing instead to retain its entire workforce. Toyota also retained its dealers in most countries, even if they were underperformers. As with employees, the company has a long-term, stable relationship with its dealers, many of whom are second-generation operators.

The Corolla is a symbol of stability for Toyota. This basic family car was initially outfitted with a 1,100cc engine that, over the past 40 years, has grown to 1,800cc. At the same time, its fuel efficiency has steadily improved, with the latest tenth-generation hatchback model achieving 40.5 mpg (17.2 km/l), the best in its class in Japan. Corolla has been the best-selling model in Japan for 36 of the past 40 years, and accounts for 16 percent of all units sold by the company worldwide on a cumulative basis.[18]

At the same time, Toyota's top executives seem to thrive on paranoia. They constantly hammer in messages like "Never be satisfied" or "There's got to be a better way." One of the favorite sayings of former Chairman and President Hiroshi Okuda is "Reform business when business is good." In his inaugural address, Okuda said, "doing nothing and changing nothing" is the worst thing to do in the new century. Likewise, President Katsuaki Watanabe is fond of saying, "No change is bad."[19]

Thus, when Watanabe was appointed president in 2005, he instilled paranoia across the company by announcing his dream list of expectations during his term. They included a car that can make the air cleaner as it runs; a car that will not hurt drivers and pedestrians and never get into an accident; a car that can make drivers healthier the longer they drive it; a fuel-efficient car that can go from one coast of the United States to the other on one tank of gas and eventually around the world.[20]

"You have to put your life on the line in order to make something good," said Watanabe a few months after becoming president. "If you compromise in the process, nothing good will come of it. If you listen to this person's and that person's opinion, your spiky horns get dull. You have to keep sharpening your horns."[21] He is going to extremes in suggesting that employees put their lives on the line or keep their horns sharpened, but such remarks resonate within the organization.

Watanabe seizes every opportunity to instill an atmosphere of urgency. When a string of recalls put a dent in Toyota's reputation for quality during the summer of 2006, he made several public apologies and described the problems as a "crisis." Toyota used the quality issue to shake up the whole organization, its subsidiaries, and its suppliers. Watanabe acknowledged: "There are so many challenges we need to address."[22]

Hierarchy and Freedom to Dissent

Watanabe remembers how he came up the ranks fighting with his bosses and is fond of saying, "Pick a friendly fight." The voicing of opinions contrary to those of top management or headquarters is an everyday occurrence at Toyota. Dissenting against your bosses, not blindly following their orders, bringing bad news to them and generally not taking them too seriously are all permissible behaviors at Toyota, as discussed in Chapter 7. In fact, we were surprised to hear so many dissenting opinions during our interviews with Toyota executives. Those voicing concerns about the status quo did not seem to feel any fear or stigma about bad-mouthing the company. They appeared to be confident that they were doing the right thing by providing constructive criticism. The targets for their critical comments shall remain anonymous, but ranged across a wide spectrum from headquarters to younger workers. Here are some typical comments:

- There [are] definitely two camps within the Toyota organization. There are those who have grown up on the international side of the business and those who have come through the domestic side. And often, these organizations don't know each other, probably don't trust each other, and probably don't like each other because of battles over scarce product.

- We have a generation of young Toyota Motor Sales, U.S.A., associates[23] who are coming up the ranks, who have never known anything other than good times. They never had to deal with cars arriving at the docks that haven't been well received by the public and had to sell their way out of that. . . . All they have known is the good times.

- As an organization, we may have had various fears. . . . Toyota did very well in the twentieth century, and I suppose there are things we must try not to forget at the start of the new century. But I'm seeing signs of forgetting. There is always the danger of forgetting.

- As the company has grown and in areas where we have lost the original guiding principles, you may find elements of our problem. There are warning signs that Toyota may not be as good 20 years from now.

From an outsider's perspective, the organizational structure of Toyota appears very hierarchical, constituting silos up to the executive vice president level, despite efforts to flatten the organization that began in the late 1980s. In 1988, the company instigated a move to limit the number of stamps of approval (*hanko*) required within each department from seven or eight to three. Since 1989, it has flattened the seven layers of official status within each division to three—staff manager, department manager, and general manager. These reforms helped to eliminate functional bureaucracy within departments but did not eliminate the silo mentality between departments such as the production control department, the purchasing department, the finance department, or the personnel department.

Simplified and Complex Communication

It is an unwritten rule at Toyota that you simplify your words when communicating with others. As Human Resource Director Akio Matsubara explained:

> In my work, I am constantly being told to describe myself in easily understood terms. This is particularly relevant in IT-related work. I understand that they are working very diligently, but I have no idea what they are saying. In other words, in that world, you have to be someone who has done that kind of software work in order to understand them. So we are constantly asking people to break things down to a manageable level and discuss them using a simple language.[24]

Another common practice is the use of A3 (11 x 17 inch) paper as a simplified format for presentation, with subheadings for background information and clear statements of objectives, analysis, action plan, and expected results. These sheets, which include process flowcharts and histograms, are then posted on the walls for everyone to see in a practice known as *mieruka*, to broaden communication throughout the company.

At the same time, Toyota maintains a complex web of communication networks that aim to connect everybody in the company. The lofty aspiration is to reach a state where "everybody knows everything." To approach this ideal, intracompany communication links are established horizontally across functional and geographic lines and vertically across hierarchical divisions, as well as diagonally or informally across personal and professional interests, hobbies, educational background, birthplace, and other potential areas of linkage. As a result of these interwoven links, employees at Toyota belong to large numbers of committees (*iinkai*), self-organizing study groups (*jishuken*), and informal groups (close to 20 such groups exist within Toyota).

Toyota's communication networks extend beyond the company to its business partners, most notably its dealers. In the case of the Lexus in the United States, communication with the dealers occurs through channels that include daily data transmissions, telephone and intranet communications, and frequent visits from area offices and by the Lexus Division managers. The most time-consuming form of communication is face-to-face meetings, including the National Dealer meeting, the Fireside Chat meeting, the National Dealer Advisory Council meetings, and the Lexus Dealer Advertising Association meetings (see Chapter 7).

Embracing Contradictions as a Way of Life

So what accounts for Toyota's steady move to the top and now its ability also to leap forward as a global leader of the auto industry? Much has been made of the Toyota Production System (TPS), its logistics management, and its fast product development. But these systems or hard innovations do not fully account' for Toyota's continuing success. Looking at the soft side of Toyota, we see rigid hierarchies and financial and human resource practices more often associated with inefficient global companies, making its success even more puzzling. Nevertheless, it is the soft side of Toyota that is more revealing of its core strength, and on closer examination, it offers a peek at a unique approach to organizational behavior in the era of the knowledge worker.

After six years of research and over 220 interviews, we have come to understand that it is the way Toyota combines the hard and soft sides that allows it to continue outperforming competitors. Both sides depend on each other to work. They are like two wheels on a shaft (Figure 1.1) that bear equal weight and together move the entity forward in the right direction. It is Toyota's relentless focus on the human being as the center of production and consumption that drives this company's continuing success. It is a model of the new global company that is also a mirror of human creativity—always growing and always incomplete.[25]

This brings us to the theoretical basis of this book, which is how Toyota symbolizes the transition of the global economy and society from the industrial age to the knowledge age. In the

FIGURE 1.1   The Two Sides of Toyota.

Toyota's Hard Side
Toyota production system
Logistics management
Research and development

Toyota's Soft Side
Human resource management
Dealer management
Corporate culture

industrial society, contradictions, opposites, and paradoxes were commonly viewed as characteristics to be avoided or eliminated. The renowned management scientist Frederick Taylor prescribed scientific methods and procedures such as time and motion studies to eliminate conflict and contradiction in the workplace and increase efficiency on the factory floor. No one is a better practitioner of Taylorism than Toyota. But contemporary studies in human cognition show that we learn by doing and by being forced to reconcile our unique perspective with those of others who disagree with us. The opposing insights of others are necessary for us to understand the organic whole. This is how new knowledge is created.[26] We believe Toyota embraces this understanding in its view of the organization and production by cultivating contradictions and challenges in human interactions and channeling the resulting creativity into the production process.

Conclusion

The first step to better understanding Toyota is to recognize that contradictions, opposites, and paradoxes are a way of life within the company. Toyota relentlessly pits opposing forces against each other to realize continuous innovation and constant renewal. We identified the six contradictions that characterize the relationship between the hard and soft sides of Toyota and pervade its culture. But what is it that pushes

Toyota onward and upward to the never-ending next phase of development? If contradictions, opposites, and paradoxes are simply recognized and embraced without any movement to a higher-order resolution of these tensions, then the organization stalls. The two wheels joined by the shaft (Figure 1.1) must produce movement forward in the right direction. In the case of the Lexus, if the development team at Toyota had recognized the need to achieve both fuel efficiency and high-speed capability but could not resolve this apparent conflict by moving to a higher-order resolution (in the philosophical language of Hegel, this is a dialectical resolution called *aufheben*),[27] the Lexus LS400 would not have been a class leader in both fuel efficiency and performance and would have been subject to the gas-guzzler tax, preventing the Lexus from becoming the number one selling luxury car brand in the United States.

Contradictions, opposites, and paradoxes within Toyota are self-generated and deliberately imposed. Toyota strives to remain "extreme," a state of disequilibrium where radical contradictions coexist, pushing it away from the comfort zone to create healthy tension and instability within the organization. This tension becomes the catalyst for movement forward. The organization finds new solutions beyond opposing traits, sending it off on a new trajectory. This trajectory moves upward in an expanding spiral as the firm continuously pursues innovation and self-renewal in the resolution of opposites. This resolution is not a compromise or balance, but a transcendence of opposites, leading the firm to higher levels of performance.[28]

In Chapter 2, we show how the cultivation of contradictions inside Toyota that spur innovation is guided by a larger pattern of expansive and integrative forces operating on the company that respectively drive it to the outer reaches of achievement and pull it together as a unified organization.

Six Opposing Forces That Drive the Company's Expansion—and Keep It from Breaking Apart

Deconstructing Toyota in the course of our research was like peeling back the layers of an onion but never reaching the center. The degree of contradiction and paradox was distracting as we looked for the fundamental reasons for Toyota's success.

The breakthrough came when we realized these paradoxes were central to our investigation. Very quickly, a larger pattern of expansion and integration began to emerge. We tracked this pattern through six case studies and in interviews with Toyota employees, distributors, and dealers across the United States, Europe, Asia, and Japan. Eventually we identified three expansive and three integrative forces unique to Toyota.

The expansive forces lead Toyota toward new challenges and greater diversity and complexity, whereas the integrative forces allow the company to weave together and internalize these experiences and perspectives and make sense of the complicated environment in which it operates (Figure 2.1). The six forces are as follows:

Expansive Forces
- *Impossible goals:* Toyota sets goals for itself that most would consider impossible to achieve, and it does this knowing full well that the means to achieve them may not yet exist.

FIGURE 2.1   The Six Forces in Toyota.

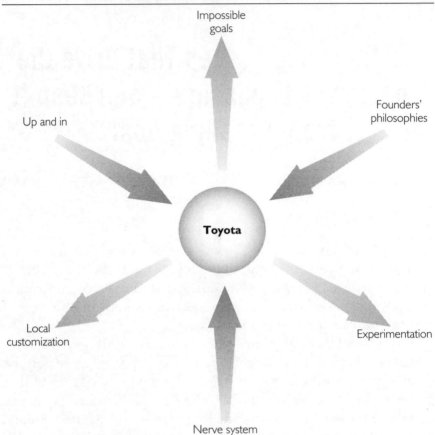

- *Experimentation:* Toyota encourages a high level of experimentation and learning from failure.
- *Local customization:* Toyota customizes products and operations to incorporate the sophistication and diversity of local markets around the world.

Integrative Forces

- *Founders' philosophies:* Historic words of the founders represent the core values, shared and practiced by all, that are the foundation of Toyota's unique corporate culture.

- *Nerve system:* Toyota's intricately layered network of open communication promotes a cross-pollination of knowledge and practice that ensures "everyone knows everything."
- *Up and in:* Toyota's human resource management policy guarantees job security while emphasizing continuous development of individual creative potential through learning and improvement. This approach is in stark contrast to the more conventional "up or out" management policy where those who fail are out the door.

In the following sections, we describe each of the forces in detail, illustrate how the six forces work together to move the company both incrementally and in leaps and bounds, and show how they are supported by the company's capital resources.

Forces of Expansion

"This is how we do things here," is a common refrain in every organization with its own operational momentum. Preordained practices help a company keep moving along planned trajectories with routine methods that are known to have worked in the past. These methods become standardized and create efficiencies that prevent reinvention of the wheel. Over time, they become part of the corporate culture. Those methods can also lead to rigidities that interfere with necessary modifications or the adoption of new practices that could improve operations.

Such rigidities are challenged by the pressure exerted on an organization to reach new customers as well as new market segments and geographic areas, not to mention the challenges of competitors, new ideas, and new practices. Toyota embraces these pressures to instigate continuous change and improvement, resulting in expansion and diversification of its activities into even more layers of complexity. The company grows by deliberately subjecting itself to expansive forces for change (Figure 2.1).

Impossible Goals

Impossible goals infuse the organization with the motivation to break free of established routines and try new things. This is usually what starts a cycle of evolution at Toyota and is normally expressed as a social value. When Kiichiro Toyoda, the founder of the Toyota Motor Corporation, decided to enter the automobile business, his goal was to produce automobiles independently, without relying on an overseas partnership. This was at a time when the big Japanese conglomerates (*zaibatsu*) such as Mitsui and Mitsubishi were hesitant to enter the automobile business.

This social value proposition has its parallel today in Toyota's goal of "continuous optimization" in the face of contradiction. In Toyota-speak, this means that a solution must be found that is not a compromise or an easy way out of conflicting demands but is optimal. It is accomplished by seeing the problem from new perspectives and developing new approaches that transcend contradiction.

When Toyota rivaled General Motors as the world's largest carmaker in unit sales in 2007, it was not because Toyota had set for itself the goal of becoming number one. Rather, this was a by-product of its aim for a 15 percent global market share by the year 2010, a goal it had set in 2003 and called the "Global 15." As former Toyota President Fujio Cho explained, the Global 15 was actually a dream goal meant to inspire employees rather than express a commitment to a specific numerical target.

In late 2002, when this objective was being formulated, Toyota held almost 11 percent of the global market in terms of unit sales, while General Motors and Ford accounted for 15 percent and 12 percent, respectively, so reaching 15 percent amounted to toppling the top two. Year after year, Toyota's market share crept upward, aided by incremental sales averaging 650,000 units per year since 2002. At this rate, the inspiring Global 15 dream is expected to become a reality by 2010 and demonstrates how effective impossible goals are as a driver of Toyota's expansion.[1]

Other impossible goals at Toyota are described in Chapter 3 and include meeting the needs of every customer by having a full line of vehicles in every market; developing the Lexus as "the finest car ever built" with "the finest dealer network in the industry" and ensuring that a Lexus with 50,000 miles on the odometer would not look, feel, sound, or perform any differently from one fresh out of the factory; bypassing Japan to globalize vehicle production with the creation of the Innovative International Multipurpose Vehicle (IMV) in Thailand, Indonesia, Argentina, and South Africa.

Experimentation

Toyota's eagerness to experiment is an expansive force that has helped it scale the hurdles in achieving its impossible goals. First, it breaks down the big goal into manageable challenges. Then it tries to come up with new initiatives, practices, and processes for handling the more difficult challenges in each component. The goals may be audacious, but the experimentation is pragmatic and limited in scale.

These initiatives become opportunities for exploration and learning. They operate on the premise that every original plan for a project is imperfect and incomplete, and will only be completed by the project's successors. If the original plan does not work, they learn from the experience, modify the plan, and try again. If it does work, they create a new routine from this successful practice and share it across the organization, aware that even new routines eventually will become obsolete. The organization then turns to chasing another challenging goal.

The force for experimentation underpins two sets of paradoxes in Toyota operations: gradualism versus the big leap, and stability versus paranoia. It tackles impossible goals through small, incremental experiments to achieve a significant evolution and institutionalizes new routines into existing, stable practices, fully aware that they will become obsolete. This approach drives the continuous search for new practices. The force of experimentation fosters learning and the willingness to try new things—key factors that continuously push Toyota out of its comfort zone toward new horizons.

In Chapter 4, we use the Prius, the Scion, and the IMV projects to elaborate on the experimentation process, including the values that serve as its enablers at Toyota. The experimentation process includes the eight-step problem-solving process, the practice of defining objectives and breaking down complex tasks using the A3 analysis, and the institutionalization of new practices in the organization.

Local Customization

Local customization acts as an expansive force on Toyota in ways that are different from other firms because it doesn't just adapt to local needs. It customizes its products and operations to match the level of consumer sophistication in each locale. The opposite approach to localization is global standardization as practiced by Porsche of Germany. This method achieves lower production costs, increased profits, and a strong brand image by minimizing local customization and selectively satisfying only those customer demands that are common across markets. Porsche has benefited from this approach because of the economies of scale derived from standardizing products and operations, and it has yielded high levels of profit for the company. The determining factors for a successful global standardization strategy are simplicity and efficiency.

In contrast, Toyota's strategy of local customization increases operational complexity because it addresses specific customer needs unique to each market and centralizes that process. A quicker way to implement local adaptation is to acquire an existing local manufacturer and allow it to function autonomously, as General Motors has done. This approach seeks to reduce complexity but increases redundancy and operational costs. Toyota's customization approach concentrates product development and manufacturing preparation processes at its headquarters in Japan, while bringing in a high level of local input to tailor products for each market. This increases the operational complexity of the organization exponentially, while expanding the boundaries of Toyota's knowledge base as it incorporates intelligence gathered from the various markets into the central process.

Among the top 10 automakers in 2006, Toyota's unit sales were the most diversified geographically because of its policy of extensive customization in each market. While North America was its largest market in sales terms, it represented only 31.8 percent of total units sold worldwide. By contrast, the largest market of each of its rivals represented 58.2 percent of total sales for DaimlerChrysler, 56.6 percent for VW Group, 52.0 percent for General Motors, and 50.5 percent for Ford.[2]

Does Toyota achieve local customization without sacrificing economies of scale? The numbers say yes. In 2006, Toyota led the Japanese market in units sold per model (24,700 units per model). In North America, Honda led but Toyota ran a close second with 90,300 units per model, over 40 percent more than third-placed Ford. In Europe, Toyota led its Japanese rivals by a margin of over 20 percent with 33,400 units per model. Toyota sells both locally customized models and "global cars" or standardized models like the *Corolla*, the *Yaris*, and the IMV *Hilux*, achieving more production units per model than its rivals while offering a broader product line through customization.[3]

In Chapter 5, we show how Toyota customizes its products and operations to incorporate the sophistication and diversity of local markets around the world, as in case of the IMV in Asia, the Yaris in Europe, and the Scion and the *Tundra* in the United States.

All three expansive forces have encouraged Toyota to find new customers, try new processes, and develop and use new technologies. Along the way, it becomes a more complex organization as it internalizes a greater variety of perspectives from the growing numbers of employees and customers in its many markets. A drawback of exponential expansion is that effective communication deteriorates, and it becomes increasingly difficult and costly to efficiently coordinate operations. How does Toyota cope with the hazards of constant expansion and growth? What is the glue that keeps it together? We had to dig deeper inside Toyota to find out.

Forces of Integration

While the expansive forces extend Toyota's organizational and knowledge boundaries, a set of integrative forces weave the company together and keep it from spinning out of control. These are: the founders' philosophies, the nerve system, and up-and-in human resource management (Figure 2.1). These forces combine to center Toyota and perpetuate its culture while stabilizing its continuous expansion and absorption of new perspectives.

Founders' Philosophies

The following individuals—Sakichi Toyoda, who created the parent company (Toyoda Automatic Loom Works), Kiichiro Toyoda, the son of Sakichi (founder of Toyota Motor Corporation), Taiichi Ohno, (creator of the Toyota Production System), Eiji Toyoda (first cousin of Kiichiro and former President), Shotaro Kamiya, (developer of Toyota's domestic and global sales network), Shoichiro Toyoda, (son of Kiichiro and also a former President), Robert B. McCurry (former Vice Chairman of Toyota Motor Sales, U.S.A.), and Alex Warren (former Senior Vice President of Toyota Motor Manufacturing, Kentucky)—share a common trait: they cultivated and passed on the practices and values that define Toyota's corporate culture. These include the mindset of *kaizen* or continuous improvement, the values of respect for people and their individual capabilities, teamwork, humility, putting the customer first, and *genchi genbutsu* or seeing things firsthand. These simple philosophies are the basis of Toyota's corporate values and have profoundly influenced its evolution.

While Toyota is not alone in having core values originating with its founders, it is unique in the way it inculcates and ritualizes them in practices designed to test and reinforce their relevance every day. The Toyota Production System, with its emphasis on kaizen, epitomizes this practice. The values are disseminated in stories and on-the-job training, and the accumulated anecdotes are retold and reflected on through history. Toyota began to organize and document these stories as global expansion accelerated, and it eventually published them in *The Toyota Way 2001* handbook as a tool for instructing employees worldwide in the company's core values. The continual retelling of these stories and their reinforcement in practice help Toyota employees cope with the uncertainties of constant change, providing a common framework to guide strategic decision making.

In Chapter 6, we describe four shared beliefs and values: tomorrow will be better than today; everybody should win; customer first, dealers second, and manufacturer last; and genchi genbutsu. These values have withstood the test of time to define, shape, and give stability to Toyota's corporate culture.

Nerve System

The nerve system refers to an intricately layered network of open communication, through which Toyota tries to preserve a small-town feel throughout its vast organization by ensuring "everybody knows everything." Employees often work in cross-functional teams requiring communication that traverses departmental layers and functional reporting lines. This creates multiple layers of formal and informal communication that interconnect organizational units in myriad and often geographically dispersed ways. This tendency is encouraged by the company philosophy that sends all employees to the frontlines to see things firsthand, as well as by product development teams making frequent visits to customers and dealers to improve their understanding of markets (genchi genbutsu).

The internal structure of Toyota supports the free exchange of ideas, emphasizing the communication of differences to improve operations and resolve problems. Toyota executives are seriously committed to listening to all stakeholders and continuously have their ears to the ground. Every stakeholder's opinion is respected and taken at face value in line with the core philosophy of respect for people. Their example facilitates the free movement of information among all employees. In essence, the nerve system of Toyota serves as the human version of the World Wide Web by which it senses and becomes aware of what is going on in all parts of the organization. By enabling effective listening and action, the nerve system has helped fine-tune Toyota's sense of the different markets and their peculiar needs. And it synthesizes all this input to offer both customized and standardized "global cars."

The elements that underpin the nerve system at Toyota are described in Chapter 7 and include open communication and lateral dissemination of know-how throughout the organization; the freedom of employees to voice contrary opinions; frequent face-to-face interaction; efforts to make tacitly understood knowledge explicit to others; and the provision of formal and informal support mechanisms, including training centers and clubs within the company.

Up-and-In Human Resource Management

In the conventional up-or-out human resource management practice, employees are expected to achieve, and poor performers are weeded out. Toyota's up-and-in treatment of employees guarantees them the long-term employment that was once typical of Japanese management practice, and it emphasizes continuous development of employee skills and experience. Individual skills are developed to serve long-term goals. This means employees are allowed to fail, and performance evaluation emphasizes learning over immediate results.

Toyota is committed to developing the potential of every employee. Junior staff are routinely trained on the job, paired with superiors who assign their tasks and coach them. The performance evaluation system is unique, even among Japanese companies doing long-term team-based evaluations. It assesses the ability to handle issues creatively, resilience, and *jinbo* or trust from other employees, among others.

Issues are resolved in *genba* (in the field), placing a high level of authority and responsibility with local personnel. This is the flip side of up-and-in management—delegation and local empowerment—a practice that is only possible because employees are trusted to do the right thing. This trust stems from the founders' philosophy of respect for people. Jim Press, former President of Toyota Motor North America, observed that local empowerment was particularly noticeable in sales and marketing:

> The company has really understood its role and focused on engineering to produce the very best products and manufacturing processes, and it does not get involved in [local] sales and marketing, letting that grow in other countries. [This] has been a real key to success.[4]

But only those who accept and fit in with Toyota's values and up-and-in culture will find opportunities to grow. These are the employees who maintain the corporate memory in their heads and hands as they rise up through the ranks.

In Chapter 8, we dig deeper to describe the enablers of Toyota's up-and-in human resource management system, looking at the conditions needed for it to function effectively. These include a commitment to stable and long-term employment, continuous employee training, action orientation, team play, and learning-based evaluation.

So how do the three integrative forces work together to keep the company on a stable footing? First, they strengthen the existing corporate culture. Continuous sharing of the founders' philosophies instills a sense that the company's values are permanent and will stand the test of time. Up-and-in human resource management ensures the stability of the workforce and fortifies corporate memory, as employees stay longer within the organization. Second, Toyota's culture of information sharing and open dialogue makes sense of an increasingly complicated reality through knowledge sharing and coordinated decision making. This is supported by multilayered and intricate face-to-face communication that serves as a powerful integrator of ideas and opinions dispersed throughout the organization. These three integrative forces—founders' philosophies, the nerve system culture of dialogue, and up-and-in management—maintain the organic whole in its endless pursuit of expansion and transformation.

Six Forces Working Together

As their natures suggest, the six forces complement each other in their opposition. When expansive forces become too strong, integrative forces are triggered to maintain cohesion. It becomes more difficult for the nerve system to function effectively when expansive forces are adding new markets at greater distances across the globe. Toyota's accelerated expansion after 2002 saw increased investments aimed at nourishing the nerve system to increase opportunities for employees to meet, get to know each other, and work together in formal and informal ways. Toyota also published its handbook, *The Toyota Way 2001,* to reinforce the founders' philosophies of genchi genbutsu, respect for people, the customer first, and kaizen in the behavior of global managers.

Another example of how the forces support each other is in the interaction of the expansive force of experimentation with the integrative force of kaizen as a founders' philosophy. Whether improvement is day-to-day as in kaizen or occurs in a leap, both are methods of experimentation for learning how to make things better than before. Experimentation is bolstered by the nerve system and the philosophy of respect for people, both integrative forces. Mutual respect cultivates open and honest communication for better-informed experimentation. And the integrative force of up-and-in human resource management is another support for experimentation as it views failure in terms of what has been learned from it and trains and evaluates employees for individual resilience and the ability to define and solve problems while also functioning as team players.

Generally, the six forces, in combination, create complex dependencies that strengthen each of the forces and keep Toyota in a state of disequilibrium, where radical contradictions coexist, generating healthy tension and instability within the organization. Any change in the predominance of one of the forces disrupts this state, pushing the organization away from the comfort zone and sending it off on a new trajectory. The trajectories change along with the combination of forces, as is the case at any organization over time. The difference is that Toyota instigates this process of continuous instability interrupted by continuous change. Figure 2.2 illustrates how the company evolves incrementally, grounded in kaizen, while periodically moving in leaps and bounds.

Resource Base

Constant change in any organization is time consuming and expensive. This is difficult to manage, especially in a mature industry where standardization and scale are the key drivers of profitability. By definition, a mature industry is one that has stable earnings yet low potential for growth, and the auto industry, with a compounded annual growth rate of just 3 percent from 1999 to 2006, is a typical example. Yet Toyota does not view the auto business as mature and doesn't hesitate to spend without restraint on endeavors deemed critical by top management toward enhancing company growth. This brings us to the issue of resources, both capital and human, and how they can catalyze or amplify the effects of the expansive and integrative forces on Toyota (Figure 2.3). The resource base is crucial to influencing the forces for optimal interaction.

Toyota keeps a significant amount of disposable capital. Its research and development spending grew from $4.4 billion in 2000 to $6.9 billion in 2006, outpacing growth in research spending for the entire industry during the same period by a factor of two. However, while available resources are important, equally critical is how they are allocated to achieve the goal.

FIGURE 2.2 Evolution at Toyota, induced by the interaction of expansive and integrative forces, which results in a state of perpetual change.

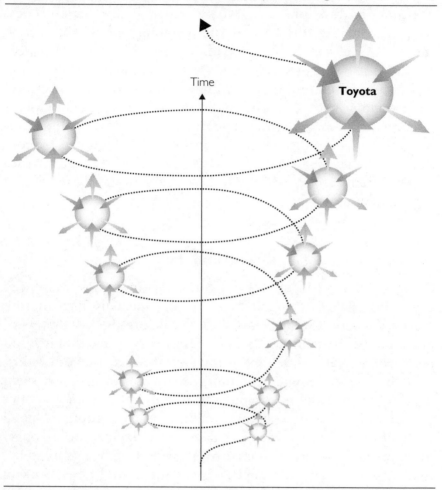

Note: The progress of this evolution, which is typically incremental, is also characterized by big leaps and bounds as the company evolves into a larger and more complicated entity with the passage of time.

All companies facing a shortage of resources will carefully and creatively allocate them to maximize returns. The danger lies in an overabundance of resources. Then "careful" falls to the wayside and "creative" allocation dominates the picture. In this respect, Toyota has been both frugal and indulgent, especially

FIGURE 2.3   The allocation of resources to catalyze or amplify the effect of the Six Forces acting on Toyota.

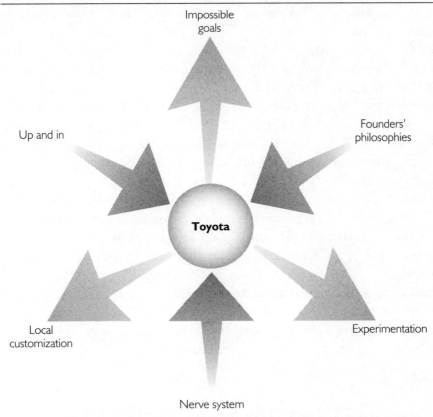

when it allocates resources into activities deemed financially risky yet critical to meeting an identified demand.

Toyota allocates significant resources to employee training, which plays a critical role in strengthening both the hard and soft sides of the company described in Chapter 1 (Figure 1.1). Training for the Toyota Production System, the centerpiece of Toyota's hard side was once the domain of each manufacturing plant. It is now centralized at the Global Production Center established in 2003 at Toyota's second oldest plant in Motomachi, Toyota City, Japan. In 2006, this was reinforced with the establishment of the North American Production Support Center and the European and Asia-Pacific branches of the Global Production Center to provide training in every manufacturing process.

Training employees in soft-side skills is a more arduous task. Unlike the hard side, where processes are defined and consistent regardless of location, the soft side, with its emphasis on people, can vary in nature and degree from one market to the next. There are no shortcuts to accelerate employee acquisition of soft skills. For this reason, Toyota established two institutions of learning in 2002: the Toyota Institute and the Global Knowledge Center. There, best practices in sales and marketing sourced from operations around the globe are disseminated to the workforce. These endeavors are both time consuming and expensive, and Toyota, more than any other automotive manufacturer, has shown the willingness and commitment to invest the enormous resources required to train employees and dealers at these institutions. As described in Chapter 9, Toyota relies on a pool of readily available capital based on a policy of maintaining cash reserves that have been frugally accumulated over the years. And the company allocates these resources appropriately and without reservation to develop organizational capability and people.

Six Forces in Action: Case of the Lexus

In this section, we examine the six forces in action in the case of its luxury brand Lexus. Initially developed for the U.S. market, the Lexus has become the new benchmark there in the luxury car market, consistently rating highly in customer and dealer satisfaction since its 1989 launch and now selling in Europe, Africa, the Middle East, South America, Japan, Asia, and Oceania.

So what convinced customers to purchase the *LS400* when it was launched in 1989? Was it technical achievement or the relentless pursuit of perfection in marketing? The most likely answer lies in the tailoring of the car to the specific demands and desires of the U.S. luxury car consumer, guided by the founders' philosophy of putting the customer first and the nerve system that effectively disseminated customer needs. It was also the emphasis on local customization that delivered an unforgettable experience at Lexus dealerships, from sales to service.

It was the 1980s, and facing a political backlash in the United States to rising Japanese imports, Toyota was adhering to voluntary import restrictions. This created a dilemma. How could it increase revenue from the United States with limits there on imports? One answer was to start manufacturing locally. But there was another, more radical possibility: enter the luxury segment and increase the average revenue and profit on each vehicle sold.

The problem was that outside the Japanese market, Toyota did not have a luxury car and would have to develop the technology it needed from scratch. To build such a car for the U.S. market in the mid 1980s, Toyota had to make it faster than the top speed of any Japanese luxury car. It also had to make it accelerate much faster to get onto the highway, and the car had to have much better fuel efficiency to avoid the gas-guzzler tax. Most U.S. luxury cars were privately owned and driven by their owners, whereas in Japan most were company owned and driven by chauffeurs. Nevertheless, Toyota was determined to build "the finest car ever built." It forged ahead with no history in the U.S. luxury car market and worst of all, no car. By any measure, this undertaking began as the pursuit of an impossible goal.

Developing technology for the Lexus proved difficult. The engineering team wanted to create a car that was ahead of every existing luxury vehicle on the market and had to tackle difficult technical conflicts like speed versus fuel efficiency, without settling for trade-offs. This called for some courageous experimentation. For six years, the engineering team persisted in addressing problems by identifying their root causes and relied on institutional practices of continuous improvement and teamwork to perfect the design of the groundbreaking first Lexus LS400 sedan, putting a $1 billion dent in capital resources (refer to Chapter 3 for a more detailed description of the Lexus LS400 development).

All events leading up to this point were favorable. The right combination of trade barriers, demographics pointing to the rise of affluent customers, and the willingness at Toyota to try new things, all made fertile ground for germinating the Lexus seed. But there were no guarantees that U.S. consumers would buy a luxury vehicle with no heritage or brand recognition. Toyota Motor Sales, U.S.A. (TMS), the U.S. sales subsidiary of Toyota, proposed creating an entirely new, independent dealer franchise dedicated solely to selling the Lexus—an enormous undertaking considering the investment required to build, staff, and support a new network of dealers, and build a new brand. This risky proposition met resistance at every level at Toyota. It was only the Chairman Eiji Toyoda who finally broke the tension. In a meeting in 1986 with senior executives and the president of TMS, he declared, "Let's do it according to the TMS plan." A new impossible goal was approved.

The first step in developing the sales, marketing, and service strategies for the Lexus was to acquire a deep understanding of the targeted customer's needs. In 1985, four years before the Lexus was launched, a team was formed to identify these needs by going to the field and witnessing customers' lifestyles firsthand. The next step was establishment of the dealer network, including the field offices that would support them and form part of the Lexus franchise. Capital resources were used to develop a comprehensive communication network to support the Lexus, including a proprietary satellite communication channel and IT system for dealer training and to enable quick diagnosis of technical faults locally.

In 1987, while the dealer network was being established and the Lexus LS400 was still under development, a divisional general manager in the United States authored the Lexus Covenant (see Chapter 6 for the full text) as a public declaration of the Toyota philosophy and commitment to their goal of providing a superior product. It promised delivery of the "finest cars" and unparalleled service that would treat each customer as "a guest in our home." The declaration expressed Toyota's core values in concrete terms as an integrated practice for all managers, associates, and dealers on the Lexus team. This helped to guide and coordinate activities for the new brand in a way that reinforced the founders' philosophies.

The LS400 was launched in September 1989 to glowing reviews and, to Toyota's relief, sold extremely well. However, a recall just three months later had the potential to ruin the new brand. To prevent this, Toyota organized a massive, coordinated effort of all Lexus personnel to complete the recall process within 20 days (the recall is detailed further in Chapter 6). There were worries that the recall might have eroded dealers' trust in Lexus, but dealers and customers alike expressed a high level of satisfaction with the process and the results, and at the next Lexus Dealer Advisory Council, the first remark from the association's chairman was, "Thank you for the recall."

The recall was a pivotal moment in the infancy of the company's first luxury brand. Everything had depended on the success of its latest experiment in customer service, and the Lexus project proved Toyota's commitment to putting the customer first by teaming up with the dealers. Lexus dealers experimented further with the unique marketing and service innovations developed for the recall that later became industry standards, such as provision of same-class loan cars during repairs (refer to Chapter 3 for additional information on dealer service innovations). Lexus field managers learned about these innovations on routine dealer visits and disseminated them to other dealerships in the nerve system. If field managers encountered dealers with unsatisfactory track records, they would help those dealers improve their performance in line with up-and-in human resource management.

The roots of service innovations at the dealerships can be traced to dealers' interpretations of the Lexus Covenant while they were designing their operations. Dealers and their service personnel were entrusted to make decisions on customer service in line with the policy of local customization and the founders' philosophies of putting the customer first and having respect for people. As a result, few competitors in the luxury brand market could match the experience of a Lexus purchase.

For Toyota, building the LS400 was the *check* move in a game of chess, and the experience that owning a Lexus provided was the *checkmate*.

In the mid-1990s, the Lexus saw its first drop in sales. To boost demand, Toyota encouraged dealers to offer discounts to new buyers. This caused uneasiness among the dealers, who saw discounting as contrary to the luxury brand image. When dealer anxiety grew, the nerve system kicked, in and Toyota held a series of "Fireside Chat" meetings to share its business plans and hear dealers concerns and suggestions about how to handle the decline (additional types of face-to-face interactions, similar to the Fireside Chats, are described in Chapter 7). The open and earnest discussions with dealers, especially when business was poor, were powerful experiences that helped weather the slowdown. From 1997 on, the Lexus was back on a growth track. By 2000, it was the number one brand in the U.S. luxury car market, a distinction it has held onto ever since.

Conclusion

As the Lexus case shows, a radical proposition becomes reality through the interaction of the six forces operating on Toyota. In the following six chapters, we look at each of the forces in detail to show how they capture the innovation process, starting with impossible goals.

CHAPTER 3

The Force of Impossible Goals

Like the navigators of early times who grew restless when at port too long, Toyota is restlessly in pursuit of new horizons and conscious of the ship's potential to run aground. This explorer spirit dates back to Sakichi Toyoda, the founder of Toyota's parent company, Toyoda Automatic Loom Works. He was fond of saying, "Open the window. It's a big world out there."[1] This expansive pressure stimulates employees to set goals that seem difficult or even impossible to achieve, pushing them beyond conventional practices and driving Toyota's continuous self-reinvention and growth.

Eiji Toyoda and Shoichiro Toyoda, fourth and sixth presidents of the company, opened the window to overseas markets during Toyota's early history, while in recent history, senior executives have been looking out the window exploring new frontiers to create the company's next big jump. Senior Toyota Advisor, Yoshio Ishizaka, pondered out loud the initiatives of Toyota's most recent presidents Hiroshi Okuda, Fujio Cho, and Katsuaki Watanabe:

> [When] Okuda-san became president we were talking about "harmonious growth."[2] Even though [the 1990s] was the lost decade in Japan, we managed to get out the Lexus, and around the middle of 1990s, we took on the challenge of the hybrid car. All this in just 10 years. When Cho-san took over, we were talking about "Global Vision," to capture a 15 percent [global market] share by 2010. And in the Watanabe era, I believe we will continue to come up with

[new] things again. This means we are not just thinking about our day-to-day evolution as a company but also have in the back of our minds the possibility of another big jump forward, and this becomes a kind of spark for determining our overall direction, which is something we should all be considering carefully.[3]

Make no mistake. With "continuous improvement" (kaizen) as a pillar of the organization, Toyota remains a stickler for detail in day-to-day operations. As Sakichi's son Kiichiro Toyoda, also a former President, used to say, "We are working on making better products by making improvements every day."[4] At the same time, the company is eyeing its next revolutionary step forward.

As Executive Vice President Yoshimi Inaba described it, even when business is successful, senior executives are out exploring for the "next booster rocket" to power evolutionary change. A former President of Toyota's U.S. operation, Toyota Motor Sales, U.S.A. (TMS), Inaba was always wary of TMS' success in replicating the Toyota model and remained on the lookout for potential new disruptions. "The number one enemy of TMS was its own success," he said. "It had a long history and some of the top managers had thirty-year careers [there]. It was even more Toyota-like than Toyota [in Japan]. . . . I called it a 'conventional model at its prime.'"[5] Since TMS was doing so well and contributing a significant amount of profit, it was easy to try to avoid doing anything that might disturb that. But as Inaba saw it, "If you sketch out the wrong idea for the next booster rocket or if you do nothing, you are guaranteed to decline. What are you going to do next? I think the question of what picture you are going to draw [next] is critically important."[6]

With the explorer mindset, someone at Toyota opens the window, looks outside, and draws a picture of what the future holds. That someone could be a chief executive or one of many middle-managers or engineers. Setting tough goals to actualize the future may not be unique to Toyota. What is unique is how it sets those goals and resolves contradiction to achieve them. We examine this process by looking at three impossible goals among many that have driven Toyota's evolution. The first is Toyota's customer-first policy that seems to defy economic common sense by aiming to meet every customer need and provide a full line of vehicles in every market; the second is its development of a new standard of luxury automobile ownership with the Lexus, the finest cars that never age and sold by the finest dealers; the third is its unique strategy of globalization that bypasses Japan to make a global car.

Meet Every Customer Need

It is, of course, impossible to meet every customer need in every market. To do so would require Toyota to incorporate millions, even billions of modifications into their cars to suit each potential customer, which does not make economic sense. Philosophically, however, Toyota is bent on meeting the needs of every customer, as stated in its internal document *Toyota Value:* "For Toyota to carry out [the policy of] 'customer first' globally, it is essential . . . to respond to the needs of every customer quickly and thoroughly."[7] This philosophy extends beyond the customer to include the supply partners, the workers on the assembly line, and the distributors, dealers, and service centers.

Toyota attaches a strong social value to meeting the needs of every customer and enhancing satisfaction with the product. It publicly declares its impossible goals to raise the social consciousness of its employees, as in the following statement in the closing section of *Toyota Value:*

> We are always optimizing[8] to enhance the happiness of every customer, as well as to build a better future for people, society, and the planet we share. This is our duty. This is Toyota.[9]

The goal of developing new cars for every customer segment in each country or region arises out of this sentiment.

It is contrary to conventional wisdom in strategic management, which espouses the merits of staying focused and making trade-offs. According to Michael Porter, a leading scholar in the field at Harvard University, the essence of strategy is choosing what not to do.[10] Targeting all customers, meeting all their needs, and producing all varieties of the product, are aims that run counter to the essence of strategic business practice. Toyota knows that its reasoning goes against conventional wisdom.

Nevertheless, Toyota caters for all customer segments with no trade-offs, especially in its two most developed markets, Japan and the United States. It makes the *Corolla* for the utility-minded customer, the *Sienna* for the family-oriented customer, the *Prius* for the environmentally conscious customer, the *Lexus* for the luxury-seeking customer, the *Scion* for the young customer, and so on. This approach stems from the firm belief that a car helps make people happy. It is reminiscent of Henry Ford's philosophy of the three Ps—People, Products, and Profit[11]—and his vision to make the car affordable to American families of moderate means, so they could enjoy "the blessings of happy hours spent in God's great open spaces."[12]

Similarly, the current President of Toyota, Katsuaki Watanabe, stresses the social value of automobile manufacturing as building a better future for people, society, and the planet. Thus, his oft-repeated aim to build a dream car that cleans the air, prevents accidents, makes people healthier and happier when they drive it, and gets you from coast to coast on one tank of gas.[13] According to Watanabe, permeating these lofty ambitions throughout the organization is management's most important task. "These days, I am asking [employees] to develop communities instead of cars," he said. He stimulates those around him by prodding them to consider how cars can make communities safer, for example by emitting clean air. "We must develop such [clean] cars to live our mission and be accepted by society. Although there is a long way to go, we can make it, and our employees are working hard to realize this goal."[14] This socially responsible approach was core to the company's founders, and it guides Watanabe's actions:

"I always keep a copy of the *Toyoda Koryo* [Toyoda Precepts] in my pocket. This tells us to stay ahead of the times through creativity and curiosity, and contribute to the good of society through the company."[15]

Driven by the strong social value of customer first, Toyota has made inroads into three key market segments in the United States that seemed impossible at the outset, with the Lexus in the luxury segment, the Scion in the youth segment, and most recently the Tundra for the pickup truck driver, the last stronghold of U.S. automakers. Despite the hurdles of creating its first luxury vehicle and adding a new franchise in the United States in more than 40 years, Toyota quickly captured the hearts and minds of American customers with the now legendary Lexus, LS400. We explain the Lexus strategy in more detail later in this chapter, but first let's look at how impossible goals have carved a space for Toyota in two other market segments.

The U.S. Youth Segment

Toyota entered the U.S. market in 1957 with small cars that became popular among baby boomers in their 20s. By the late 1990s, however, the children of boomers saw the Toyota as Mom or Dad's car and tended to shy away from purchasing one. In fact, the average age of a Toyota buyer in the United States was 48, the oldest among Japanese car buyers.[16] Toyota had tried to attract young customers in the United States but faltered. It revamped the *Celica* coupe and *MR2 Spider* roadster in 2001, but neither sold well. Nor did the *Echo* (known in Japan as the *Platz*), which was the first Toyota subcompact aimed at the youth segment.

In response, Toyota introduced the Scion in 2003, targeting youth born between 1980 and 1994, known as "Generation Y." They were more difficult to please as consumers because they had been exposed to marketing techniques from childhood and were more skeptical of the messages coming from TV commercials and magazine advertising than previous generations. They also tended to view cars more as a means of self-expression, and they were more dissatisfied with the car purchasing process than any previous generation.

On the positive side, Generation Y was more responsive to new brands than their parents had been, as long as the product met their needs. To cater to this segment, the early model Scion *xB* had a square, unconventional design and a luxury-level sound system already installed, as well as some 40 optional accessories that allowed young customers to personalize their car. It was priced transparently to eliminate tough sales negotiations at the store and promoted in grassroots, viral marketing that relied heavily on word of mouth, sponsorship of musical events and art exhibitions, and blogs. The car became a supercharger that allowed Toyota to reach what was until then an untouched youth segment. In Chapters 4 and 5, we show how Toyota has succeeded in getting the Scion into the hands of Generation Y customers at a level of demand far exceeding supply of 130,000 units in 2007.

The U.S. Trucker Segment

With the launch of a full-size pickup truck in November 2006, Toyota advanced on the last stronghold of the Detroit Three, with a product researched, designed, engineered, tested, and produced in the United States and promoted in TV ads as the "all-new, built-in-America Toyota truck." Jon Gertner in the *New York Times* described the depth of research conducted for the Tundra by the project's Chief Engineer, Yuichiro Obu, and the Project Manager, Mark Schrage:

> In August 2002, Obu and his team began visiting different regions of the United States; they went to logging camps, horse farms, factories, and construction sites to meet with truck owners. By asking them face-to-face about their needs, Obu and Schrage sought to understand preferences for towing capacity and power; by silently observing them at work, they learned things about the ideal placement of the gear shifter, for instance, or that the door handle and

radio knobs should be extra large, because pickup owners often wear work gloves all day. When the team discerned that the pickup has now evolved into a kind of mobile office for many contractors, the engineers sought to create a space for a laptop and hanging files next to the driver. Finally, they made archaeological visits to truck grave-yards in Michigan, where they poked around the rusting hulks of pickups and saw what parts had lasted. With so many retired trucks in one place, they also gained a better sense of how trucks had evolved over the past 30 years—becoming larger, more varied, more luxurious—and where they might go next.[17]

Based on this level of research into customer needs, Toyota targeted the full-size Tundra (pictured in Figure 3.1) to the person working on a ranch or at a construction site, someone who might go fishing for bass on weekends or head out to a NASCAR race or a country-music concert, and might even be the owner of a motorcycle. This was the customer that Toyota called the "true trucker," and they decided to pursue that segment as a

FIGURE 3.1 The full-sized *Tundra*.

Source: Photo courtesy of Toyota Motor Sales, U.S.A., Inc.

breed of customer that might exist in other markets besides the United States. The Tundra is Toyota's third attempt at trying to crack the U.S. pickup truck market. The *T100*, its first big truck entry into the United States, failed in the 1990s. So did the earlier and smaller version of the Tundra in 2000. Following its launch in 2007, the full-size Tundra generated significant interest among truckers, enabling Toyota to reach its projected sales of 200,000 Tundras during the year, almost 60 percent more sales than the earlier Tundra model.

"Meet the needs of every customer" was the driving force behind development of the Lexus, Scion, and Tundra for the U.S. market. But a more fundamental mission of Toyota is to "enrich and serve society through the building of cars and trucks." These goals are meant to encourage employees from the assembly line worker on up to the chief executive to go beyond the status quo, to ignore conventional wisdom, to repudiate existing practices, and to break frame.

Meeting the Needs of Customers in Other Markets

In Japan, where Toyota commands a market share of more than 40 percent, the company comes closest among the top 10 automakers to marketing a full line of vehicles. In 2006, Toyota had 94 models in Japan, far ahead of Nissan with 35 models, Ford (excluding Mazda) with 34 models, General Motors with 31 models, and Honda with 30 models.[18]

In Europe, where Toyota has been a slow starter, the company's main offerings include the *Yaris* and *Aygo* (a joint venture with Peugeot-Citroen) for the low-end segment, Corolla for the middle segment, the Prius for the hybrid segment, *Avensis* and *Camry* for the high-end segment, and Lexus for the luxury segment. Scion and Tundra have not yet been introduced in Europe, where the priority has been to increase dealer profitability.

In the Asia-Pacific market, Toyota is the top brand in Thailand, the Philippines,[19] Vietnam,[20] and Brunei, but the company still has a long way to go towards meeting the needs of all customers in these countries. Given the large growth potential of China and India, as well as the rise of new local competitors from this region, the Asia-Pacific market is fertile ground. It remains to be seen whether Toyota can transplant its social values in this region as it has in the United States and Japan.

The Finest Cars, the Finest Dealers

In Chapter 2, we had a glimpse of the Lexus story to illustrate the six forces at work. Here, we revisit the Lexus to show how setting impossible goals and resolving contradictions in development and production can become self-sustaining energy within the company that powers its growth. The following three goals that Toyota set for the Lexus were not only difficult, but seemed irrational:

1. To develop "the finest cars ever built"
2. To build "the finest dealer network in the industry and to treat each customer as we would a guest in our home"
3. To ensure that a Lexus with 50,000 miles on its odometer wouldn't look, feel, sound, or perform any differently from one fresh out of the factory: the anti-aging standard

The Finest Cars Ever Built

When Toyota decided to develop a luxury car for the U.S. market in the mid-1980s it faced some serious obstacles. The most expensive car it sold in the United States was the *Cressida*, at $16,000 retail. Luxury cars in Japan, such as Toyota's *Crown* and Nissan's *Cedric*, were classified as compact cars in the United States and lacked speed. Japanese safety regulations required that the cars have limiters built in to prevent speeds above 111.8 mph (180 km/h). Thus, the Lexus required Toyota to move into areas where it lacked knowledge and experience, forcing a reexamination of its basic technologies, from manufacturing and body techniques to procurement. In addition, the United States was the most competitive market in the world, dominated by American and European brands. Armed with cutting-edge technology, quality, and a sophisticated brand image, Mercedes-Benz and BMW cornered the high end of the U.S. luxury car market. Their expensive price tags also kept them at the high end as the foreign exchange rate doubled their European price. Two American brands, Cadillac and Lincoln, occupied the low end of the luxury market.

Toyota established far-fetched targets for the Lexus LS400 that surpassed the existing best-selling luxury brands and pushed the envelope with respect to speed, fuel efficiency, noise level, air resistance, and weight. To build "the finest" car, Toyota had to achieve high fuel efficiency without sacrificing speed. As shown in Figure 3.2, European cars provided high speed, but, because of their low fuel efficiency, were subject to

FIGURE 3.2 Lexus *LS400*'s envelope pushing speed and fuel efficiency performance compared with other luxury cars in 1985.

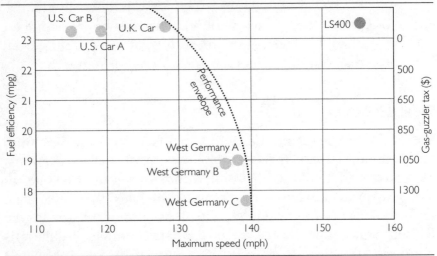

Note: The LS400 was designed to achieve a fuel efficiency exceeding 23 mpg (left axis) while running at over 150 mph (horizontal axis), making it exempt from the gas-guzzler tax (right axis).
Source: Emi Osono, "Lexus: The Challenge of the U.S. Luxury Car Market" (ICS case no. 10610E, Hitotsubashi University, Tokyo, 2006), 21.

a gas-guzzler tax of $1,000 and more for each car. Conversely, American cars avoided the gas-guzzler tax by compromising the ability to perform at high speeds.

Ichiro Suzuki, Chief Engineer of the LS400 development project, realized that his team would have to overcome several contradictions. Improved fuel efficiency would require a lighter vehicle, while low road noise required more insulation material. He created a list of six technical contradictions that had to be resolved to build the car:

1. Outstanding high-speed control and stability/excellent riding comfort
2. Fast and smooth ride/outstanding fuel efficiency
3. Superb noise reduction/lightweight
4. Elegant styling/outstanding aerodynamic performance
5. Warm ambience/functional cabin
6. Outstanding high-speed stability/excellent air resistance (low coefficient of drag)

Suzuki insisted that all the contradictory elements had to be achieved. No compromises or trade-offs. To start, he had to create a new mindset on the development team. He accomplished this with two guiding philosophies: "Action at the Source" and the "Not Yet Philosophy." Action at the Source encouraged everyone to go all the way to the root of a problem and solve it at the source. The Not Yet Philosophy cultivated an uncompromising spirit on the team. These philosophies were instrumental in creating a team culture that never took no for an answer and in establishing an environment where additional members with different functional backgrounds (e.g., R&D, production, engineering, sales) could join in working toward the common goal. Devising even partial solutions to the "mission impossible" at hand, especially in the early stages of development, created cohesion on the team. Once they could see that they could resolve contradictions, they were motivated to higher levels of achievement.

The Finest Dealer Network

Building the finest car ever was one thing, but building the finest dealer network, with all its inherent variables of brand personality and market conditions, was quite another. To launch a new dealer network for the brand, Toyota would have to build a succession of models along with a new sales and service process dedicated to maintaining high customer satisfaction. It would also have to invest in information technology (IT) and in marketing to establish the brand. Given the time, money, and effort this required, most Toyota employees thought a new dealer network was an impossible challenge. But by the end of 1988, Toyota management in Japan had concluded that launching a luxury car in the United States would require an entirely new business model and a new dealer network. A new brand meant new pricing and financing schemes, and new internal systems to support it. Yoshio Ishizaka, former President and Chief Executive Officer of Toyota Motor Sales, U.S.A. (TMS), recalled the heavy resistance from Toyota executives in Japan at an executive committee meeting at Toyota headquarters:

> They were not confident in TMS' ability to establish a new dealer network. We could only do our utmost to convince them, then it was up to Chairman Eiji [Toyoda] to decide. Everyone held their breath. He looked at us and then at everyone in the room and said: "Let's do it according to the TMS plan."[21]

Given the high stakes, TMS felt a moral obligation to build the finest dealer network in the industry. It drew up the Lexus Covenant as guiding principles and in addition to providing the "finest cars," promised that Toyota dealers would "treat each customer as we would a guest in our home."

Treating customers like guests in one's home is a lofty ideal, especially in the United States where car dealers are among the least trusted people in business. To make sure this commitment became a reality, Lexus introduced a number of firsts in the industry with respect to customer service. These included the offer of a loaner car of the same class during repair and service calls, free freight service in case of failure, 24-hour emergency roadside assistance, free car washing, customer shuttle service, and complimentary gas fill-up. The floors of dealer service divisions were kept clean at all times, and service work took place in full view of waiting customers. Some dealers provided services beyond the call of duty, such as owning fuel trucks to supply gas to customers who had run out of gas and giving meal coupons to customers waiting for their cars to be serviced.

Anti-aging the Lexus

It is surely bold to declare publicly that a Lexus with 50,000 miles on its odometer will not look, feel, sound, or perform any differently than one fresh from the factory. To achieve that target, people in the plant had to approach manufacturing from an entirely new perspective. Plant workers went out to the field to carefully inspect and observe rival European cars. In Japan, some were even mistaken for thieves because of their overzealous inspection of Mercedes-Benz and BMW cars parked at golf courses.

Paint and interior materials were developed for special durability that resisted normal wear, even after 10 years. Six coats of paint were applied to the Lexus body, and the thickness of chromium plating was increased eightfold. To prevent interior materials from fading, a special laminated glass that filtered sunlight was used for the rear window, and materials that faded at half the rate of conventional materials were used in the interior. To avoid subtle variations in interior color, the team tried to purchase all the synthetic resin used in cabin interiors from a single vendor, contrary to standard practice of using multiple vendors to minimize procurement costs.

To meet the more stringent precision manufacturing standard for the Lexus, the engineering arm of Toyota had to develop entirely new precision instruments. For example, mounting the drive shaft to prevent vibration at high speeds required accurate positioning of the mounts supporting the transmission and differential gear. Although expert craftsmen could achieve the new level of accuracy, Toyota's existing machine press technology could not. So before building the first Lexus LS400 prototype, Toyota had to learn how to retrofit its machine presses to consistently manufacture components at precise tolerance levels. Only then could it reduce the rejection rate of parts produced outside the required specifications.

Collaboration between engineering and production began 36 months before production started, 12 months earlier than usual. Production of the Lexus LS400, pictured in Figure 3.3, initially required 40 to 50 percent more labor compared with the *Supra,* Toyota's high-end car at the time. Postassembly inspection for the Lexus was also more thorough. Customer delivery inspection items numbered 200, with all components in the car started up, and it required 24 man-minutes, compared with the industry average of 5 to 10 man-minutes. The first Lexus rolled out of the factory after production of 450 test cars in more than one million miles of test-driving. This ability to command abundant resources of time, labor, and investment is part of the equation of achieving impossible goals at Toyota.

FIGURE 3.3   The Lexus *LS400* in 1989.

Source: Photo courtesy of Toyota Motor Corporation.

Bypassing Japan to Make a Global Car

In 1998, an idea emerged that would literally turn the whole company, suppliers included, upside down. It was the project to create the Innovative International Multipurpose Vehicle (IMV), a family of global cars in a production network that bypassed Japan to produce at bases in Thailand, Indonesia, Argentina, and South Africa. The IMV would render the concept of "Made in Japan" irrelevant to the Toyota brand. Many Toyota executives and middle managers thought it was either too risky or impossible. Former Senior Managing Director Zenji Yasuda,[22] then Director of Overseas Planning Operations and one of the originators of the IMV, recalled trying to convince Toyota's board:

> The issue raised most actively [against the IMV] was the risk of starting production in overseas factories without the experience [of producing it first] in a Japanese factory. I argued that while the financial world and the mass media were operating in a global network, no one in the manufacturing world was. So, if we gave life to the [IMV] concept, we would be able to globalize manufacturing.[23]

Yasuda reminded the naysayers that they would never accomplish anything if they just harped on the risks. He said he wanted Toyota to develop the world's first global manufacturing system. "We wanted Toyota to be global, not just in sales, but in manufacturing too. I persuaded everyone by saying that this was a good chance to homogenize the Toyota Production System globally."

Before the IMV project, factories in Japan were central to international production. Toyota prepared mass production of new models in Japan first and then transferred the know-how and equipment to overseas factories. Product development, manufacturing technology development, and production planning know-how were largely centralized at headquarters. Although the IMV was designed at headquarters, it was the first major vehicle produced at overseas plants that had not been produced first at Japanese factories. Figure 3.4 shows the centralized production model before the IMV and the interdependent production system after it.

The concept of the IMV that many inside Toyota had viewed as too complicated, too risky, unrealistic, and even impossible, was formally recognized as a companywide project in September 2002. Production of the IMV series began in Thailand in August 2004, followed by Indonesia in September 2004, Argentina in February 2005, and South Africa in April 2005. In 2005, Toyota produced 520,000 units of the IMV in all four countries, representing the second largest overseas production volume behind the Corolla (approximately 1,000,000 units), and ahead of the Camry (approximately 500,000 units). The project was a success. The chief obstacles they had to overcome were the mindset of "Made in Japan," local procurement of components, and concerns about quality and cost.

Many thought it was risky to relinquish the "Made in Japan" label, which had become synonymous with quality around the world and had been the emphasis of Toyota marketing activities. At the time, Akio Toyoda, the grandson of Kiichiro Toyoda, was in charge of both sales and production in Asia as Senior Managing Director. He realized that changing the mindset of Toyota people alone would require a major campaign, and he made it a personal crusade to convince people that the days of "Made in Japan" were over, replaced with a "Made by Toyota" label in the era of global production:

> I was adamant about not fixating on the idea of "made in Japan" or "made in Thailand." Instead, I was trying very hard to establish the idea of "made by Toyota" and tried to impress upon the local Thai [factory] workers that they were Toyota people. . . . I heard things like, "I have no problem selling cars made in Japan, but when it comes to selling cars made outside of Japan, I'm not so sure." My answer was that these vehicles were all "made by Toyota." Our cars are made by Toyota associates around the world,

FIGURE 3.4 Conceptual model of the Global Production System (a) before and (b) after IMV.

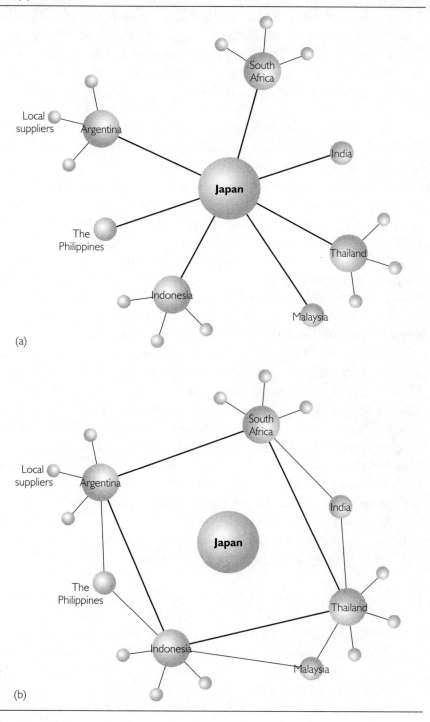

associates who share the same values with regard to what is important in manufacturing, regardless of ethnicity or nationality. . . . The IMV's success was acknowledgment by both the customer and the market of the "Made by Toyota" concept. It made me very happy.[24]

For IMV production to succeed, components for the vehicles had to be procured locally. Toyota developed a logistics network of international parts production, concentrating production of major components such as engines, molds, and part-unit production in a few key locations to gain economies of scale. Gasoline engines were produced in Indonesia, diesel engines in Thailand, and molds in Taiwan and South Korea. To manage unstable production capability in some countries, it spread the manufacture of a specific part among several countries. For example, manual transmissions are manufactured in both India and the Philippines. To maintain quality, the company dispatched people from Japan in two phases.

When the IMV Project Office was established in late 2002, several leaders skilled in production were transferred to Thailand and Indonesia where they worked with local managers and workers to redesign and improve their production processes. When it was time to start production, Toyota dispatched several hundred members of the Japanese production preparation team to plants in Thailand and Indonesia, who coached both workers and local suppliers. The company also asked the Japanese suppliers to do the same at their local factories.[25]

Executive Managing Coordinator of the IMV Project Office in Thailand, Hiroshi Nakagawa, credited that office with achieving total quality management (TQM):

The IMV Project Office controlled everything, from development, production planning, quality management, and procurement, to information technology systems, logistics, marketing, risk management, and beyond, from start to finish. In this regard, the IMV project differed significantly from most other projects.[26]

Nakagawa also emphasized the impact of their slogan, "One team, One aim, Working together," in getting everyone on board:

We were all working together toward the same goal to break down the barriers to success, rather than working independently by function. If a problem arose in facilities, the maintenance team from our factory would jump right in to resolve the issue before the equipment was installed. If a design problem arose, our quality control team would jump in and help implement appropriate measures. We were able to respond like this in a very smooth way.[27]

Lastly, Toyota embarked on initiatives to reduce costs. For one, it used the same platform and shared parts where possible, to lower design and production costs. The same platform was used in three types of vehicle—trucks, minivans, and sport utility vehicles. It also limited the number of IMV models to five (see Figure 3.5 for photos of the five models) by incorporating the market preferences of each country at the planning stage and minimizing the changes in specifications for each country.

Producing at overseas plants rather than in high-cost Japan is a major cost saving in itself. Although doing away with initial production in Japan was a first, it eliminated the cost of duplicating the process in the producing countries. Bypassing Japan had an additional cost benefit. Cars designed on the assumption that they would be produced first in a Japanese factory included parts that could not be produced in local factories overseas and had to be imported, raising procurement costs. The IMV project eliminated this cost as well.

The project achieved additional economies of scale by using the four main assembly plants in Thailand, Indonesia, South Africa, and Argentina as the export bases for supplying markets in 140 countries. This is what enabled the IMV to achieve the second largest volume annually in overseas production (520,000 units) in just 17 months. IMV cars produced in these four centers were exported to countries in Asia, Europe,

FIGURE 3.5 The five IMV vehicles: (a) *Hilux* Single Cab, (b) *Hilux* Extra Cab, (c) *Hilux* Double Cab, (d) *Innova* Minivan, and (e) *Fortuner* SUV

(a)

(b)

(c)

(d)

(e)

Photos courtesy of Toyota Motor Corporation.

Africa, Oceania, Central and South America, and the Middle East, as shown in Figure 3.6. Plants in India, the Philippines, and Malaysia manufactured vehicles for their respective domestic markets.

FIGURE 3.6 The four IMV production centers and the product destination areas.

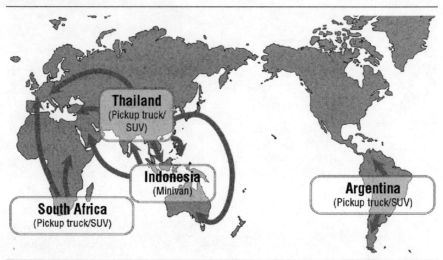

Source: Toyota Motor Corporation Sustainability Report 2006, 22, from Toyota company web site, www.toyota.co.jp/en/environmental_rep/06/download/pdf/e_report06.pdf (accessed April 2007).

Conclusion

Impossible goals are not just inspirational guideposts at Toyota. They become achievable because they are defined by a creative culture that both seeks continuous improvement and undertakes revolutionary change. The "frame-breakers" in the organization, such as Yasuda, recognize when incremental improvement is at a pivotal point and are willing to take risks even under intense criticism and pervasive pessimism because they believe it is the right way to go. Champions higher up in the organization willing to support the frame-breakers and stand by them, especially when things turn sour, are essential. Akio Toyoda, head of Asia operations at the time, championed the IMV project as a turning point for the company in a new era of transnational business, stepping in at a crucial stage to keep the process moving.

Producing the IMV in Thailand, Indonesia, Argentina, and South Africa for sale in more than 140 markets meant the vehicles had to satisfy design safety regulations in each of those markets. By September 2003, the accumulation of compliance requirements had resulted in so many design changes, the design team could not meet the schedule. Just as many people began to concede that a postponement of commercial production was inevitable, Akio Toyoda stepped in. As Yasuda recollected:

> He took responsibility for everything, including vehicles that would be produced in Thailand but sold in Europe, so we could just go ahead and do what needed to be done. He was very persistent. People who were practically at the point of meltdown found a second wind, and the younger employees were ready again for a challenge. I remember the scene vividly and its still impresses me.[28]

Reflecting on that time, Akio Toyoda said he would have assumed full responsibility with headquarters for failure of the project, because even a failure would have been a huge learning opportunity: "I felt that even if the [IMV] ended in failure, there was no better way of learning, because everyone was working so hard."

> While Toyota is often perceived as a success story, we have also had numerous failures. We have used these experiences as learning tools for our people. That's how I was trained. [29]

Toyota has a long history of putting bold ideas into action. Mistakes are inevitable. Setting goals that are bold and seemingly impossible works hand in hand with a culture of experimentation, where the real reward is not success or failure, but the knowledge accumulated from many high-quality learning experiences. In Chapter 4, we examine Toyota's culture of experimentation.

CHAPTER 4

Eagerness to Experiment

"Let's give it a try." "Don't be afraid to make mistakes." These are the mottos that Sakichi Toyoda put into practice as President of Toyoda Automatic Loom Works, and they explain why Toyota the automaker has been an experimenter since the day it began. It was this sentiment that drove Toyota to ship two prototype cars to the United States in 1957. Then President of Toyota Motor Sales Company, Ltd. in Japan, Shotaro Kamiya, was under no illusions about the company entering the U.S. market:

> Even if our cars don't quite measure up at the moment, we don't have time to just stand around and watch. We need a bridgehead. Initially, we may experience some setbacks in entering the market, but all the time we'll be gaining precious experience and gradually improving our business performance.[1]

Kamiya knew from the start that their bridgehead model, the *Toyopet Crown* (Figure 4.1(a)), might take a beating. Sure enough, it could not handle U.S. long-distance highway conditions because the body was too heavy and the car lacked power and stability at high speeds. As a result, exports were halted and unsold inventory withdrawn. But 10 years after this initial setback, Toyota was exporting more cars to the United States than to any other country. *Corona* (Figure 4.1(b)) sales in the United States shot up from 3,800 units in 1964 to 40,700 units in 1967.

FIGURE 4.1   (a) The *Toyopet Crown* (1957) and (b) *Corona* (1964).

(a)

(b)

Photo (a) courtesy of Toyota Motor Sales, U.S.A., Inc. Vehicle in photo (b) owned by the Toyota Automobile Museum.

Eiji Toyoda, who became President of Toyota in 1967, reflected on their initial foray into the U.S. market:

> It was a wild risk to take, but the timing was pretty good. Our initial bad experience merely strengthened our determination to make cars that would sell in the States. We knew that TMS [Toyota Motor Sales, U.S.A.] would collapse if we didn't have decent products to sell. The first time we tried, we failed. So we took up the challenge and tried again, redoubled our efforts, and the second time we succeeded. . . . In the end, the risk was worth taking.[2]

The explorer mindset goes hand in hand with experimentation. Setting impossible goals encourages Toyota to try new things, reach out for new customers, and move its operations to new countries. However, having this mindset and actually following through on it are two different matters. The force of experimentation drives Toyota to act on impossible goals, but in a highly disciplined way. Experimentation is the way one tests a hypothesis when there is no assurance that it is correct, and it enables learning from the failures as well as the successes. By experimenting, Toyota learns what works and what does not work, gains insights about customers and technology, and develops new processes and practices that help the company continue its journey of discovery. Toyota people consider themselves to be in the business of discovering something better, so they are constantly on the lookout for things that challenge the status quo.

Current President Katsuaki Watanabe contrasted how lofty ambitions force people to break mold and explore, while easier goals do not encourage exploring or taking on new challenges. From his experience, he noted:

> Employees can easily improve 5 to 10 percent. This is why I don't like goals that can be measured as 100 percent complete or not. I prefer setting challenging goals where people achieve less [than 100 percent] and evaluate how they tried achieving them, even if they did not make it in time.[3]

Zenji Yasuda, former Toyota Senior Managing Director, stressed how Toyota's goals are directive but not restrictive, allowing employees to aim their creative energy in whatever direction they deem appropriate. According to Yasuda:

Watanabe's "car that makes air cleaner" goal is fittingly vague. If he makes it more concrete, employees won't be able to exercise their full potential. The vague nature of this goal confers freedom to the researchers to open new avenues of exploration, procurement to look for new and unknown suppliers who possess needed technology, and sales to consider the next steps needed to sell such products.[4]

The goals may be audacious, but the experimentation is limited in scale and pragmatic. The *Prius* hybrid is the most recent example of this audacity combined with the discipline of experimentation that is the Toyota Way.

Development of the Prius illustrates how the discipline of experimentation at Toyota is partial and incremental, but also thorough. Experimentation is serious business at Toyota, with the huge investment of time and money in hybrid technology as testament. Why did it invest so much money and effort in hybrid cars when most of their competitors considered the hybrid system an unproven technology of questionable market appeal? Toyota began selling the Prius in Japan as early as 1997 and introduced it to the U.S. market in 2000. At the time, the company was keenly aware of the coming transition to alternative power-train technologies, and knowing that it could only provide a partial solution did not deter it. For Toyota, the partial solution achieved through experimentation is a meaningful endeavor because it can lead to a better solution.

The solution that Toyota and other automakers were seeking had to address concerns about environmental pollution and the conservation of resources. In the early 1990s, automakers were confronting the fear that without a crucial, technological breakthrough in fuel efficiency, the automobile had no future. Toyota set up what it called the G21 project in 1993, to develop a new type of car for the twenty-first century that was both environmentally friendly and user friendly. The G21 team first came up with a comfortable four-seat car that was fully equipped with power features and provided a 50-percent improvement in fuel efficiency. But Toyota executives rejected this prototype. They said the car concept was "all right." But a 50-percent increase in fuel economy was not enough. This was their formal response: "Your aim for the car of the twenty-first century is too low. If that's the best you can do, the project should be cancelled."[5]

Then Executive Vice President in charge of research and development (R&D), Akihiro Wada, demanded a 100-percent improvement in fuel economy, which was unachievable with the most advanced gasoline or diesel engine technology or even fuel cell technology, which was still in its infancy. "The only way past this limitation was the hybrid car," recalled Takeshi Uchiyamada, the leader of the G21 team.[6] The new target to double the achievement in fuel economy left Uchiyamada no choice but to tap the still uncertain and untested hybrid technology that was in the research phase at Toyota. And he didn't have much time, because an additional target set by the executive board was to showcase the G21 concept car at the Tokyo Motor Show in 1995.

With no choice but to push ahead with uncertain technology, failures had to be expected. The engine in the first Prius prototype wouldn't even start. When it finally did, the car only moved a few hundred yards down the test track before coming to a stop. Later on, the battery pack shut down when it became too hot or too cold. Nevertheless, the company was determined to go forward with an unproven technology, and do it entirely in-house. "We put everything into the development of this car," recalled Uchiyamada.[7] In the end, it took 1,000 Toyota personnel and $1 billion to develop the first Prius (see Figure 4.2).

The experimentation process at Toyota, in pursuit of impossible goals such as the Prius, was governed by routines and practices as described next. These are the tools or "hardware" of experimentation, and they reflect Toyota's underlying values, the "software" of experimentation that makes it practical and meaningful.

FIGURE 4.2 The *Prius* models: (a) first generation released in Japan only (1997), (b) second generation (2001), and (c) third generation (2003).

(a)

(b)

(c)

Source: Vehicle in photo (a) owned by the Toyota Automobile Museum. Other photos courtesy of Toyota Motor Corporation.

Experimentation Hardware: The Eight-Step and A3 Processes

Toyota's eagerness to experiment is embedded in the problem-solving routines or processes that have become a normal part of everyday business. The company evolved the Plan-Do-Check-Act (PDCA) model (shown here), which is a generic, continuous improvement process practiced widely throughout the business world, into the eight-step and A3 reporting processes, which are unique to Toyota. These are both an expression of the culture at Toyota, in which problem solving is considered to be a critical capability that is implanted in all employees early in their careers through rigorous training.

- *Plan:* Develop an action plan
- *Do:* Put solutions into action
- *Check:* Verify results
- *Act:* Make necessary adjustments to the action plan and solutions

According to the Senior Managing Director in charge of Human Resource Management, Akio Matsubara:

> Up until an employee's tenth year with the company, we repeatedly administer a three-stage training process designed to develop problem-solving skills. All Toyota employees, domestic or overseas, learn problem-solving skills as the basis of Toyota's fundamental approach to getting work done. Toyota's philosophy is that, when an employee solves a problem, they make a contribution to corporate policies that ultimately are connected to user satisfaction. We inculcate our employees with the idea that learning to solve problems well is the absolute minimum requirement for success at Toyota.[8]

The eight-step process, referred to as the Toyota Business Practices (TBP), helps employees develop the necessary problem-solving skills. According to former President Fujio Cho, TBP is a "standard and a common language for all at Toyota."[9] The eight steps are:

1. Clarify the problem

2. Break down the problem

3. Set a target

4. Analyze the root cause

5. Develop countermeasures

6. See countermeasures through

7. Monitor both results and processes

8. Standardize successful processes

The A3 reporting process is named for the 11 × 17 inch size paper known in Japan as the A3. Only the most essential information needed to solve a problem is summarized on this one sheet of paper and communicated throughout the company. A3 paper was the largest size that would fit into a facsimile machine, which was the common method of communication within Toyota until the advent of the personal computer. A lot of information can be condensed onto a sheet of A3-size paper (see Figure 4.3), but simplified in A3 form, the information

FIGURE 4.3   Conceptual A3 proposal for the IMV project.

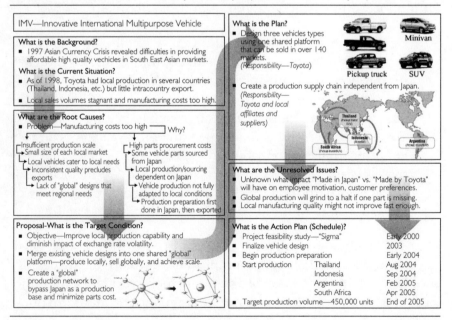

flows according to the problem-solving process, from "problem definition and description" in the top left corner to "future steps" in the bottom right corner (see Figure 4.4).

The eight-step process and the A3 reporting process lay out the path for employees who are challenging the status quo, testing a hypothesis, and discovering what works and what doesn't work. Toyota has discovered that the most practical way to realize mission impossible is to think deep but act small, taking measured steps, and never giving up—the quintessential traits of an experimenter. What sets Toyota apart from other companies as an experimenter is the way it thinks in this process and organizes it, as follows:

- Think of the "objective of the objective"
- Break down large, complex problems into smaller or more concrete problems

FIGURE 4.4   Basic structure and flow of the A3 report.

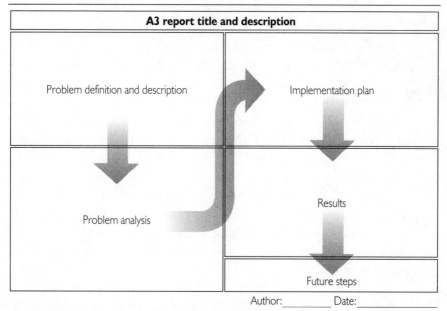

Adapted from Jeffrey Liker and David Meier, *The Toyota Way Fieldbook: A Practical Guide for Implementing Toyota's 4Ps* (New York: McGraw-Hill, 2006), 381.
Source: Developed by authors.

- Start small and take incremental steps
- Repeat experiments even if they fail
- Institutionalize successful practices
- Continue to raise the standard

Each of these practices is applied in new product and business model development at Toyota, as shown with the IMV, Scion, and Lexus.

The Objective of the Objective: The Starting Point of an A3 Analysis

Many of the Toyota managers we interviewed emphasized that the most important step within the eight-step process is the first—to clarify the problem—which involves clarifying the ultimate objective in relation to the more immediate aims. Toyota employees are trained to think about the true objective, or the "objective of the objective." Executive Vice President Akio Toyoda recalled how he was trained in the A3 reporting process in his youth, and he emphasized the importance of the objectives:

> One management tool that helps us to always be aware of this value is the discipline of summarizing things on a single sheet of A3-size paper. An A3 always began with an explanation of the background—why the topic was being brought up at that particular time under that particular theme. Next came the objective. The objective should have the public and society in mind. Otherwise, the managers would ask things like, "Do you really expect to be a full-fledged member of this company with the kind of objective you've written down?" When you do this [A3 process], you really need to think through what the true objective is. Senior associates would be critical of us in a severe but constructive way, pointing out the need to have clear, concisely thought-out objectives.[10]

Development of the Scion as a new business model provides a useful example of how thinking about the objective of the objective actually works. The stated objective of launching the Scion in the United States was to attract young customers. Another objective, however, was to change Toyota's sales process, which ranked low in terms of customer satisfaction. Customers were complaining about the complicated options packages and the long and tedious price negotiation process. Toyota realized that reshaping its sales operation would take time, given its size, its history of success, the risks involved with failure, and the lack of incentive among dealers to change.

Yet another objective of launching Scion was to shorten Toyota's product development process. To achieve this objective, the executive in charge of product development mandated the team to develop the *bB*, later adapted for the U.S. market as the Scion *xB*, at half the development cost of similar cars. This forced the team to eliminate expensive prototyping and make extensive use of computer simulations instead. As a result, the bB was developed in just 15 months, rather than the usual 24 months. These examples show how Toyota chooses the most realistic approach to changing Toyota. After experimenting with change to develop the Scion, they were able to transfer whatever improvements this yielded to the rest of the company.

Development of the Innovative International Multipurpose Vehicle (IMV) is another example of how thinking about the objective of the objective yields greater results. The IMV started as a response to the simple question: how can Toyota lower the sales price of its *Hilux* pickup truck and the Toyota Utility Vehicle (TUV)? The Hilux and the minivan series TUV had been developed for several Southeast Asian countries such as Thailand, Indonesia, the Philippines, and Malaysia. Rigorous analysis of why these vehicles did not sell more outside the region led to analysis of root causes and ultimately, to development of what would later become the IMV project by Zenji Yasuda, who was Director of Overseas Planning Operations at the time. Yasuda said the idea for the IMV first surfaced in 1998:

> We first thought about using common parts for TUVs and the Hilux. The idea came from an unexpected source.

I had begun to wonder why Ford was able to sell its *F150* [pickup truck] at such a low price. Hiroyuki Watanabe and Kazuo Okamoto told me that it was because the F150 was selling at 750,000 units annually. If we could sell 750,000 vehicles, we could also make them affordable. But we were making too few vehicles in each country so there was no way we could keep costs down. The IMV concept came together out of this wrangling amongst the three of us as we tackled this challenge.[11]

Yasuda, Hiroyuki Watanabe, who was director of product planning, and Kazuo Okamoto as director of engineering, all pursued the objective of the objective to understand how they could sell more of these vehicles. They determined that the hidden objective was to provide customers in industrializing countries with better products at reasonable prices, even though consumers in the region were hardly in a buying mood after the Asian Financial Crisis of 1997 had sent local currency values plummeting.

Breaking Down the Problem

After identifying the true objective, Yasuda and his colleagues asked what else would make a car expensive besides low manufacturing volumes and varied platform designs and parts. They broke down the larger problem into smaller, more concrete issues and pinpointed the specific cause of each. This kind of questioning ultimately led to countermeasures such as deciding not to do final assembly in Japan, which decreased the production of components where manufacturing costs were higher. They also increased local sourcing by concentrating production of the more expensive components to one or two countries.

In the second half of 2000, IMV project leaders initiated a survey called "IMV Sigma" to identify all possible problems they might encounter implementing their new plan. Once every two months, more than 50 people representing every function in the project, including representatives from

Thailand, Indonesia, Argentina, and South Africa, gathered for a two-hour meeting to list and analyze issues concerning every aspect of the IMV project. They identified all the problems arising from platform integration and decided on a product strategy to meet market needs with limited variation. They also conducted surveys to confirm the capabilities of local plants and suppliers in countries that were likely to become production centers, checked local and international transportation infrastructures, and identified possible problems in international logistics management.

Every function and local unit that would be involved in the IMV project was invited to these meetings, regardless of whether the particular issues directly affected them or not. Yasuda considered it critical that every function in the project be represented and that local operations understand all the potential problems they might encounter. He called the meeting "Sigma" with reference to its meaning as the "summation" of ideas and opinions from the various viewpoints, from product development and production to procurement.[12] Throughout this process, Toyota was breaking down the problem into manageable pieces and conducting thorough analysis, while sharing and developing an integrated understanding of a large and complex project.

Start Small and Take Incremental Steps

A historically proven approach to experimentation is to start small and take incremental steps. Toyota's launch of Scion in the United States reflected this thinking. The launch (Figure 4.5) was executed using a cascade approach: first in California in June 2003, then in the South and on the East Coast in February 2004, and finally in the Midwest, or central region of the country, in June 2004. As the leading market for automakers and the most receptive to new things, California was the ideal place to introduce the Scion. It was also the easiest place for Toyota Motor Sales, U.S.A. (TMS) to implement a new sales policy, with only 105 dealerships and many of them in close proximity to TMS headquarters. The company allowed for an eight-month

FIGURE 4.5   The cascade launch of the Scion brand in the United States.

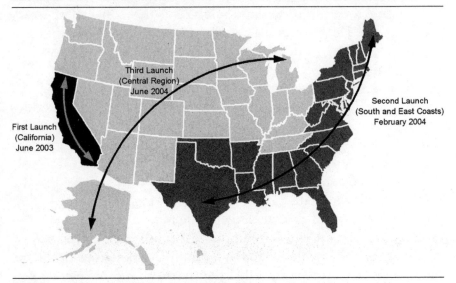

Source: Emi Osono, "The Birth of Scion: Can Toyota Attract Young Customers?" (ICS case no. A040010E, Hitotsubashi University, Tokyo, 2004), 30.

interval between the first launch in California and the second in the South and on the East Coast.

During that time, Toyota conducted thorough marketing research to find out how customers had become aware of the Scion, how it was being sold and delivered, and what customers thought about the overall experience of discovering, buying, and owning one. Along the way, Toyota learned what worked and what didn't and made many incremental improvements.

Repeat Experiments Even if They Fail

Scion was not Toyota's first foray into the youth market. Two other experiments preceded it. The first was the Will brand in Japan, launched under an initiative called the Virtual Venture Company (VVC). The VVC was the project of a group of companies from different industries, focused on developing innovative products and services. Toyota launched a VVC project to develop cars that appealed to young customers. To do this, it set up a VVC design office in August, 1998 in Tokyo, rather than at Toyota headquarters in Aichi Prefecture. Toyota wanted the VVC project to ignore established customs and routines and concentrate on creative innovation. VVC took charge of product planning, while development was handled by the Engineering Department at headquarters. Three Will brand models (shown in Figure 4.6) were launched in the initiative. They attracted a lot of attention because of their unique design and a pricing system that combined fixed fee and charges for distance driven, which was tracked by Toyota through its G-book in-car communication system. That attention, however, did not translate into sales; the initiative was dissolved, and the last Cypha was sold in July 2005.

The second experiment that preceded the Scion was the Genesis project, launched in 1998. A cross-functional team of ethnically diverse employees from marketing and general affairs, was tasked with developing marketing strategies that would convince U.S. youth to buy the *Echo* subcompact, the *Celica* two-door sports coupe, and the *MR Spider* convertible sports coupe, which had been strong sellers in Japan. The Genesis team developed novel marketing techniques, including the sponsorship of concerts, extreme sports events, and advertising specifically targeting the MTV, VH1, and Comedy Central audiences.[13] By November 1999, just two months after these initiatives, the average age of new customers for the newly launched Celica fell from a high of 42 to 33, and for the Echo from 43 to 38.[14] But by 2003, the average age of Celica and Echo customers had risen again, to 37 and 45 respectively. Genesis failed to keep attracting young customers. Toyota had learned that marketing alone would not be enough to corral the U.S. youth market. This gave a stronger voice to TMS when the time came to choose which Scion models would represent the brand.

Institutionalizing Successful Practices

Toyota builds benefit from success and failure. When an experiment is successful, it devotes time and effort to institutionalizing

FIGURE 4.6 The three Will brand models: (a) Will *Vi* (2000), (b) Will *Vs* (2001), and (c) Will *Cypha* (2002).

(a)

(b)

(c)

Photos courtesy of Toyota Motor Corporation.

the successful process and building it into daily work routines. When an experiment fails, it learns from the experience, modifies the plan, and tries again.

In the case of the Lexus, the Fireside Chat meeting was institutionalized as a regular practice. It began as a set of meetings between the heads of the TMS Lexus Division and Lexus dealers, initiated when sales had stagnated in the mid 1990s as the yen appreciated against the dollar. The objective of the meetings was to ease the minds of dealers by disclosing the company's plans for surviving the crisis in sales. Toyota discovered that a candid exchange of opinion in small groups was very effective as a method of communication and building relationships with the Lexus dealers. It called these face-to-face discussions "Fireside Chats," the term President Franklin D. Roosevelt had used to describe his radio broadcasts to the nation during the Great Depression. Toyota began to hold its own fireside chats once a year between January and February. The head of the Lexus Division at TMS and operational executives would visit the CEOs and other executives of up to 20 dealerships in each area to discuss anything and everything face-to-face.

In the case of the Scion, Toyota consulted with the dealers to find out what practices worked and institutionalized those practices. The Scion field office had found that some dealers were communicating more effectively with young customers by assigning a few young associates to Internet marketing, and this was subsequently recommended to other dealers. The field office had also discovered that some dealers were carrying cars preequipped with accessories and displaying them as product samples, even though the official Scion policy was to install customized accessories after the car was bought. Toyota realized that preloading accessories gave customers a better visual image of the product, allowing them to make a more informed purchasing choice. These practices were not made official for Scion dealers, but sharing them as recommendations allowed Toyota to gently institutionalize such successful new practices while ensuring dealers the freedom to discover what worked best for them.

By establishing successful practices as new standards, Toyota ensures that they are shared throughout the organization. This sharing increases the chance that another level of continuous improvement will emerge somewhere in the organization. In contrast, many companies do not put enough time and effort into embedding effective new practices into their processes. By not institutionalizing something that is known to have worked, it becomes lost organizational memory, resulting in wasteful reinvention of the wheel. The difference in organizational capability in a company like Toyota that institutionalizes new practices by building them into daily routines, compared with a company that does not, becomes more significant over the long term (see Figure 4.7).

Continue to Raise the Standard

While Toyota institutionalizes what works, it does not assume that those new practices are effective forever. Both the eight-step TBP and the A3 reporting processes emphasize the importance of monitoring the effectiveness of a successful practice. In the case of the Scion, Toyota management established a new

FIGURE 4.7 The two conceptual trajectories of improving organizational capability: institutionalizing successful new practices versus not doing so.

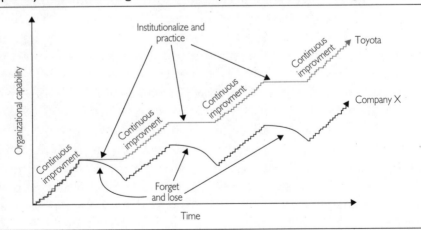

practice of providing accessories only in response to customer requests. The dealers were also told not to "push-sell" against the customer's will. These practices proved very successful, with many customers accessorizing their vehicles online before picking them up at the dealership. But management was also flexible in allowing dealers to accessorize display models for the customer's benefit. As Jim Farley, the former leader of the Scion team at TMS, observed: "Scion is a laboratory, a work in progress that will continue to evolve along with the quick-changing demands of a new generation of consumer. . . . Where we are today may be far from where we will be tomorrow."[15]

Toyota's leaders were saying that the company would never be satisfied with its achievements. In personal communication, they told us that not doing anything would be the worst thing for the company. Naomi Ishii, Group Manager at the Toyota Institute, emphasized the importance of always raising the bar:

> Once we solve a problem and reach a new level we have to raise our standards, otherwise they deteriorate as the environment changes and new problems arise. . . . When new problems suddenly become visible, we have to reconstruct our indicators and renew our objectives [and raise the bar]. If we don't do this, then after ten years, Scion will have lost all meaning. The same is true for Lexus.[16]

Speaking of Lexus, when the brand was launched in Japan in 2005, a new standard for truly personalized service was enacted and described as "selfless devotion to hospitality." Toyota created the new standard by building showrooms that looked more like luxury hotels than dealerships. Lexus dealers were offered a stay at the Ritz-Carlton Hotel in Osaka to get a feel for the level of service they would be expected to offer their customers. In addition, they spent two days at Fuji Lexus College located at the foot of Mt. Fuji near Tokyo, to study the core elements of the hospitality philosophy. They return to the college twice a year for a refresher course on hospitality and to share best practices with Lexus dealers around the globe.[17]

Experimentation Software: Values

The preceding practices constitute the hardware of experimentation. The values and principles supporting these logical routines are the software, and they can be traced back to the founders of Toyota. The values expressed by Sakichi Toyoda in his mottos for the Toyoda Automatic Loom Works, "Let's give it a try" and "Don't be afraid to make mistakes," are integral to the corporate culture that enables experimentation.

In this section, we show how five values in particular serve as the enablers of experimentation: (1) taking decisive action, (2) tolerating failure, (3) being honest, (4) doing good, and (5) never giving up.

Taking Decisive Action

The mindset of experimentation requires a willingness to take decisive action to produce results. Toyota employees are constantly encouraged to get their hands dirty with the motto, "If you're 60 percent sure, take action." Taking action and not succeeding is considered okay, because doing nothing is worse. The high worth attached to decisive action originates with the founders, Sakichi and Kiichiro Toyoda, who were fond of saying:

Before you say you can't do something, try it.

—Sakichi Toyoda[18]

An engineer who has the ability to criticize but does not take action is not able to make cars.

—Kiichiro Toyoda[19]

The value of decisive action has been reinforced over time through the practice of Plan, Do, Check, Act (PDCA). As part of the continuous improvement routine used extensively at Toyota since the late 1950s, PDCA is aimed at facilitating action and producing results, in a culture of "learning by doing."

Tolerating Failure

Toyota has a high tolerance for failure. In fact, failure is viewed as an everyday event at the company, a sentiment originating with the founders about learning the hard way. As Sakichi Toyoda recalled:

> I have experienced many twists and turns in my life; many hard fought battles and half won skirmishes. For the most part, I have seen more failures than successes.[20]

Toyota does not just tolerate failure—it embraces failure as a mechanism for learning, recognizing that you have to fail to progress. When something goes wrong, it is viewed as an opportunity to take corrective action and learn from that experience. Akio Toyoda described his experience with the IMV in such terms:

> I felt that if this [IMV Project] failed, the failure itself would be a huge learning opportunity. That is to say, while Toyota is often perceived as a success story, we have also had numerous failures. We have used these experiences as learning tools for our people. That's how I was trained.[21]

Likewise, IMV proponent Zenji Yasuda recalled one incident early in his Toyota career when he made a very costly mistake. After he tendered his own letter of resignation to his boss, he was surprised by what ensued:

> When I brought him the letter, he did not even look at it. He told me to consider it an expensive "learning lesson." After that [costly mistake], his attitude toward me never changed.[22]

This view of failure supporting the expansive force of experimentation is complementary with the integrative force of up-and-in human resource management, described in detail in Chapter 8. Under this management system, Toyota invests in people with a long-term view, understanding that its investment will pay cumulative returns years later. In addition, the broader view of failure provides opportunities for employees to improve their skills and develop their potential over the long term. Toyota allocates substantial resources to increase employee capability, described in Chapter 9. Furthermore, as Senior Managing Director Akio Matsubara pointed out, this system provides opportunities for all employees to experiment, learn, and grow, allowing them to develop their potential, regardless of age, background, or function:

> It is inevitable that some associates will be able to deliver results in certain circumstances and others will not. However, we believe it is important to consider that those who did not succeed with one set of circumstances, might succeed with another.[23]

Being Honest

Toyota relies on the results of experimentation to learn what works and what doesn't, but this process cannot succeed if employees feel they have to hide bad news or fabricate positive results. Senior Toyota Advisor, Yoshio Ishizaka, described why the culture of experimentation works in the context of PDCA:

> From my 40 years of experience with PDCA at Toyota, [I can say that] it's about not telling lies. This may not be so obvious, but it's all about being honest. Toyota culture emphasizes honesty.[24]

The problem-solving processes described in this chapter— the PDCA model, the eight-step process, and the A3 reporting process—are built on the assumption that problems, errors, and flaws will always exist. A unique feature of Toyota's work culture is the way it encourages all employees to admit that problems exist, to make them visible, to see them as opportunities for improvement, to identify their root causes, and to take concrete countermeasures to prevent problems recurring over the long-term. At the same time, this culture embraces the notion that to err is human—people make mistakes and have weaknesses and limitations. The company finds that the most constructive way to address these limits is by encouraging employees to be honest about their mistakes and weaknesses.

When a problem arises, whether in sales or on the factory floor, Toyota employees are trained in the eight-step process to pinpoint the problem with their own eyes and continually ask "why" until the root cause is found. Taiichi Ohno, creator of the Toyota Production System and originator of the famous "five-why analysis" (ask "why" five times about every problem to identify its root cause), urged his associates to pursue the facts by seeing things firsthand, rather than relying on cold, statistical data compiled by someone else. "Data, of course, is important," he would often say, "but I put the greatest emphasis on facts."[25] Data can be skewed to reflect a variety of interpretations, but facts are facts. They do not lie; they keep you honest.

Doing Good

Trying new things and staying ahead of the times form the basic rationale for experimentation. Sakichi Toyoda, when he founded the Toyoda Automatic Loom Works, saw these practices not only as a motivating force, but as a duty of employees that enabled the company to be of service to humankind. For Sakichi, the ultimate purpose of the company was not only to make money but to do good for society. Former sales chief in Japan, Shotaro Kamiya, echoes this thinking:

> We have to avoid the foolishness of working for Toyota's profit alone, no matter what, recognizing that the company is only one element in the construction of society, just as Japan is only one member in the community of nations. We must strive to be in tune with society both in Japan and internationally.[26]

Sakichi Toyoda's values and convictions were codified as the "Five Main Principles of Toyoda" on October 30, 1935, commemorating the fifth anniversary of his death. They are translated into English as follows:

1. Always be faithful to your duties, thereby contributing to the company and to the overall good.
2. Always be studious and creative, striving to stay ahead of the times.
3. Always be practical and avoid frivolousness.
4. Always strive to build a homelike atmosphere at work that is warm and friendly.
5. Always have respect [for the existence of a higher spiritual being], and remember to be grateful at all times.[27]

Known today as the "Toyoda Precepts," these principles constitute the foundation of Toyota and the manner in which it functions daily. They serve as the guidelines for company policy and activities, as well as management and staff behavior. The current President, Katsuaki Watanabe, carries a small sheet of paper around with him that lists the five principles, and he makes frequent reference to them in his speeches. In a recent interview, he commented on the enduring relevance of the Toyoda Precepts:

As president, I sometimes quote the Toyoda Precepts when I make a speech or public address. They are old words, but their content is very applicable today. When I was asked to become president, I thought about the various resources that form the backbone of Toyota, and I invariably came back to the Precepts. That's why I carry them around with me on a small sheet of paper and read them occasionally. For example, the [third] principle, "Always be practical and avoid frivolousness," tells us to eliminate *muda*, *mura*, and *muri* [waste, unevenness, and overburden], which is the fundamental thinking behind the Toyota Production System.

This leads to continuous searching to reveal problems and never being satisfied with the status quo.[28]

Never Giving Up

By their very nature, experiments at the outset draw more naysayers than believers because there is no assurance of success. There is also no assurance that they will be designed or performed correctly to reveal the best result. Even though Toyota is highly tolerant of failure, it's still not easy for employees to initiate an experiment, and it's even more difficult to shut down an experiment that is ridden with setbacks. The key that determines whether worthwhile experiments will have a reasonable chance of any measure of success is the Spartan determination and commitment of project leaders, who never give up in the face of adversity.

Former President of Toyota Motor Sales, U.S.A., Yoshimi Inaba, stood his ground in support of the Scion experiment in the face of increasing resistance from both headquarters in Japan and the American dealers. He recalled the experience:

> In reality, there were only a small number of true believers in the Scion at TMS. The majority were traditionalists. This is always the case. I think this was true at Toyota even in Japan. The Japanese side was even less believing. It was probably because we were so confident that we could really make it happen that we never gave up trying to convince Japan. Just starting the Scion [project] was no easy task, and if we were to try to start [such a project] now or on any other occasion, I'm not sure we could.

> After communicating with the dealers over and over again, some opinion leaders among them began to visualize the idea of the Scion, and their reaction changed to, "Hey, this is going to work." But other dealers remained either opposed or skeptical. After all, it was a difficult proposition for the dealers because their margins [from selling

new cars] would come out to about half of what they normally were.[29]. . . By discussing dealers' concerns over and
over again until we had ironed everything out, we gradually attained, little by little, a kind of alignment with them.
I believe this is how it happened.[30]

One of the leaders of the IMV experiment, Zenji Yasuda,
also had to overcome obstacles and opposition throughout
the life span of the project. While it was sometimes difficult
to get through everyone's negativity, he never gave up, and his
persistence paid off. Here are his reflections on how the project
got started and where it would end up in the future:

> Those who aggressively supported our idea [in the begin-
> ning] were definitely a minority. . . . My sense was that one-
> third of the people felt it was new and exciting, one-third
> came along for the ride, and one-third strongly opposed
> the idea and felt it should be tossed out.[31]

> When will the IMV project be completed? I would say
> "never." The reason we have had good results so far is
> because [the first group of] people worked so hard. They will
> eventually hand over the reins to others. Right now, I'm con-
> fident that the new people who take over will continue the
> work and take the project to the next stage and beyond.[32]

Toyota's eagerness to experiment forces the company to
explore the world outside, to take risks, and to tolerate failure.
It never gives up. This quality of persistence is a key criterion
for evaluating employees that is unique to Toyota, as discussed
in Chapter 8, where we look at the up-and-in system of human
resource management.

Conclusion

In this chapter, we have looked at Toyota's eagerness to experiment as an expansive force operating in the company, and how
this is practiced and integrated with other forces. The mindset

of experimentation is supported by a culture that tolerates and embraces failure as a learning experience, allowing the company to move incrementally while also pushing it to explore extremes in the search for new possibilities. Toyota innovates and improves in small steps, incrementally, using tools like PDCA, eight-step, and A3 reporting routines. At the same time, the force of experimentation occasionally builds up to produce a huge leap, as with the Lexus, the IMV global production platform, and the Scion. These leaps seem radical and counterintuitive in a company where incremental improvement is ingrained. They seek change boldly rather than step-by-step. Yoshimi Inaba shared his thoughts about this contradiction:

> Toyota, the epitome of gradualism, was an unlikely place for the Lexus to be born. However, in 1989 it started. Then, in 2003 the Scion started, which was a surprise even for me if I look at it objectively. These initiatives made Toyota unique and enhanced the creativity of the organization. I would like us to have such an initiative once or twice a decade.[33]

Experimentation requires a shared set of values among the employees revolving around decisive action, tolerance for failure, honesty, social duty, and persistence. These soft skills are built into the working culture at Toyota through continuous communication and practice. It has taken Toyota years to inculcate these values in its workforce, in a process guided by the initial direction set by the company founders. Thus, we have identified the founders' philosophies, which we describe in Chapter 6, as the first of the three integrative forces acting on Toyota that play a critical role in the culture of experimentation.

Toyota's way of combining the hard and soft tools of experimentation differentiate it from other companies. In Chapter 5, we examine Toyota's unique combination of the global and the local as the driver of experimentation and international success.

CHAPTER 5

Local Customization

Toyota began as a small, local company, producing its first automobiles in the Mikawa region near Nagoya in the provincial town of Koromo-cho. The town eventually renamed itself Toyota City. The first Toyota passenger car, the *A1* prototype, was produced there in May 1935 followed by the model *AA* in September 1936 (Figure 5.1). One month later, the AA was renamed the *Kokusan Toyoda Goh*, meaning "domestically produced Toyota."

Toyota today conducts its worldwide business from the same location, administering 15 plants within Japan, eight of them in its hometown, plus 53 manufacturing companies in 27 countries and regions, selling automobiles in more than 170 markets around the world (as of March 2008). Despite its global presence, Toyota remains a local company at heart. Its headquarters are still in its hometown, and many of its executives boast about being "country folk from Mikawa."[1] When venturing overseas, it tries hard to become a local company, as Akio Matsubara, Senior Managing Director of Human Resource Management, explained:

> When we operate in other countries, we are sensitive to the needs and requirements of the countries and regions we have entered. For example, to get a sense of the true situation on the ground in the United States, we ran a test at NUMMI,[2] in California, a joint venture with GM. After that, we started factory operations in Kentucky. The issue then was how to successfully assimilate into the region. We tried to become an extremely local-friendly company, because in

FIGURE 5.1   (a) The *A1* Prototype and (b) a Toyoda *AA*.

(a)

(b)

Photo (a) courtesy of Toyota Motor Corporation. Vehicle in photo (b) owned by the Toyota Automobile Museum.

many cases our company significantly affects the local economy and the lives of the people in the region in question.[3]

This sensitive approach to local operations is a creative contradiction as Toyota strives to be global and local at the same time and exerts an expansive pressure in the organization. We call this third expansive force "local customization." The process starts with the way Toyota innovates for individual markets. It then rolls these innovations into a global process that benefits every market, while maintaining local preferences and demands. Toyota incorporated local customer tastes into the development and design of the single-platform Innovative International Multipurpose Vehicle (IMV) in Asia, the subcompact *Yaris* in Europe, the youth-oriented Scion, and the full-size *Tundra* pickup truck in the United States. In each case, Toyota developed new products and business models that addressed the demands of new local customers and then globalized local best practices throughout the organization in a process of dissemination that is now centralized at the Global Knowledge Center.

By catering to unique sets of local preferences, Toyota is pushed to new customer targets, new business relationships, new ways of marketing, and new supply chain management systems and process technologies. Like the expansive force of impossible goals and experimentation, local customization also drives Toyota to try new things in response to the demands of local markets around the world.

According to Executive Vice President Tokuichi Uranishi, local customization provides an outlet where local employees can direct their creative energy toward "satisfying the specific needs of customers and fulfilling the aspiration of growing local business." This, he emphasized, was a key difference between Toyota's approach and global standardization:

> Local customization comes first, followed by model integrations, shared platforms, and common parts to reduce complexity. It should not be the other way around, nor should it be at the same time. A global company that surveys every potential market need and chooses one optimal solution will be very efficient, but along the way it sacrifices the creative potential of its employees in the local operations.[4]

Local customization has pushed Toyota out of its comfort zone at home, where it is dominant, and into overseas markets where it has often been the underdog. Doing unconventional things in local markets is a process of discovery for Toyota that leads to new practices and processes.

The Underdog Even at Home

In the 1930s, Toyota was the underdog in its own, domestic automobile market, which was dominated by Ford Motor Company, General Motors Corporation, and other foreign automakers. Japanese consumers were not just curious about foreign-made automobiles, they were buying them up at a furious pace; Ford and Chevrolet models sporting 3,000cc engines topped the list.

It was against this backdrop that Toyoda Automatic Loom Works began preparing to enter the Japanese automobile market. Kiichiro Toyoda, back from a tour of automobile plants in the United States and Europe, had set aside a corner of the loom plant and started developing a small gasoline engine in March 1930. But after several years of trial and error, he decided to make a car with a big engine. "I'm thinking of making a popular car," he said.[5] To Kiichiro, a popular car was the latest, best-selling 3,000cc Ford or Chevrolet. It was an unexpected choice considering the average income level in Japan and the numerous narrow roads that littered the landscape. Rival Japanese automakers Kawasaki, Mitsubishi, Nissan, and Nippon Sharyo had contemplated entering the small passenger-car market with a 1,000cc engine, but none had dared to challenge the imports head-on. History would prove Kiichiro's choice was the right one.

Toyoda Automatic Loom Works announced its first passenger car, the A1 prototype, in May 1935, and started commercial production of the model AA in September 1936. To do so, it had to increase its capitalization to 3 million yen although it was not even a car company yet.[6] This changed in August 1937 with the establishment of Toyota Motor Company, Ltd. Toyota was weak in financial resources because it was not part of the multi-company industrial conglomerates known in Japan as *zaibatsu*.

As Toyota's first President, Kiichiro Toyoda foresaw an increasing sophistication among Japanese consumers in the taste for cars. The AA was the first instance in which Toyota incorporated the sophistication of a local market into the development and design process. While Ford, Chrysler, and Chevrolet continued to ship popular American-designed cars to Japan that were not a good match to local needs, like maneuvering through narrow roads and parking in tight spaces, the AA was the first to break that pattern by offering tighter turning characteristics and additional mirrors to improve visibility. Toyota learned early in its history that local customization pays dividends globally, over the long term.

Customizing the IMV in Asia

In the mid-1970s, Toyota made its first attempt at local customization in the Philippines and Indonesia with its so-called Asian cars. All development and design processes for these low-priced multipurpose vehicles—known as Basic Utility Vehicles (BUVs)—were done locally. Production of the BUV began in the Philippines in November 1976 and in Indonesia in May 1977. In Indonesia, it was called the *Kijang* (Indonesian for "deer"). Producing the Kijang required minimum investment in stamping and other new production equipment, so, overall investment in the local production plant was small. Toyota also encouraged local development of parts manufacturers to reduce the need for expensive parts imports from Japan. To boost productivity and encourage employees to help one another when necessary, the motto on the shop floor was *gotongroyong*, meaning "mutual assistance."[7]

The BUV was the precursor to the launch of the Innovative International Multipurpose Vehicle (IMV) project in September 2002. But developing the IMV was much more challenging because it had to meet the diverse needs of consumers in more than 140 countries in Asia, Europe, Africa, Oceania, Central and South America, and the Middle East. Road conditions, including unpaved roads, varied from country to country. One set of customers might need vehicles that could accommodate large families, while another set wanted to transport building materials or vegetable produce. In Middle Eastern countries, vehicles had to withstand sandstorms, while in Asian countries they had to deal with floods. Toyota also had to consider the rate of diffusion of the automobile in different societies, driving habits, the availability of local repair shops, the capabilities of local dealers, various import restrictions, and local competition.

The IMV incorporated the main preferences of all the major countries in a single platform for three types of vehicle—trucks, minivans, and sport utility vehicles (pictured in Figure 3.5 of Chapter 3). Based on its understanding of the needs of customers in Thailand, Indonesia, the Philippines, South Africa, Argentina, and Saudi Arabia, Toyota designed a platform that broadly addressed the need for a vehicle that was both smooth to drive and rugged enough to handle difficult driving conditions. It produced five IMV models in the four main assembly countries of Thailand, Indonesia, Argentina, and South Africa, while countries such as India, the Philippines, and Malaysia manufactured IMV vehicles for their respective local markets. By using a single platform and limiting the number of models, Toyota minimized the design and production costs of the IMV.

The Challenges and Benefits of Local Customization

The challenges of local customization are the same for every car manufacturer. Success hinges on proper handling of the economics of product development and manufacturing. The chief hurdle is figuring out how to scale vehicle design and manufacturing to yield cost benefits, while satisfying local needs for customization. Toyota achieves both without compromising one or the other. As pointed out in Chapter 2, Toyota enjoys better economies of scale per model than its competitors in the two major markets of Japan and the United States.

However, 14 of its 54 overseas models sell in less than 10 markets (Australia, Canada, China, Hong Kong, New Zealand, Singapore, Taiwan, Thailand, United Arab Emirates, and the United States). These 14 models are *RAV4 EV* (electric vehicle), *Mark II, Alphard, Liteace, WISH, Comfort*, the IMVs (considered one model), Scion *xB*, Scion *tC, Century*, Tundra, *Sequoia, Highlander*, and Lexus *GX*. They account for one-fourth of all Toyota overseas models and were developed for a limited number of countries in order to customize them to local needs, yet they all share chassis frames and have common parts with car models sold in other markets to reduce design complexity and production cost.

As challenging as local customization may be, it has benefits in auto manufacturing. For one thing, it exposes Toyota to the diversity of perspectives it needs to overcome the limitations of its own provincial origins. Learning to understand and accept these differences is the first step in facilitating local customization. Akio Matsubara emphasized the importance of this approach in human resource management:

> In our training courses we try to impress upon people the importance of standing in the shoes of your counterparts [in other countries], and thoroughly studying them, their national spirit and rules [of behavior]. I believe there is no other way . . . . As we become confident in the work we do, I think we tend to impose our own rules on others regardless. These days I am trying to warn against this. We need to be curious, to welcome others' curiosity about us, and to grant each other enough leeway to be able to understand one another as we move forward.[8]

Local customization also exposes Toyota to conditions unheard of in its home market that help it to further stretch the envelope in vehicle engineering. In the mid-1970s Toyota engineers drove vehicles across the Arabian Peninsula in temperatures up to 140° (60°C) to test air conditioners and antidust devices. These tests were instrumental in developing steering wheels and dashboards that could withstand high temperatures and gauges that accurately measured those temperatures rather than mistakenly indicating overheating. These innovations were the foundation for Toyota developing vehicles to meet the unique requirements of the Middle East.

Finally, local customization exposes Toyota to the sophistication of local tastes, as in Europe, where it was a latecomer. In Europe, Toyota discovered how high the bar had already been set by local producers. Virtually all new European cars introduced after the 1979 Frankfurt Motor Show were FF models; front-engine front-wheel drive cars offering excellent handling and driving performance in a refined package of color-coordinated interiors, comfortable seats contoured to snugly fit driver and passengers, and loaded with options. The wide array of competitive products in Europe put Toyota on the defensive. To survive, it had to develop products that met local market demands on all these fronts.[9] They felt a sense of déjà vu. Back in the 1930s, Toyota was the underdog in a Japanese market dominated by foreign imports. Fifty years later, it was the underdog in a European market dominated by superior local producers. Toyota proactively incorporated sophisticated local demands into its products and operations in the European market with development of the Yaris in 1999. The Yaris is to Europe what the AA was to Japan.

Customizing the Yaris for Europe

The Yaris was the first Toyota whose appearance was designed in Europe, by a European designer, specifically for the European market (Figure 5.2). When it was launched, its curvaceous exterior appealed instantly to European tastes. *BusinessWeek* praised the Yaris for its Mediterranean look: "Thanks to its new design studio in southern France, near Nice, Toyota's recent models look distinctly Mediterranean. Its whimsical Yaris, which starts at $12,000, exudes Latin flair with its cute snout and peppy stance."[10]

FIGURE 5.2 (a) The first- and (b) second-generation *Yaris*.

(a)

(b)

Photos courtesy of Toyota Motor Corporation.

In addition to a stylish exterior, the Yaris offered more advanced technology, greater safety, and roomier interiors than its European competitors, setting new benchmarks in its class. Its low emission, fuel-efficient engine was the best in that market segment—a 16-valve engine with intelligent variable-valve timing usually found only in more expensive cars. For safety-conscious

Europeans, the Yaris ushered in a new safety standard for small cars by introducing dual air bags.[11] This level of technology and safety was unusual in the highly cost-competitive class of cars in which the Yaris competed. Consequently, the car was a hit in Europe, competing successfully against the VW *Polo*, the Ford *Fiesta*, the Peugeot *206*, and the Renault *Clio*. After its introduction in 1999, the Yaris broke annual unit sales records six years in a row, with demand continuing to outstrip supply.[12]

Underlying the success of the Yaris is local customization, Toyota style. In Italy, it "fit the Italian car demand profile perfectly," said Norio Kitamura, former President of Toyota Motor Italia.[13] "Nicknamed 'The Little Genius,' it was positioned as a stylish car for a fashionable person living in a trendy city in Italy," he said. Instead of historical and conservative Rome, fashionable Milan was chosen as the launch pad for the Yaris. The press conference invited not only automotive journalists, but also opinion leaders and social trendsetters. One hundred brand-new Yaris cars were lined up in a showroom in the most fashionable part of Milan, and guests were invited to try one out at no cost for three months with the opportunity to buy the vehicle at a specially discounted price. This marketing program was a tremendous success, with 75 percent of the guests eventually buying a Yaris.[14]

In France, Toyota tried to match local preferences by positioning Yaris as a "car built in France by French workers."[15] Cognizant of the French disdain for import brands, Toyota France emphasized the location of the Yaris plant in northern France at Valenciennes. In November 2005, it aired a television commercial showing a large number of workers surrounding a second-generation Yaris, with the message that 1,000 jobs had been created at the Valenciennes factory to produce the new car.

The pan-European tagline for the second-generation Yaris (Figure 5.2b) was "bigsmall" to convince consumers that there was a surprising amount of room inside the compact exterior. Toyota Motor Marketing Europe had advised Toyota France not to translate the tagline and to use it as it was, but French managers argued that the message didn't get through to the

French consumer. Toyota France chose *Vraiment Optimale* (truly optimal) as its tagline, retaining the original concept but putting it in the French vernacular.[16]

In Germany, the Yaris was positioned to win over a new type of customer. In contrast to Toyota's existing German customers, who were typically older, less affluent, and not highly educated, Yaris was aimed at attracting the young, educated, and financially well-off consumer. University students were offered new financing schemes with lower down payment requirements, longer loan periods, and discounted insurance policies that included free repairs.[17]

Customizing the Scion for the United States Youth Segment

The youth segment, especially in the United States, represented a burgeoning market for automakers. At the turn of the century the so-called Generation Y, born between 1980 and 1994, purchased only 5 percent of new cars in the United States but this was expected to grow rapidly, adding 4 million first-time buyers each year until 2010. By then, Generation Y was expected to be the buyer of 25 percent of new small cars sold in the United States, jumping to 40 percent by 2020.[18]

Numerous marketing studies have found Generation Y in the United States to be very different from previous generations. These consumers, especially the women, are more educated than any previous generation. They are more ethnically diverse, with more than one-third represented by nonwhites, and they are optimistic about their income prospects including economic support from their parents. Their overexposure to contemporary marketing techniques makes them more demanding as consumers and more skeptical than other generations about the messages in television commercials and magazine advertisements. They are also more sophisticated in their awareness of technology and their expectations of design, quality, and safety standards in a car. In this generation, the car is a symbol of self-expression for more people than it was for previous generations.[19]

Capturing the interest of this highly attractive segment was not easy for automakers, Toyota included. It was a demography that strived to be different, not only from previous generations, but from one individual to another. It also demanded to be entertained and to be given an opportunity to explore, while expecting hassle-free products and services in addition to the usual product performance criteria. Business as usual was not an option for this group of customers; innovation was the order of the day. Toyota tackled the challenge of capturing this elusive market with the Scion, which forced the company to drastically rethink its conventional business model. This led to new practices and processes in all areas, from new product development, parts logistics and supply systems, to new pricing, marketing, and interaction with the retail customer.

The Custom Features

Toyota based the first generation of Scion cars on the existing *bB* and *ist* models, both previously developed for the Japanese youth segment. The bB was a small, boxy wagon that looked like a World War II ambulance, and the ist was a small hatchback that combined an SUV-like flair with the large wheel wells of a muscle car. The bB and ist models had undergone several minor changes. Bumpers and headlamps were upgraded to make them more crashworthy; tires, braking, and suspension systems were revamped to improve handling, and seat and dashboard materials were given a more luxurious, high-tech look.[20]

Changes in product specifications for the Scion were kept to a minimum to prevent the price from rising. But the vehicle's sound system got a major overhaul under the direction of Scion Chief Engineer, Tetsuya Tada. Market research in the United States had revealed that Generation Y had a serious attachment to its music. Tada conceived the "speakers on tires" concept and argued for a high-performance sound system for the car, ignoring the conventional view that the quality of the sound system should be determined by the level of equipment suited to the Scion's target price range.[21] Toyota tapped a venture company that it had no previous business with to obtain a new semiconductor technology for processing music signals. It combined this technology with the advanced speaker system and noise-absorption materials used in the Lexus, and offered these as standard equipment, with the option of adding a subwoofer. With these changes, the bB and ist were transformed into the Scion *xB* and *xA*, respectively (Figure 5.3).

Scion models xA and xB were launched with few variations, with a choice of body color and transmission type only. Although

FIGURE 5.3 The *Scion* (a) *xA* and (b) *xB*.

(a)

(b)

Photos courtesy of Toyota Motor Sales, U.S.A., Inc.

tuning (modifying the performance and appearance of cars) was broadly practiced among young Japanese car owners, it was limited to a niche group of enthusiasts in the United States. But Tada predicted tuning would prove popular among Generation Y, so the Scion came with a large number of options—up to 40 accessories, compared to 15 for the average Toyota vehicle— allowing customers to personalize their cars. Options included a choice of red or blue floor lights, chrome-plated shift lever knobs, and crystal clear taillights.[22] For the first time in its history, the Toyota Engineering Department shared vehicle drawings with the Specialty Equipment Marketing Association in the United States before the Scion launch to encourage independent accessory manufacturers and tuners (specialists who modify the performance and appearance of cars) to develop accessories for the Scion.[23]

Customizing Operations

Most of the innovations that came out of the Scion project were linked to practices developed during the customization process. They included a new ordering and inventory system, a new pricing scheme, a new dealer interface process, and a new marketing program. These practices were not all necessarily new to the industry, but they were new to Toyota. In hindsight, the Scion project was a major experiment for the company in the most sophisticated youth market in the world—the United States.

With Jim Farley as the first head of the Scion operation, the team experimented with a new ordering and inventory system that was a complete reversal of prevailing practice. Under the new system, purchasers would specify their desired options in advance and wait a few days before picking up their custom vehicle at the dealership. Prior to this system, the customer drove the new car home on the day of purchase with accessories preinstalled. Often those accessories did not fully match customer demands because choice was limited to those accessorized vehicles in stock at the dealership. The project team had discovered, however, that Scion buyers were willing to wait up to seven days to get what they wanted.

Under the new system, dealer inventory was halved to a 15-day supply relative to other Toyota cars. Most of the inventory could remain at port, allowing the dealers to reduce the level of stock on site. In a sense, on-site inventory was now simply for display and didn't have to be shoved out the door to make room for new models. The new system not only reduced overhead costs for the dealer, but also gave the customer complete choice in the customization of their vehicle. The Scion team developed an information system that allowed dealers to track the available inventory at port and replenish out-of-stock accessories as needed and inform the customer which day their accessorized vehicle could be picked up at the dealership.

The new ordering and inventory system also reduced the need for price negotiations to some extent. In the past, dealers would negotiate price on the basis of the stock they had on hand and the demand level in the market—low stock and high demand drove prices up—and customers often had to haggle to get the exact car they wanted at an acceptable price. The same occurred when dealers cleared excess inventory, often using incentives and discounts, leaving customers unconvinced they got a fair deal or the best price. Every marketing report, however, was pointing to the same conclusion: customers, especially young customers, did not like negotiating price to purchase a car. The Scion team decided to go one step further and eliminate price negotiations from the sales process altogether. Instead, they devised a scheme they called "pure pricing" in which dealers set their own retail prices and posted them on the Internet or the storefront, and they honored those prices with the customer. Under pure pricing, no deviation from the published price was allowed. It gave customers advance knowledge of the retail price and made the sales process transparent, reducing customer anxiety about the purchase.

The Scion team also streamlined the dealer interaction with the customer. The previous practice often took four hours as the customer was required to interact first with a receptionist, then a sales associate, followed by the sales manager and the finance manager or store manager, and had to renegotiate the deal each time with each dealer representative. The Scion team asked dealers to assign one specially trained sales consultant to preside over the entire sales process in a separate space in the showroom for consulting with Scion customers. Two additional spaces were set aside for the Scion in the showroom: one, to display the vehicle on a flat panel television screen with accessories in display cases; another labeled the "discovery zone," equipped with personal computers and printers allowing purchasers to customize their own vehicle on the Internet. The Scion space was like a separate dealership within a dealership (Figure 5.4), where potential customers could gather their own information and also have questions answered by specialized sales consultants.

Toyota used the new grassroots marketing approach for the Scion known in the trade as "viral" or "guerrilla" marketing, to

FIGURE 5.4   The Scion dealership within a dealership showroom.

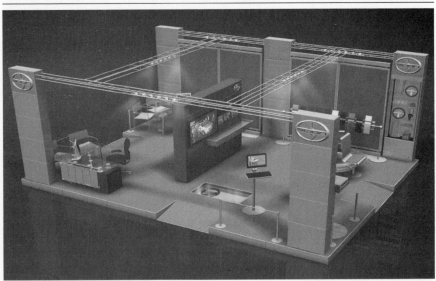

Photo courtesy of Toyota Motor Sales, U.S.A., Inc.

get around the skepticism of Generation Y about conventional mass marketing on television and other media. The objective was to get the word out on the street. The Scion team used multiple, alternative communication channels to insert the brand into the Generation Y lifestyle. One year prior to launching in California, posters featuring slogans like "No Clone Zone" and "Ban Normality" were produced and distributed, and the same images were projected onto buildings at night to stimulate consumer curiosity. The Scion name did not appear anywhere on the posters. There were also test-drive events, like a tent with banners set up near an entrance to the expressway or at hip-hop events. Pamphlets featuring Scion were published as inserts in popular culture magazines like *Urb, Asian Culture*, and *Tokion*. Music CDs, gift certificates for hip-hop apparel brands, and remote-controlled model cars were given out to potential customers who had demonstrated a strong interest in the Scion. By May 2003, two months before the launch of the xA and the xB, 19 percent of the population in California under the age of 35 recognized the Scion brand.[24]

After the launch, the Scion team worked to generate further ways to grab the attention of youth and stimulate their interest in the car. They linked the Scion to popular music, art, and fashion by associating it with nightclub events, tattoo art (Figure 5.5),

FIGURE 5.5 The Scion tattoo.

Photo courtesy of Toyota Motor Sales, U.S.A., Inc.

fashion magazines, break dance tournaments, graffiti painting, street rallies, and music programs on cable TV (see Figure 5.6). They also approached the car performance and appearance tuning culture, sponsoring 17 tuning events in 2003 in cooperation with tuners and accessory makers. On weekends, Scion sales

FIGURE 5.6 Posters of Scion-sponsored events: (a) wall painting and skateboarding exhibition (2003), (b) live music release party (2004), (c) Scion art tour exhibition (2005), and (d) the post neo explosionism art exhibit (2005).

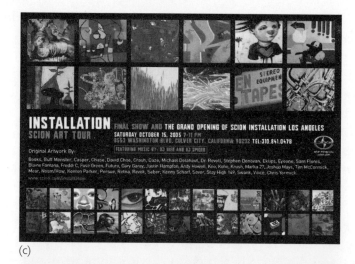

(c)

(d)

Photos courtesy of Toyota Motor Sales, U.S.A., Inc.

associates paraded eight Scions, four xAs and four xBs, through the districts where young people hung out. All these grassroots initiatives were supported by announcements and feature articles on the Scion web site.[25] By September 2003, two months after the launch, brand recognition in California among those under 35 years of age had risen to 53 percent, according to a company-sponsored survey. Two-thirds of respondents in that group said they had seen Scion cars at events or on the road, while 12 percent said they had heard about the vehicle from friends or had read about it in magazines.[26]

Former head of the Scion operation at Toyota, Jim Farley, reflected on the importance of listening to Generation Y in grassroots marketing: "You have to take off your tie and listen to them where they are and on their terms . . . which is why we have gone to tuner events, colleges, and auto shows." Targeting the trendsetting Generation Y in the United States has had a global impact for Toyota in the process knowledge gained from the experience, said Farley:

> We are targeting trendsetters. They define what is cool and trendy. Not us. What we have to do is offer the right product and dealer experience to this target and then learn, listen, and make effective use of their feedback. One thing that is portable to other [countries] is the intensity with which we are listening . . . that is portable.[27]

The Scion experiment pushed Toyota to explore new frontiers. The Scion Covenant shows how the company deviated from usual practice:

The Scion Covenant[28]

- Display all prices clearly and stick to those prices. Prices should be the same wherever they appear (in the store, on the Web, and in the media).
- Provide accessories only in response to customers' requests.
- The Scion Corner should be built in Toyota showrooms.
- Never mix Scion inventories with Toyotas; Scion must be displayed distinctively.
- Provide designated and trained Scion staff.
- Advertising (following Scion guidelines) should be separate from Toyota.
- Prepare information folders on vehicle registrations, accessories, and so on.
- Provide this information to all field associates.

Customizing the Tundra for the United States

The full-size Tundra was targeted to the "true trucker" segment in the United States. This is not the average owner of a pickup truck. True truckers demand the most from their vehicle because they depend on it daily for work. These drivers are the real opinion leaders among full-size truck owners. Toyota knew that if true truckers bought the Tundra, the others would follow, but first they had to find out what true truckers were, by exploring their hobbies and general areas of interest, such as hunting and fishing, country music, NASCAR races, ranching, and construction. Then they had to convince them to switch from whatever model they were driving to the Tundra. The Big Three Detroit automakers still had a tight grip on the trucker segment, forcing the underdog Toyota to innovate in the extreme.

The Tundra was launched as "the all-new, built-in-America Toyota truck," but as former Scion head Jim Farley pointed out: "It wasn't just the launch of a new product. We were entering a new market, with new customers—it was about a whole new way of doing business."[29] To prove that the full-size Tundra was all new, Toyota created a nationwide test-drive program called "Tundra Prove It!" It showcased the truck at 350 trucker-type events over 10 months, offering drivers the chance to get behind the wheel and run the Tundra through the roughest and toughest of road tests, on off-road trails, and in acceleration runs, braking exercises, and hauling and towing demonstrations. These tests were aimed at creating a perception of the new Tundra as "bold, powerful, and capable."[30]

Another new approach Toyota adopted for the Tundra launch was creative collaboration with a diverse group of external companies to develop marketing materials. "We outsourced point-of-sale materials to Bass Pro, a company that runs sporting and outdoor goods stores. Brochures were created by designers of CD album covers for country music, while for advertising, our agency worked with companies that had worked on Harley-Davidson motorcycle and Caterpillar equipment marketing," explained Jim Farley.[31]

On the manufacturing side, the idea of actually situating parts suppliers inside the San Antonio plant was also new. Toyota spent $1.28 billion building its San Antonio plant, with the capacity to produce 200,000 Tundra trucks a year, and it allocated part of the 2,000-acre site to house 21 parts suppliers. This co-location scheme not only brought down costs but also improved reaction time in the "just-in-time" production system and improved communication between Toyota and its suppliers.

The Tundra is not only all-new as a truck design, but it is also all-American in the sense that it is the most American-style product in Toyota history. From design and engineering to manufacturing and marketing, the truck is built by Americans, for Americans. To hone in on its all-American image with the Tundra, Toyota launched literacy programs in San Antonio's south side, where the factory is located:

> There [Sky Harbor Elementary School], in the Toyota Family Literacy Program Room, Hispanic families are learning to read and write English. "The south side had not been receiving much attention," says Jada Pitman, who runs the program. "But now you have homes and roads being built to accommodate Toyota. Their presence is really being felt in the community."[32]

Disseminating Local Best Practices throughout the World

Toyota has developed new practices and processes as a result of incorporating the unique demands of customers in specific local markets. Local customization has worked because Toyota recognizes the value that diversity brings to the whole company and therefore entrusts its local operations with significant autonomy. The challenge for Toyota was how to preserve that diversity and autonomy while encouraging each country to share its best practices for mutual benefit. As the automobile industry became globalized, Toyota had to pursue both localization and global commonality.

Toyota established its Global Knowledge Center in July 2002 in Torrance, California, embracing the opposing requirements of localization and commonality of practice. The task of the center was to disseminate innovation from specific local markets into a global process to benefit the whole company. Prior to establishment of this center (discussed in more detail in Chapter 7), there were few avenues within Toyota for transferring customer knowledge across countries or sharing local best practices in sales and marketing worldwide.

The lack of opportunity to share knowledge and best practices across countries stemmed from the perception that Toyota's marketing and human resources practices—the soft side of management—were a local phenomenon and since market conditions differed from country to country, no single set of sales and marketing rules could apply to all countries in the world. The laws governing automobile dealers differed from country to country, which limited the transfer of single best practices across countries. The same logic was applied in relation to other soft issues, including remuneration, business modeling, and employee evaluation. In remuneration practices, U.S. dealer sales employees were paid on a commission basis only, while in Malaysia, remuneration was 50 percent salary, and the remainder based on sales volume and commission. Europe and Australia also had different pay structures. There was no single, best practice in pay structure that could be applied in all countries in the world.

There is some truth to this logic, but as the world is becoming "flat"[33]—characterized by a competitive environment where companies compete on increasingly equal terms due to the effects of globalization—the conventional wisdom about sales and marketing being incompatible across markets may be overturned sooner than expected. New model introductions in Southeast Asia were typically delayed by a few years after the model was first launched in the United States, Japan, or Europe. But today's customers are better informed about product introductions in other markets, and they demand timely access to those products in their own markets. Automakers who delay introducing products from one market to another will lose out to competitors who offer the latest models. This was one of the reasons Toyota started the IMV. As car markets across the globe become equally sophisticated, distributors will adopt proven methods to improve their business, regardless of where those practices originated.

Toyota successfully incorporated local consumer tastes and demands into the development, design, marketing, and sales for the IMV in Asia, the Yaris in Europe, and the Scion and Tundra in the United States. To keep its distributors one step ahead of the competition, Toyota makes these success stories available in the form of case studies documented by the Global Knowledge Center, Toyota's repository of best practices in sales and marketing worldwide. The center is a neutral organization, with no direct authority or control of any territorial division or department within Toyota or its distributors. As a result, it can encourage distributors around the world to use its educational programs, but the decision to do so is up to each distributor.

"What we can do is provide local staff with a lot of ideas and examples that they can adapt to local requirements," explained Executive Vice President Yoshimi Inaba.[34] By not forcing the adoption of specific practices, the Global Knowledge Center ensures distributors retain the flexibility to use the documented best practices as they best see fit. Echoing Executive Vice President Tokuichi Uranishi's words, this freedom allows the distributors "creative energy" to take charge and, inspired by the best practices, leads them to new and better ways of running the business. The spirit of local customization has permeated the Global Knowledge Center, where all distributors are free to source innovations generated from specific local markets and apply them to their own respective benefit, allowing local best practices to grow into global best solutions tailored to each local market.

Conclusion

Toyota customizes its products and processes by incorporating tastes and demands unique to each local market, and this pushes Toyota to new frontiers. In the case of the Scion in the United States, new frontiers were opened up with respect to ordering and inventory systems, a pricing scheme (pure pricing), the process of dealer interaction with the customer, and a grassroots marketing program. In the case of the IMV, local customization went beyond sales and marketing activities to include innovations in development and production.

Local customization goes hand in hand with the two expansive forces described in Chapters 3 and 4—impossible goals and the eagerness to experiment. The impossible goal of "developing the finest cars ever built and building the finest dealer network in the industry" was realized in the United States with the Lexus, and the impossible goal of "bypassing Japan to make a global car" was realized in Asia with the IMV. Development of the Scion brand and the Tundra were successful, localized experiments in the United States aimed at winning new customers in the youth segment of Generation Y and American truckers. These three expansive forces drive Toyota to reach new customers, try new processes, and develop new practices and technologies. Ultimately, they push Toyota to grow exponentially in an upward spiral increasing the complexity of the organization. In Chapters 6 through 8, we describe the integrative forces that serve as the glue to keep Toyota from spinning out of control. The founders' philosophies are the first integrative force underlying the shared values that define Toyota's corporate culture.

CHAPTER 6

The Founders' Philosophies

What prevents Toyota from fracturing at the edges or spiraling out of control under the expansive forces that drive its growth? The power of the founders' philosophies is the glue that binds employees, dealers, and suppliers and connects their aims. It acts as an integrative force in concert with Toyota's two other binding forces, the nerve system and up-and-in human resource management, which we deal with in subsequent chapters.

The founders' philosophies are the linchpin of integration and are ingrained at Toyota globally. The company's relentless pursuit and dissemination of the values expressed in these philosophies by people like Shotaro Kamiya, Taiichi Ohno, and others (see Figure 6.1) has effectively aligned the core values of Toyota employees, dealers, and suppliers. We have identified the following founding philosophies that have served over the years to pull together the organization and its various external constituents:

- Tomorrow will be better than today
- Everybody should win
- Customer first, dealers second, and manufacturer last
- Genchi genbutsu (go and see things for yourself, firsthand)

Each of these statements of philosophy functions within the company to align the values of executives, associates, partner companies, and the rank and file.

FIGURE 6.1 The Founding Proponents of Toyota's Philosophies: (a) Sakichi Toyoda, who created the parent company Toyoda Automatic Loom Works; (b) Kiichiro Toyoda, the son of Sakichi and founder of Toyota Motor Corporation; (c) Taiichi Ohno, who created the Toyota Production System; (d) Shotaro Kamiya, who developed Toyota's domestic and global sales network; (e) Eiji Toyoda, a first cousin of Kiichiro and former President; (f) Shoichiro Toyoda, son of Kiichiro and former President; (g) Hiroshi Okuda, Senior Toyota Advisor and former President; and (h) Fujio Cho, Chairman and former President.

(a)

(b)

(c)

(d)

(e)

(f)

(g)

(h)

Photos courtesy of Toyota Motor Corporation.

Tomorrow Will Be Better than Today

The shared belief at Toyota that tomorrow will be better than today grows out of institutional memory from the difficult experience of entering the international automobile market about 50 years behind the dominant American producers and almost 100 years behind the established European manufacturers. Though it seems unimaginable today, in 1950 Toyota was facing oblivion because of a shortage of cash. In the early 1960s, it was having difficulty penetrating the European market because dealers there were unwilling to handle the unknown Toyota brand. Such hardship shaped the view that any obstacle could be overcome, starting with those at home.

After Toyota's founding in 1937, it weathered the storm of World War II and the severe economic conditions that followed, then the crippling labor dispute of 1950 that forced it to close its factories for two full months. The company almost went bankrupt. It laid off 1,500 employees, 25 percent of its workforce. To show their remorse, the entire management team, including President Kiichiro Toyoda, resigned. Akio Matsubara, Senior Managing Director in charge of Human Resource Management, said these early hardships shaped the company's core values and corporate identity:

> At that time we really had no financing and money was extremely tight. We were so strapped for cash that we became obsessed with eliminating waste and accelerating return on investment so we could immediately reinvest back into the business. So, we could not keep an inventory of parts, and if we produced a defective product, it was a catastrophe.

> The system we now know as TPS [the Toyota Production System] was born of this environment and has survived to the present day. These days, TPS is part of our corporate identity, but it was certainly not present from the beginning. It was created in response to a couple of threats; one was the labor dispute and the other was the sense of impending

doom felt by Kiichiro Toyoda and the management team that remains to this day. More than just an institutional memory, I believe [this fear] was imprinted by the company's turbulent origins.[1]

To penetrate the European market in the early 1960s, Toyota initially targeted peripheral countries like Denmark, Norway, and Finland because they lacked domestic auto manufacturers and their markets were not that large. After succeeding in northern Europe, Toyota set its sights on the continent, but it was not easy to find distributors willing to handle their vehicles. Dealers hesitated because Toyota was an unknown player, and the regulations in some countries prohibited dealers from selling more than one brand. Toyota's first sales agreement was with Aera Auto Import, in 1963, to import to Denmark, Sweden, and Norway, followed by a contract with Louwman and Parqui of the Netherlands in 1964. By the late 1960s, agreements were reached with distributors in Belgium, Switzerland, Great Britain, France, Italy, Austria, and Greece. Sales grew very slowly, with only Finland, Belgium, Denmark, Switzerland, and the Netherlands registering annual sales exceeding 3,000 units. Toyota's selling points at that time were its novelty and mechanical simplicity affording relatively trouble-free operation.[2]

The German, British, and French distributors faced bigger obstacles with Toyota as these countries had their own automakers, making competition more severe. Unable to find a distributor in Germany that was willing to handle its products, Toyota affiliated with a bank to create its own distributor, Deutsche Toyota Vertriebs, in 1970. When the bank filed for bankruptcy in 1974, Toyota became sole owner of the distributor and renamed it Toyota Deutschland GmbH.

Even with its own distributor, Toyota could not make progress with German dealers, so it approached agricultural machinery dealers, gasoline stations, and car repair shops, building its first sales network mainly in rural areas. The rural market was familiar ground for Toyota given its origins in rural Japan.[3]

Seeing Obstacles as Challenges to Be Overcome

In the early 1990s, Toyota hit another major obstacle with the steep appreciation of the yen. This made its vehicles more expensive to overseas buyers and exacerbated a growing trade row with the United States over imports and Japan's growing trade surplus. On top of this, Japan's bubble economy had burst, decimating domestic car sales in the ensuing recession. Profits fell by almost 60 percent from 1991 to 1994. Meanwhile, the environmental impact of vehicle emissions was a growing concern. Toyota began to slouch its collective shoulders, feeling that the industry was under siege, and wondering how selling more cars made the world a better place to live. It was during this tumultuous period that the company engaged in deep and wide-ranging discussions about its future. The result was a vision statement in 1992 known as the "Toyota Earth Charter" that made environmental issues the top priority. Executive Vice President Tokuichi Uranishi described the sentiment behind this vision:

> Unless we solved the environmental issues, there would be no future for the car. But if we did resolve this issue, we would be making a contribution to society and could sell our cars with pride. So, we forged ahead, taking a drastic approach to tackle environmental issues. This led to the Prius, and even when the doubters told us that two power sources would be inefficient and would never be profitable, we forged ahead anyway. Another priority was to contribute to society at a local level by expanding production locally. We wanted to share the reasons why we wanted to grow with other [countries], to show that it was not just to generate more income, but to have the feeling that we were all contributing to society.[4]

Toyota has persevered through hardship, and over the long term, because of a naiveté in the mindset of people who see obstacles only as challenges; they genuinely believe that they can overcome all obstacles. Hence, obstacles become a source of power to energize people, who are, by nature, optimists at heart. This naive optimism leads the company to set impossible goals, and it has been passed down from the founders of Toyota, whose slogans are filled with this spirit of naiveté and optimism. As Matsubara recalled:

> As far as our corporate DNA is concerned—and this is not written down in any textbook—there are two phrases that still leave an impression on me after spending more than 30 years leading the life of a Toyota Man. One is the phrase that hung in Sakichi's home: "Endure a hundred times, strengthen yourself a thousand times, and you will complete your tasks in short order." I believe this is one element of our founding, corporate DNA, and the phrase itself is one manifestation of the beliefs of our founders, who were filled with the . . . spirit of overcoming obstacles. The other is, "To do what you believe is right, to do what you believe is good, and doing these things right then and in that way is a calling from on high. Thus, do it boldly, do as you believe, do as you are." These are very heavy words [from Eiji Toyoda, who became company president in 1967], but the point is, you have to be brave and persevere whether there is opposition or not; you have to think hard and come up with solutions until you succeed, and once you have done your best, most thorough work, you will find things turning on their heads, and that in itself becomes a source of power.[5]

Never Being Satisfied with the Status Quo

Behind the phrase "tomorrow will be better than today" is the attitude that Toyota will *make* it a better day, and this is embodied in the routine practice known as *kaizen,* a Japanese word meaning "continuous improvement" that is now part of the vernacular of manufacturing industries around the world. Kaizen is a habit of mind that dates back to the founder of the Toyota

Motor Corporation, Kiichiro Toyoda, who said, "We are working to make better products by making improvements every day."[6] John Kramer, Toyota Motor Sales, U.S.A., Vice President and head of the Global Knowledge Center, described the underlying sentiment of kaizen:

> [W]e're a big company, but it's really a small company attitude. There is a kind of hunger there, a fire in the belly that makes us always want to be a little bit better, do our jobs better, and if you can learn something every day and try to make a difference you're going to be successful.[7]

Kaizen is the habit of wanting to do a little better every day by eliminating waste and continuously becoming more efficient. It is an attitude of never being satisfied with the status quo, which helps to explain why Toyota is continuously and persistently conducting experiments. Tony Fujita, Toyota Motor Sales, U.S.A., Vice President and first head of Toyota's Global Knowledge Center, described it this way:

> I can't imagine Toyota being satisfied with any facts, any situation, any era, or any success. It's impossible. It shows in Mr. Watanabe's policies. I think it is Toyota's culture not to be satisfied, not to allow itself to be satisfied. The company always demands progress. Kaizen is not only a word; it is everything to Toyota. It's implanted.[8]

To support kaizen, Toyota cultivates a sense of crisis in the organization as described by Tokuichi Uranishi:

> If we become satisfied with the status quo, things start to go wrong. To prevent this, we have to instill a healthy sense of crisis [among employees]. If we don't reduce the environmental burden through technical innovation in our cars, we will not survive in the future. This is a long-term sense of crisis. But unless you are facing a real crisis, it's very difficult to maintain a sense of crisis among employees.

Toyota has been good at fostering this, and implanting [a continuing sense of crisis] in the organization remains one of management's most important tasks.[9]

Everybody Should Win

The second philosophical value that serves as an integrative force within Toyota is the notion that everyone should win. As a guiding principle, it moves everyone forward together. For Kiichiro Toyoda, the word *everyone* included society at large, and this is central to the mission of the auto company he founded, which is, "To contribute to society through the manufacturing of automobiles." Everyone also included the entire automobile industry. When Toyota opened its first automobile factory in Koromo-cho[10] on November 3, 1938, Kiichiro pledged to build a great automobile industry with these words:

> We must discard our narrow self-interests and endeavor to serve the greater good. Neglect your duties and you'll bring ruin upon yourselves; fulfill your responsibilities and you'll find yourselves enhanced. If each person makes the most sincere effort in his assigned position, the entire company can achieve great things.[11]

Everyone also included countries other than Japan. In 1988, when Toyota opened its U.S. automobile manufacturing plant in Kentucky, Kiichiro's son Shoichiro Toyoda, now honorary Chairman, echoed his father's commitment:

> Here at the start of this new venture, I am confident that Toyota Motor Manufacturing will certainly live up to your expectations. We are aware of what being a good corporate citizen means and [we] are determined to press forward toward a bright future, hand in hand, with the people of America.[12]

The year 1988 was a difficult year for Toyota and the Japanese automobile industry in general. The yen had appreciated from a low of 260 yen to the dollar in February 1985 to double that value (129 yen) by February 1988. Japan-U.S. trade frictions were headline news. "Toyota—Moving forward with America" was the theme of the opening ceremony at the Kentucky plant, emphasizing good corporate citizenship in alliance with workers.

Today, Toyota is trying to be a good corporate citizen in more than 170 countries. Senior Managing Director Akio Toyoda said the company has always been motivated to act "for the country"—first in Japan, then in the United States and Europe, and now in Thailand and Indonesia. This philosophy has been a driving force for local adaptation and customization:

> We intentionally used the expressions "for Thailand" and "for Indonesia." The Toyota Group was built "for the country." Cars imported from Japan were sold and we gained a good market share. This was done for Japan. Then, "for the country" evolved to mean local production and referred to the particular country where production took place. Since its founding, Toyota has maintained this "for the country" philosophy, weaving it into our values through the generations.[13]

Factory Workers as Knowledge Workers

On a microlevel, Toyota succeeded in getting its factory workers to buy into its aim "to contribute to society through the manufacturing of automobiles." In the rural town where Toyota began, there was nothing around for miles. The only resources were human resources. As Matsubara argued, what differentiates Toyota from its rivals even today is its view of the factory worker not only as a pair of hands on the assembly line, but as a knowledge worker who accumulates *chie*, the wisdom of experience that can only be gained on the factory floor:[14]

Looking at workers on an assembly line, the Western automakers just want those workers to follow a fixed set of procedures and they do not expect them to use their brains. That is the work of the line manager. At Toyota, we expect every assembly line worker to direct their wisdom toward originating ideas for improving base costs, quality, and safety. Here the job of the line manager is to create an environment in which line workers easily make suggestions and are supported to implement those suggestions.[15]

Dealers as Partners

Not only has Toyota made factory workers into knowledge workers, it has done the same with independent automobile dealers. Toyota views dealers as the "Radar for All of Toyota." This mission gives dealers the responsibility to communicate their knowledge of their specific market and customer needs to the rest of the Toyota group. From the beginning, dealers were brought into the process and shown how they could contribute their expertise to benefit themselves as well as the company. In contrast to the atomistic view of business relations that builds silos and limits interaction, it is a broadly interactive approach that recognizes interdependency in a business ecosystem. Dealers are partners at Toyota. Toyota managers maintain close relationships with the dealers, visiting them frequently, hearing their views, asking for their input, and ensuring they are involved in key decision-making processes. Every Toyota employee, from top management to young associates, makes the effort to visit a local dealer when traveling overseas.

In St. Petersburg for an international conference in 2007, Toyota Chairman Fujio Cho took the opportunity to meet with a local dealer and visit the site of a new Toyota factory under construction. At the dealership, he noticed a long lineup of Toyota vehicles waiting for repairs. Worried that problems in manufacturing quality had surfaced, he went to the manager but was relieved to find that 90 percent of the cars were brought in for repairs to scratches and dents, not functional defects. "I instantly understood from the explanation of the manager and from my personal experience taking a car from the St. Petersburg airport to the hotel that drivers in this city are aggressive and will cut into your lane with only the slightest opening. During that one-hour ride there were four or five times when I thought our car was going to collide with another."[16]

Senior managers take every opportunity to interact at the front line, and all employees work hard to make dealers an integral part of the organization. Global Marketing Division General Manager, Katsuyoshi Tabata, described one of the ways they do this from his experience while working at Toyota Motor Sales, U.S.A.:

By sharing our future plans, in good times or bad times, dealers feel that they are trusted by the distributor and that the distributor is trusted by TMC [Toyota Motor Corporation]. This will increase their commitment to Toyota, and it makes a difference especially when we can't provide new models for a while or when we want dealers to invest more in their facilities or people.[17]

John Kramer echoed Tabata in describing the value of close relations with dealers:

At Toyota we also deeply understand the fact that we are just not all that smart; we have to work very hard. We have to rely on other people to do the very best job they can, every day of the week and every month of the year, in order for us to achieve mutual success. And the bulk of that responsibility lies with our dealers, our retailers. That's a relationship that we have always valued. I don't think we will ever let that slip away. We stay very close to the dealers. We ask for their input when we are about to take on any new ventures or change our processes. We are constantly out visiting our dealers, hearing their voices, and making them part of our process.[18]

As someone who has also worked for an American auto company, Kramer recalled how dealers in the United States were viewed:

> I remember, when I began with a competitor in the United States in 1972, the relationship with the dealers was always bad. . . . I can't tell you how many times I've been to meetings where we would, I guess, denigrate our dealers, either for the fact that they were so stupid and didn't realize that they should be doing this or that, or because they were making a lot of profits and we weren't.[19]

Profit sharing with the dealers is a founding principle at Toyota. President of Toyota Motor Sales, U.S.A., Yukitoshi Funo, explained the rationale behind it:

> Why allow so much profit to flow to the dealers? Why not let profits flow to the factory [the manufacturer]? Increasing the number of dealerships is good for the factory, but not so good for individual dealers faced with the prospect of another new dealership across the street. So, if you think of the factory first, you increase the number of dealerships; but if you think of the dealers first, the preference is to refrain from increasing the number of dealerships and put everyone's heads together to come up with ways to increase efficiency. I think this is the schematic picture.[20]

Putting dealer profitability ahead of the manufacturer is a worldwide practice at Toyota stemming from the philosophy of Shotaro Kamiya, a legendary figure at the company. Kamiya's long tenure and achievements as President of Toyota Motor Sales Company, Ltd. in Japan, from April 1950 to December 1974, earned him the nickname, "Master of Sales." He described his sales philosophy as "customer first, dealers second, and manufacturer last," with the following justification:

The priority in distributing the benefits of automobile sales should be in the order of the customer first, then the car dealer, and lastly, the manufacturer. This is the best approach for winning the trust of customers and dealers and ultimately brings growth to the manufacturer.[21]

Kamiya helped create Toyota's first dealer network in Japan back in 1935. His approach during those days became the mold for dealer relations ever since. At the beginning, there was no money to set up company-owned dealerships. Kamiya used his connections from his time at General Motors in Japan, recruiting GM dealers to sell for Toyota. He had discovered that many of the GM dealers were not satisfied with the treatment from American automakers.[22] Japan GM usually dropped dealers in financial trouble rather than help them. Kamiya promised these dealers that Toyota would treat them as equal partners and help anyone who had difficulty financing orders.[23] Sales training, promotion strategies, and pricing guidance were provided to dealers, with the Toyota Sales College offering training to middle-level sales managers. Eventually, Toyota formed the biggest dealer network in Japan.

Teamwork as a Ring of Power

To ensure that everybody wins, teamwork has been stressed at Toyota since the early days. As Kiichiro Toyoda said, "Each person thoroughly fulfilling their duties generates great power that, gathered together in a chain, creates a ring of power."[24] The shared belief at the company today has not changed—that the contribution of the team is greater than the sum of the contributions of each individual.

What Kiichiro called the "ring of power" came into play in Indonesia during production preparation of the IMV. When a growing number of senior managers at headquarters suggested postponing the launch of commercial production of the vehicle, team spirit consolidated to help them meet their original deadline. Executive Managing Coordinator Hiroshi Nakagawa was in charge of the IMV Project Office at Toyota Motor Thailand. He recalled how the slogan, "One Team, One Aim, Working Together," influenced the team's resolve:

> Everyone worked hard under this [slogan]. We were all working together to break down the barriers to success, working toward the same goal rather than independently, by function. If a problem arose in the facilities area, the maintenance team from our factory would jump right in to resolve the issue before the equipment was installed. If a design problem arose, our quality control team would jump in and help them implement the appropriate measures.[25]

When a problem arises, anyone on the team is accountable and has the authority and responsibility to find a solution. This behavior originated on the factory floor as *jidoka,* the practice of stopping the process when a problem occurs. Former Senior Vice President of Toyota Motor Manufacturing in Kentucky, Alex Warren, explained the concept:

> [In the automation process] we give humans the power to push the buttons or pull what we call the *andon* cord, which brings the entire assembly line to a halt. Every team member has the responsibility to stop the line each time they see something that is below standard. That's how we put the responsibility for quality in the hands of our team members. They feel the responsibility; they feel the power. They know that they count.[26]

Customer First, Dealers Second, and Manufacturer Last

The third philosophical value that serves as an integrative force at Toyota is "customer first, dealers second, manufacturer last." In Japan and overseas, "customer first" is a popular phrase but Toyota has been practicing it for over 70 years, ever since the idea was first articulated by the Master of Sales, Shotaro

Kamiya. This concept has shaped the company's unique relationship between distributors and dealers and between dealers and customers globally. This mindset runs through everything Toyota does, including upstream activities such as research and development. "I believe that the idea that Toyota is supported by its customers is the bedrock of our progress," said Shoichiro Toyoda.[27] The ability to listen and to hear what the customer has to say has enabled Toyota to differentiate itself from other automakers and stay ahead, according to John Kramer:

> I think the other companies have believed too much in their own message. They believed that they were so big and so powerful that they could dictate what the public wanted. . . . Fuel economy is becoming much more important; becoming a good ecological corporation is becoming much more important. As such, our designers hear out those voices over 36 or 40 months and they make design changes.[28]

The customer first philosophy also permeates the rank and file on the factory floor. Retired factory worker Kiyoshi Tsutsumi, recalled being asked by his boss one day, "Who do you think is paying your salary?" He replied that the company was paying his salary. "Wrong," he was told. "It's the customers. They buy our cars, and the company uses that money to make the next car and then sells it. Your salary comes from that transaction." Tsutsumi said that exchange had a big impact on his view of the responsibility of a manufacturer. "Since it's the customer who pays our salary, our responsibility is to make the product they want, when they want it, and deliver quality that satisfies them," he said.[29] The Lexus project best describes this philosophy in action.

The Lexus Covenant and Recall

The philosophy of customer first, dealers second, and manufacturer last is most evident at the level of the dealership. The Lexus Covenant and its first recall is an illustration of the philosophy as best practice. In 1987, while starting up the business, Lexus Division General Manager Davis Illingworth wrote the Lexus Covenant[30] (Table 6.1). It proclaims the division's strong resolve to do it right from the start by providing the finest car ever built with the finest sales network, treating each customer as though they were "a guest in our home." Every manager, associate, and dealer had to sign on to the covenant, and it soon became common practice for all new dealer associates and service personnel to sign it once their training was complete.

However, it was not until the first Lexus recall that dealers gained a true understanding of the Lexus Covenant. Three cases of defects were reported soon after the *LS400* was launched: a tail lamp that had overheated and warped, affecting the stop lamp, cruise control that would not turn off, and a battery that died.

Under U.S. federal law, car manufacturers were required to recall products for parts replacement only if it was a safety issue. Even though each reported LS400 failure had occurred only once, without incident or injury, Toyota Motor Sales, U.S.A. (TMS), chose to recall the car three months after it was put on the market. Introduced on September 1, 1989 with the claim that it was "built by 1,400 perfectionists," the Lexus recall might have been perceived as its death knell. The problem parts had been identified, but the real challenge was getting outside

TABLE 6.1   The Lexus Covenant

Lexus will enter the most competitive, prestigious automobile race in the world.
Over 50 years of Toyota automotive experience has culminated in the creation of Lexus cars. They will be the finest cars ever built.
Lexus will win the race because Lexus will do it right from the start.
Lexus will have the finest dealer network in the industry.
Lexus will treat each customer as we would a guest in our home.
If you think you can't, you won't . . .
If you think you can, you will!
We can, we will.

Source: Lexus, a division of Toyota Motor Sales, U. S. A. "The Lexus Covenant," Lexus web site, www.lexus.com/about/corporate/lexus_covenant.html (accessed February 2007).

suppliers to start production to resupply those parts. Training service personnel at the dealerships to do the replacement work was also a challenge.[31]

The recall was publicly announced on December 1 and the company took swift action. Every dealer was advised how to handle the recall. All 8,000 car owners were sent letters signed personally by Illingworth. Production of LS400 replacement parts was ramped up and service personnel were trained to fix the defects. To better handle customer inquiries, all 150 employees at the Lexus Division and all service personnel and dealer associates were informed of the problems and their remedial actions, and additional technical support was provided from Japan.

TMS proceeded to pick up every car directly from each owner's home, providing a free replacement car. The repaired car was returned washed and with a full tank of gas. For customers in Alaska, personnel from the nearest area office made house calls by plane to make the repairs. All expenses were covered by TMS. They planned to complete all repairs in 20 days, before the Christmas holidays. It was an impressive accomplishment considering that a recall of this scale normally took months to complete.[32]

The following March, when dealers assembled at the Lexus Dealer Advisory Council, Lexus associates were expecting strong criticism. They were pleasantly surprised. In his opening statement, the council chairman said: "Thank you for the recall." Dave White, General Manager of the Lexus dealership in Indianapolis, reflected on the recall: "[TMS] sent parts the day the recall was announced. The same day, they sent service personnel to teach us how to do the repairs. I had been in the business for 15 years but had never seen such an efficient operation."[33] After the recall, quite a few dealers started reciting the Lexus Covenant before the start of each working day.

Customer First in Service

Guided by the philosophy of customer first, development of the Lexus led to many service innovations that became industry standards. These included providing loaner cars of the same class during repairs, free transport of cars with engine failure, 24-hour emergency roadside service with hotel stays ($200 per night) where necessary, free car washing, shuttle services, and gas fill-up. Some dealers took the initiative to offer services beyond those demanded by the program. Half the Lexus dealers owned refueling vehicles to help customers who had run out of gas. Others supplied meal coupons to customers waiting for servicing and repairs. Lexus service personnel were entrusted to make decisions about the best way to serve their customers, with no financial restrictions.[34]

Genchi Genbutsu

The fourth philosophical value that is ingrained at Toyota is *genchi genbutsu,* which means, "go and see things for yourself, firsthand." At the St. Petersburg conference mentioned earlier, Toyota Chairman Fujio Cho explained the concept of genchi genbutsu simply as, "Have you seen it?" The inference is that if you have not seen something firsthand, then your view of that thing is not credible. This kind of thinking is especially ingrained in top executives, who feel proud to be the first ones to ask, "Have you seen it?" Chairman Cho comes to grips with the reality of the Russian market by visiting a factory and a dealership while in St. Petersburg. He commands respect not by talking about genchi genbutsu, but by walking the talk.

Genchi genbutsu infers that the root causes of problems are revealed by on-site investigation and inquiry. The following story is told over and over again at Toyota to illustrate the spirit of genchi genbutsu. One day, Kiichiro Toyoda was walking through the vast, Toyota plant. He encountered a worker scratching his head and muttering that his grinding machine wouldn't work. Kiichiro took one look at the man, rolled up his sleeves, and plunged his own hands into the oil pan, coming up with two handfuls of sludge. Throwing the sludge on the floor, he said, "How can you expect to do your job without getting your hands dirty!"[35]

Genchi genbutsu encourages people to try to solve problems with their own hands. Sakichi Toyoda, founder of Toyota's parent, Toyoda Automatic Loom Works, was fond of saying:

Before you say you can't do something, try it![36]

Never try to design something without first gaining at least three years hands-on experience.[37]

Toyota emphasizes the importance of tacit or embodied knowledge that is deeply rooted in a person's actions and bodily experience and understood in the context of their values, ideals, and emotions. Subjective insights, intuition, and hunches are an integral part of tacit knowledge. This is why Toyota views factory workers as knowledge workers capable of using their heads as well as their hands. Genchi genbutsu encourages all employees "to go to the source" and continuously analyze root causes. Taiichi Ohno, creator of the Toyota Production System, was fond of saying, "Observe the production floor without preconceptions and with a blank mind. Repeat 'why' five times about every issue."[38] Ohno cited the example of a welding robot that suddenly stopped in the middle of an operation, to demonstrate the usefulness of asking "why" five times to get at the root cause. The routine goes as follows:[39]

1. "Why did the robot stop?" Because the circuit was overloaded, causing a fuse to blow.
2. "Why was the circuit overloaded?" Because there was insufficient lubrication on the bearings.
3. "Why was there insufficient lubrication on the bearings?" Because the oil pump on the robot was not circulating sufficient oil.
4. "Why was the pump not circulating sufficient oil?" Because the pump intake was clogged with metal shavings.
5. "Why was the intake clogged with metal shavings?" Because there was no filter on the pump.

Although the genchi genbutsu philosophy originates in manufacturing, it applies equally at the retail level. Kamiya's "customer first, dealers second, and manufacturer last" philosophy can be interpreted to mean that unless you go to the front line and see for yourself, you will not understand the problem. "Unless we visit *genba* [the place where the action is], we cannot develop a good plan. Our bosses can tell if we develop a plan without going to *genba*," said Katsuyoshi Tabata:

> I understand that other Japanese carmakers emphasize *genba* too, and that this philosophy has its origins in engineering and manufacturing. But I don't know if they practice it in the sales function. I think Toyota is unique in practicing it in sales, and this is due to Mr. Kamiya whose philosophy has taken root in the Toyota sales organization in many countries, most successfully in the United States.[40]

The philosophy of genchi genbutsu also applies to the way executives at Toyota learn from their role models. Yukitoshi Funo described the importance of learning by watching over the shoulders of those at the company whom he calls the "great men":

> In my case there were many great men—Okuda-san and Cho-san are representative, but there were many others, who served as vice president and in other capacities—and we have been brought up together with them, watching how they take care of things.[41]

Conclusion

Throughout its history, Toyota employees have experienced the power of the founders' philosophies described in this chapter: (1) Tomorrow will be better than today, (2) Everybody should win, (3) Customer first, dealers second, and manufacturer last, and (4) Genchi genbutsu. These philosophies stabilize the expansive forces described in preceding chapters, helping to prevent Toyota from spinning outward in all directions fruitlessly.

These shared beliefs form the basis of the corporate values articulated in *The Toyota Way 2001*, known in the company as the "Green Book." Two of the beliefs—tomorrow will be better than today and genchi genbutsu—have been the force behind kaizen. The other two beliefs—everybody should win and customer first, dealers second, and manufacturer last—translate into the slogan "respect for people." Kaizen and respect for people are the two pillars of *The Toyota Way 2001*. This document was the first attempt to put into writing the key beliefs and values that have nourished Toyota over the years, shaping the behavior of Toyota management, employees, and external partners in the business ecosystem.

CHAPTER 7

Toyota's Nerve System—A Human Version of the World Wide Web

By all accounts, Toyota is a big company. It sold over 9 million cars worldwide in 2007, posting revenues that exceeded $200 billion. It operates more than 50 manufacturing facilities outside Japan, sells vehicles in over 170 countries[1] and employs close to 300,000 people.[2] Despite its enormous size and geographic spread, in culture, Toyota is still like a small-town company, where everybody knows everybody else's business.

Its top executives operate on the assumption that "everybody knows everything" because the culture of communication is open and personal. Information flows freely up and down the hierarchy and across functional and seniority levels, extending outside the organization to suppliers, customers, and dealers. Typical of traditional Eastern social and business practice, personal relationships are of primary importance. Consequently, Toyota's interconnected world in the digital age is primarily analog, based on the belief that e-mail cannot replace real, human communication in the flesh. This requires cultivation of the skill of listening intently to all opinions in an environment of free and open exchange and in face-to-face interaction. The result is an accumulation of relationships in an analog web that Executive Vice President Yoshimi Inaba calls the "nerve system," which, in many ways, outperforms even the most advanced computer.

Like the central nervous system in the human body, Toyota's nerve system transmits information and meaning swiftly and simultaneously to all parts of the organization, including its far-flung operations overseas. Toyota views its people as its nerve cells, the basic structural and functional units of the company that produce and transmit electrochemical signals or impulses for action. People are the neurotransmitters of its communication web.

In the factory, this means information is transmitted and received by going to the front line to communicate in person. The Managing Officer responsible for the Takaoka and Tsutsumi plants, Takahiro Fujioka, is on the factory floor every day and joins workers for drinks in the evening (*nomikai*) whenever possible, sometimes as often as four times a week. He believes real communication should take place face-to-face at the front lines, unrestricted by the limits of rank or title.[3] So he started what he calls an OASiS movement at the two factories, an acronym for *Ohayo* (good morning), *Arigato* (thank you), *Shitsurei-shimashita* (pardon me), and *Sumimasen* (excuse me; I'm sorry). He says proper habits of address are the first step in cultivating a culture that encourages people in the front lines to speak up and say what they want to say to anyone at whatever level in the organization.

Similarly, information is shared with dealers by going to their *genba* or front line. Yoshimi Inaba explained how this happens in the sales organization:

> For example, if we decided to offer sales incentives, we would communicate this to our regional offices, and the field officers in each region would communicate it to the dealers. Basically, that's all there is to it. Of course, with about 1,200 Toyota dealerships in many different regions, no single idea has a very good chance of making it all the way through to the endpoints. This is because in the dealership it has to go from the dealer's senior executive, to the general manager, to the sales manager, and then to the sales personnel. Nonetheless, I think our degree of transparency

and the speed at which these ideas are transmitted is one of our great strengths. This is what I mean by a nerve system.[4]

Before the era of the information superhighway, Toyota already had a nerve system for listening to the market and acting quickly on the views of dealers and customers. Its Master of Sales Shotaro Kamiya relied on this system to build a domestic and global sales network around the philosophy of "customer first, dealers second, and manufacturer last." Toyota has used the nerve system to avoid the pitfalls of poor communication typical of big, bureaucratic organizations where the common lament is, "If our company knew then what it knows now . . ." By ensuring that everyone knows everything, Toyota's many and disparate parts can move together as a whole, and according to Inaba, this is another source of its competitive advantage:

> Because we have such a well-developed system for absorbing market information gleaned from conversations with dealers, the nerve system so to speak, our policies for rolling out new products and for doing other things are relatively well executed compared to other players. My sense is that it is our [nerve] system that allows us to produce quality products rapidly.[5]

In this chapter, we examine how the nerve system enables everybody to know everything. As a system, it is never complete because Toyota keeps growing and producing new nerve cells that transmit different impulses in the ever-changing business environment. We have identified the following five characteristics of the system:

1. Open and lateral dissemination of know-how
2. Freedom to voice contrary opinions
3. Frequent Face-to-face interaction
4. Making tacit knowledge explicit in the Toyota Way
5. Formal and informal organizational support mechanisms

Open and Lateral Dissemination of Know-How

Toyota has traditionally placed a high value on employees communicating openly with each other in collaboration. As founder Sakichi Toyoda often said, "Entrepreneurs, managers, and staff must all work together." To facilitate teamwork, employees are encouraged to engage in *yokoten*, short for *yokoni tenkai-suru*, which literally means "unfold or open out sideways." The slogan "Let's *yokoten*," frequently heard at Toyota, encourages everyone to share their individual know-how and expertise openly with others. This fosters a kind of viral communication that results in more efficient dissemination and diffusion of knowledge in all directions. Best practices of any kind are effectively disseminated through yokoten. When a best practice in inspection at one factory becomes known, it pressures other factories to look at it and determine if it is superior to their own and quickly implement any improvements. "We need to give credit to the person or unit that came up with the idea first, but it is okay to steal best practices from others or have our best practices stolen by others," said one veteran employee in human resources.[6]

The organization has to be open for the nerve system to function. It also has to be relatively flat. Toyota Motor Sales, U.S.A., Vice President and head of the Global Knowledge Center, John Kramer, described it this way:

> The organization may seem big in numbers, but there are not a lot of layers . . . you still feel very close to the people that work for you. If people want to see me, and I think I am fairly typical of people at the vice president level, it's not difficult to get an appointment. When my door is open, people can walk in and say, "Hey, what do you think." There have been occasions when I've been working on my computer and have looked over my shoulder to find some associates there saying, "Hey, we want you to look at this."[7]

Toyota has found that one of the best ways to create an open and flat environment is to have everyone work together in a large room with no partitions. The large-room concept or *obeya* originated in Japan because of a perennial shortage of office space. The practice was transplanted through yokoten to Thailand for the IMV production project. Individuals representing the different functional groups on the production preparation team such as technology, production, procurement, logistics, marketing, and accounting, were assembled into one large room to foster open communication and teamwork. To enhance communication and teamwork, the team posted information about the project on the walls of a dedicated "situation room" obeya for everyone to see, in a process known as *mieruka,* or visualization, another best practice transferred from Japan. Figure 7.1 shows employees at the wall catching up on the progress of the

FIGURE 7.1 A View of the IMV *Obeya.*

Source: *Team Toyota 16* (internal Toyota Motor Corporation publication, Tokyo), January–February 2005, 10. Reprinted with permission.

IMV project. In 2007, Toyota Motor Sales, U.S.A., began using mieruka in a customer service obeya aimed at improving customer satisfaction in sales and service (Figure 7.2).

Practicing mieruka in a "small, closed room melts down barriers and creates a good environment for addressing issues" said Jim Mooney, Corporate Manager of Customer Service Strategy and Development at Toyota Motor Sales, U.S.A.[8] In Thailand, mieruka was more effective than computerized communication to keep employees aware and up-to-date on the project, according to Hiroshi Nakagawa, Executive Managing Coordinator of the IMV Project Office at Toyota Motor Thailand:

> Information about what was going on, the issues they were facing at any given time, and what the plan was next, was all up there on the walls, not tucked away in someone's desk. One young Thai employee suggested that we put all

FIGURE 7.2 The Customer Service *Obeya* at Toyota Motor Sales, U.S.A., Inc.

Source: "Sales Satisfaction: Obeya Solution,"*Best Practice Bulletin 42,* (internal Toyota Motor Corporation publication, Tokyo), July 2007, 4. Reprinted with permission.

this information on our server so that it could be accessed at the click of a mouse. Even though this was possible, we still insisted that everything be posted on the walls. If people have to start up their computers and strike a few keys to access information, they won't bother, and the information won't be shared. People often give up simply in the process of looking for information. Posting all information on the walls helps improve communication, and because we're human, if we share a common awareness of the issues, we will move in the same direction.[9]

Sharing information fosters a common understanding among employees of the real state of affairs surrounding them. By posting information on the walls in obeya, Toyota creates a visual image of the work that becomes a common ground for employees to make decisions and see the impact of their activities on others, according to Yasuhiro Mishima, Executive Vice President at Toyota Motor Thailand:

This may sound a bit like popular psychology theory, but everyone knew well that we had a very high goal and felt an imminent threat of danger [of being unprepared for production]. The basis of their awareness was the significant volume of information visualized [on the wall] and shared. When people from other sections came to the big office, they could see for themselves what was happening. They could also find out how their actions on issues affecting their sections were having an impact on other sections.[10]

Freedom to Voice Contrary Opinions

The organization should also be open to criticism and contradiction for the nerve system to function properly. This means everyone has to feel free to voice contrary opinions to top management and headquarters. At Toyota, employees do not blindly follow their bosses' orders, even those from top management.

Group Manager at the Toyota Institute, Naomi Ishii, said there are times when top-down directives are treated with disdain:

> When an idea comes down from the top, the folks at the bottom might say, "That can't be right; let's try this instead." This [reaction] is repeated over and over again until a final decision is made about what to do; then we adopt that plan for a year, and the process keeps bouncing around like this as it moves forward.[11]

Toyota's current President, Katsuaki Watanabe, recalled how he came up the ranks, always fighting with his bosses. "Pick a friendly fight," he said. "If you don't, you may end up with a compromise. If that happens, there is no speed, no progress."[12] Watanabe understands how knowledge improves and expands with different perspectives:

> We need a good team to make good products, and a good team is not a cozy team. We need constant feedback from customers to dealers, and from dealers to product development and manufacturing. Those providing feedback should complain, and the others should listen sincerely, and then we have a friendly fight. Combining the words "friendly" and "fight" may seem like a contradiction, but we make it work because both sides share the same goal— to produce cars that make customers happy. The first item on my list of my priorities is to make this an organization where nobody hides concerns or problems and where constructive discussion takes place routinely. Without such discussion people will tend to let problems slide with slapdash solutions that barely scratch the surface.[13]

Each individual in Toyota is expected to act according to what that person thinks is right. Authority, responsibility, and accountability rest with the person, not a title or years of seniority. This is a cultural remnant of the famous Toyota Production System (TPS) practice of jidoka. As described earlier, individual employees have the power to pull the andon cord bringing the entire assembly line to a halt if they see something that is not up to standard. Machines also stop the line when they detect abnormalities in excess of a certain level. But an employee who chooses to pull the cord is empowered by a deep understanding of the quality standard, and if everybody shares this knowledge, you can rely on people to pull the cord for the right reasons.

Title and rank are irrelevant in discussions of quality. Confronting your boss is acceptable. Bringing bad news to the boss is encouraged. Ignoring the boss is excused in the process of coming to the right decision. Naomi Ishii described how top management occasionally suffered silent rejection:

> There is absolutely nothing that is decided in a top-down manner in our company. No matter what [Fujio] Cho or [Katsuaki] Watanabe may say, if it's too bizarre, employees either modify the message or will not accept it. There's no question about that. In company lingo we call this "the silent rejection."[14]

President of Toyota Motor Sales, U.S.A., Yukitoshi Funo described how he decided to ignore orders from on high:

> When I was sent to the U.S. in 1997 [as Senior Vice President], I first made the rounds to several top executives in Japan. . . . They told me to increase the number of sales outlets. These were executive vice presidents and managing directors. They said, "Look, the number of units is going to increase, and we're going to have to increase the number of dealerships." I figured the only way to succeed was to apply the Toyota Way. So, thinking about *genchi genbutsu*, I went to the U.S. dealerships to see the situation for myself, and I thought, the reason we can't increase the number of dealerships is that we are already engaged in a kind of discount war in the metropolitan areas. Increasing the number of dealerships would simply cause more intense competition, unfair sales activities, and threaten proper management of

the dealerships. So I decided to ignore everything those top executives told me.[15]

In many of our interviews with Toyota employees, we were told how local operations had succeeded by refusing to obey the orders headquarters had advised. In the following three examples, it was the founders' philosophies of "customer first, dealers second, and manufacturer last," and genchi genbutsu that kicked in to avert any disaster that could ensue from following the wrong order from on high. The first comes from Mikio Nomura, former Vice President of Toyota Astra Motors in Indonesia from 1997 to 2001. As it was his second assignment to the country, he had developed a feel for the Indonesian market and knew that the economy would recover from the 1997 Asian Financial Crisis in about a year, and he wanted production to be ready. But Toyota headquarters in Japan believed the recovery would take another two years. As Nomura recalled:

> In 1999 we started preparing, and in 2000 we quickly launched a new car and made a profit. If we had listened to headquarters and stopped production [on the assumption that] the recovery would have taken a year longer, we would not have been ready. Indonesia made a decision that was right in the end. There will [always] be differences of opinion in important matters between headquarters and the local operations. In those instances, we shouldn't blindly follow headquarters, but do what we believe is right even if it might cause friction.[16]

The second instance comes from Taiwan, which achieved a turnaround by going against headquarters over a pricing issue. Koshiro Fukuda, was Executive Vice President of Toyota in Taiwan at the time and recalled the incident:

> I violated the constitution when I lowered the prices that had been agreed between headquarters and us. However, if we had negotiated with headquarters in the orthodox

manner, several months would have passed and with it the cumulative red ink of the dealers, bankruptcies would have been a disaster. If one dealer went bankrupt, the bank, would stop lending to all the dealers. I thought that if I could show one month of good results, then I could go back to Japan and negotiate.[17]

Pricing is often the point of conflict between the local operation and headquarters, but viewed positively, the back-and-forth on pricing is a healthy process of information exchange that leads to deeper understanding of the situation. "In the [Toyota] vernacular these information processing skills are called, 'not listening to what you are told,'" said Funo of Toyota Motor Sales, U.S.A.

The third example comes from Thailand, where the local operation swayed the opinion of headquarters that the launch of commercial production of the IMV should be postponed. Yasuhiro Mishima described the value of direct and open communication in this incident:

> Our strength lay in the fact that we had a prototype that we had actually developed, manufactured, and assembled. When we carefully examined each issue for commercial production, we developed confidence in our ability to handle the situation. We spoke very frankly about this with the various people who were worried about it, had them come and look at the trial production run so we could point out where the problems lay, and explained how we thought we would be able to solve those problems . . .[18]

Clear and unambiguous information at the scene, or genba, proved critical to deciding not to postpone the start of commercial production, said Executive Vice President Akio Toyoda:

> It is usually the people at the scene who say the schedule is too tight, but this time, it was headquarters suggesting we

postpone the start of commercial production. When we did our inspection, the line people said things like, "Are they kidding? Let's show them what we're really made of!"[19]

Frequent Face-to-Face Interaction

Although there are no reprisals if local operations ignore head-quarters' advice or if subordinates disobey orders from their supervisors, refusal to listen to others is a serious offense. "Listening thoroughly to everybody's opinion is our calling," said Executive Vice President Yoshimi Inaba. Toyota's nerve system functions only when information at the source is available to everybody in the organization. Thus, the emphasis on face-to-face interaction at the scene. As Yukitoshi Funo, President of Toyota Motor Sales, U.S.A, noted, it is only the people at the scene, at genba, who have this information at their fingertips:

> However visionary the people at the top may be, it's the people at the bottom who have the actual information about what can and cannot be done. It is at *genba* where all essential information is processed and frontline employees make the judgments that take into account local conditions and the opinions from the top.[20]

Rarely do managers at Toyota reach senior positions without acquiring and embracing the skill of listening thoroughly and intently to what employees have to say and continually questioning and probing to find the better way. John Kramer expressed the sentiment behind this practice:

> As a senior manager you're willing or motivated to listen to staff because, firstly, you respect their opinion and, secondly, you're always looking for new ideas or ways you can do better. You're never satisfied. So, it's shortsighted to think that only the senior people know the answers.[21]

It helps, of course, to have an "up-and-in" human resource management policy (see Chapter 8). Thanks to this policy, there are fewer interpersonal rivalries at Toyota of the kind that exist in most organizations where people are jockeying for position to get the job they want. In addition, managers at Toyota rarely reach senior positions if they are the preacher type. According to Funo, "A preacher is someone who doesn't listen to others."[22] The preacher is only capable of communicating unidirectionally. Toyota's nerve system aims to build multidirectional communication, not only with staff, but also with customers, suppliers, and dealers.

Much has already been written about how the Toyota Production System (TPS) embraces the knowledge of suppliers. Relatively little has been written about how Toyota taps the knowledge of dealers. To begin with, the company does not see dealers only as salespeople. As Inaba described it, they are recognized as "specialists in their chosen field, each working hard in their individual way." He said dealers have "deep smarts" and are consulted continuously because of this recognition of their tacit, experiential knowledge of the market:

> When we try something new [at the dealers], one or two meetings might be organized with a few dealers to monitor [the test], and ordinarily that would be the end of it. But we wind up [meeting] over and over again, accumulating knowledge and experience as we go. . . . Basically, the philosophy of, "What are the dealers saying," is rooted somewhere in the deepest, innermost layers of our psyche.[23]

Toyota Motor Sales, U.S.A., Vice President and first head of the Global Knowledge Center, Tony Fujita, contended that Toyota has distinguished itself from other carmakers in the United States on the basis of how thoroughly and intently it listens to dealers. "Other carmakers have meetings with dealers, but I think Toyota is unique in the frequency and the seriousness of what we discuss. What we talk about should be what we implement; we deliver on what we talk about," he said.[24]

The thoroughness and intensity of this dialogue helps to overcome any initial resistance from dealers. Inaba recalled how Toyota finally won the buy-in of dealers to the unorthodox idea for the Scion:

> Of course, I can immediately recall the faces of all the dealers who told us it would never work. After all, the Scion is a difficult proposition for them, because if you look at their margin, it's about half that of other cars. On the other hand, inventory costs are dramatically lower and dealers do well with [high-margin] accessories. In the end, the bottom line is definitely not far from the norm for Toyota. We discussed these things over and over again until we ironed everything out, and gradually, little by little, we reached a kind of . . . alignment with the dealers. I believe this is how it happened.[25]

To market the Lexus in the United States, the company had ongoing face-to-face dialogue with all dealers that was institutionalized in regular meetings, as described by Fujita:

> In the United States, we have many occasions to discuss issues with the dealers: the once-a-year National Dealer Meeting, the twice-a-year National Dealer Advisory Council, and the once-a-year award ceremony, which is followed by a session to discuss the future. For the Lexus, on top of all that, we have the once-a-year Fireside Chat, which adds up to four opportunities to discuss issues with dealers and talk about our future plans, one, two, or three years ahead, and prepare them. And Toyota not only talks, it delivers.[26]

The once-a-year National Dealer Meeting is attended by dealers from across the United States. Toyota Motor Corporation, represented by the chairman, the president, and several senior executives, along with representatives from Toyota Motor Sales, U.S.A. (TMS), use the occasion to announce slight changes in policy and seek dealer support for their plans. The presence of so many members of top management was well received and unprecedented compared with similar meetings held by U.S. carmakers who usually sent no one higher than division director.

The once-a-year Fireside Chat[27], held at several locations across the United States from January to February, includes the head of the TMS Lexus Division along with operational executives, who made 12 site visits to meet senior executives with up to 20 dealers in each location. Aimed at creating an open atmosphere for face-to-face discussion, Toyota's Lexus organization uses these meetings to explain policies on pricing, marketing, and service. Dealers can question the policies, express their opinions, and make suggestions directly to Lexus Division managers, who sit at the same table with a "we-are-here-to-listen" attitude. The Fireside Chat was initiated in 1995 during the Lexus sales slump to relieve dealers' anxieties and involve them in planning solutions that would ensure future growth.

The twice-a-year National Dealer Advisory Council is a three-day meeting in which four Lexus area office representatives record the opinions and requests of nine representatives of local dealer associations. The minutes of these meetings are published in a booklet that includes feedback from TMS and is distributed to all dealers. The Lexus Division feels that the views gathered by the council, which reflect majority opinions, complement the Fireside Chats, which focus on details that can be easily be overlooked by the council.[28]

The presidents of the Lexus dealerships established the Lexus Dealer Advertising Association (LDA) to foster consistency in advertising on national television and in regional newspapers and local radio stations sponsored by local dealerships. This was in stark contrast to past practices of advertising in stages, first by the manufacturer, then distributors, and finally dealers.[29] According to Jim Press, former President of Toyota Motor North America, the Lexus Dealer Advertising Association is "a very unique part of the culture that nobody else has."[30]

The four Lexus meetings are just a few of the many face-to-face interactions that Toyota practices. The company's largest reunion is the Toyota World Convention, a weeklong event held every four years bringing together executives from over 240 manufacturing partners, distributors, and affiliated companies representing more than 170 markets. Toyota, represented by top management including the chairman, the president, and senior company advisors, uses this convention to outline the company's future vision and keep distributors and business partners abreast of the company's activities.

Making Tacit Knowledge Explicit: *The Toyota Way 2001*

The fourth active element in Toyota's nerve system is the practice of converting deep, experiential, or tacit knowledge into explicit form, for broader sharing in the organization. Tacit knowledge is converted to explicit knowledge every time someone verbalizes or writes down the knowledge they have embodied, which is a deep understanding based on experience. Under the presidency of Fujio Cho, Toyota embarked on an initiative to put into writing the wisdom of the founders that had been passed down verbally through the generations. All their sayings and anecdotes were collected and evaluated to form a set of values, beliefs, principles, insights, and intuitions for the company. In the process, two core values were identified as the pillars of *The Toyota Way 2001*: "continuous improvement" (kaizen), and "respect for people" based on a belief in people's ordinary capabilities, as described in Chapter 6. *The Toyota Way 2001* is a 13-page document, written in English and Japanese and known internally as the "Green Book." It was first distributed to Toyota associates around the world in April 2001.

John Kramer said the aim of the book was "to commit in writing what had been passed around the village bonfire for years and years, from the elders to the next generation."[31] The growth and diversity of Toyota's overseas operations had alerted Fujio Cho to ponder the wisdom of the company elders and figure out a way to disseminate their knowledge in the new environment to help them steer those operations. What made the Toyota Way initiative more challenging was the recognition that core values evolve over time, as Toyota Motor Sales, U.S.A., President Yukitoshi Funo explained:

> The honorary chairman [Shoichiro Toyoda] insisted that the year 2001 be added [to the title]. He said that creating a work like this was a way of summarizing the past, but for the most part, not much good comes of chasing after the past. Reflecting the fact that the Toyota Way is continually changing, this version that we put together in 2001 may not be the way things are done in 2010, or in 2020. So, to ensure that message came across with no confusion, we put 2001 in the title.[32]

Senior Managing Director of Human Resource Management, Akio Matsubara, concurred that such a document necessarily remains incomplete or the company runs the risk of perpetuating values that are not in touch with reality. "I believe the Toyota Way itself is continually evolving, so we created *The Toyota Way 2001* as a document that will be revised in the future, and we are engaged in educational and other activities to communicate its contents to top managers at Toyota worldwide." He added, however, that the evolving doctrine is not, and must not, become a religion. "I have been given firm instructions from the top that there be no misunderstanding on this point: Toyota is not preaching or proselytizing."[33]

Publication of the Green Book was followed by *The Toyota Way in Sales and Marketing*, known as the "Silver Book," a documentation of the founders' philosophies that have specific relevance to sales and marketing operations. It was sent to all distributors in October 2002. Senior Toyota Advisor Yoshio Ishizaka, who was Executive Vice President at the time, took the initiative to lead in developing this document together with then Toyota Director, Yukitoshi Funo, and Global Marketing Division

General Manager, Katsuyoshi Tabata. Ishizaka reflected on the experience:

> As overseas sales grew in the late 1990s, we became aware of the need to articulate the Toyota Way in [the context of] sales and marketing. We had inherited [this knowledge] from history, but it was still only tacitly understood. We had embraced *The Toyota Way 2001* and positioned it as an important guiding force for us, but we felt there was something unique in our sales and marketing organization apart from the original Toyota Motor Corporation of Japan dating from 1950 to 1982.[34]

The two books have essentially the same content, but the Silver Book focuses more on people as the source of knowledge, and listening to what the dealers have to say. General Manager Katsuyoshi Tabata emphasized the importance of applying the wisdom articulated in the document:

> When we developed the Silver Book, we argued about what we thought Toyota's strengths were. The book contains philosophies and principles together with the statements of our predecessors, but other car companies have similar philosophies and principles, such as "customer first." So we concluded that it was not about putting those philosophies and principles into a book, but about implementing them, particularly, [in regards to] the strong and good relationship between Toyota and its distributors and dealers.[35]

Putting the founders' wisdom down on paper is the first step in the knowledge conversion process. The next and more important step is disseminating that wisdom throughout the organization in such a way that it can be embraced as embodied knowledge that is tacitly understood. Akio Matsubara described the importance of that process:

> I believe unquestionably that there is something called "Toyotaness" that is intuitive. We've always had veterans

passing this down in an aural tradition, but I had the feeling that we had reached the limits of this approach. One quickly gets a sense of the problem: How can Toyota's strengths be passed on effectively as they continue to evolve [internationally], and how do we inculcate them in the management layers of overseas operations where they may not share our values?[36]

The Toyota Way has taken root in local operations worldwide through hands-on experience. Dr. Takis Athanasopoulos, Executive Vice President of Toyota Motor Marketing Europe, stressed the embodied understanding of the core values in day-to-day experience:

The Toyota Way is not a generic company culture. I have experienced it much more as a concrete way of thinking and working. It is something that every employee can apply in his or her daily work life. It provides clear guidance and makes business decisions better and easier.[37]

Formal and Informal Support Mechanisms

Formal and informal support mechanisms have been established in the organization to contribute to effective functioning of the nerve system. The Toyota Institute was established at Toyota City in January 2002 to develop global leaders and middle managers cultivated with the values of the Toyota Way. The institute would educate 140 leaders and 300 middle managers each year. Fujio Cho, then President of Toyota, was named the institute's first president.

The Global Knowledge Center was established at Torrance, California, in July 2002 to disseminate *The Toyota Way in Sales and Marketing*. It is located at the University of Toyota, established by TMS four years earlier[38] and is a clearinghouse for the knowledge and expertise of Toyota distributors around the world. Just prior to establishing this center, Toyota organized a "Toyota Way in Sales and Marketing" forum in April 2002, gathering officers from the United States, Japan, Asia, and European regional headquarters, as well as major distributors from around the world. Speaking at the forum, Jim Press noted the challenges facing the Global Knowledge Center:

> Transferring knowledge across organizational boundaries is very difficult to do. As leaders, we sometimes get frustrated because we can't get two people or two teams that sit next to each other to fully collaborate and share information. What we're talking about now is immensely more challenging. We're talking about moving know-how across boundaries that are separated by great distances, differences in language and culture, and diversity in market conditions.[39]

At the same forum, Yukitoshi Funo said the Global Knowledge Center would help realize the vision of *The Toyota Way in Sales and Marketing* because it was "not only a place to share solutions, but to facilitate learning and build understanding of values through self-discovery."[40] As a Global Knowledge Center manager Erin Ilgen explained, the unique capability of the Global Knowledge Center is to engage distributors from across the globe in the practice of yokoten to disseminate best practices:

> This is an opportunity where Toyota is asking a third party organization, the Global Knowledge Center, although it's made up of Toyota associates, to learn how each country defines the Toyota Way in Sales and Marketing and to create the opportunity to share that knowledge. Previously, all the countries went at it solo. What happened in the United States stayed in the United States, and this applied to other countries.[41]

The Toyota Institute, the Global Knowledge Center, and the University of Toyota are formal organizational mechanisms supporting the nerve system that enables everybody to know everything. In addition to these organizations, employees are encouraged to join a wide variety of informal groups, which are common in large Japanese universities. These groups are organized by functional specialization, year of entry, education background, birthplace, managerial level, job shop within the factory, factory location, expert skills, sports and hobbies, and a host of other categorizations. It is not uncommon for a Toyota employee in Japan to belong to half a dozen of these informal groups. A retired factory worker recalled how he built vertical, horizontal, and even diagonal networks through such groups:

> Toyota employees come from all over Japan. By getting us involved in various informal groups, the company's aim is to build camaraderie. People learn how to communicate by taking part in these groups. A vertical network cuts through organizational hierarchy . . . horizontal networks broaden your contact with cohorts doing the same or different work in different locations.[42]

Conclusion

In this chapter, we have described Toyota's nerve system as a second integrative force that preserves the small-town feel of this enormous company by ensuring that everybody knows everything. The nerve system connects everyone at a personal level and in a variety of ways and links them to the realities of the business at the front line.

Can other companies emulate this? The five elements that make up the Toyota nerve system may seem simple enough, but the harder work of building an interconnected world by analog means demands a vast commitment of resources of the kind that, over time, reap compound rewards.

CHAPTER 8

Up-and-In Human Resource Management

The third integrative force that holds the expanding global enterprise together is *up-and-in* human resource management. The phrase *up-and-in* is derived from the opposite practice of up-or-out that is common in most professional firms—from consulting companies to investment banks. In the up-or-out system, a professional employee is either successively promoted up the ladder or gradually forced out of the company. Toyota rarely forces out so-called under-performers, focusing instead on *upgrading* their capabilities *inside* the company through various on-the-job training (OJT) and evaluation schemes.

To understand where the up-and-in approach comes from, we return to *The Toyota Way 2001*. We have explained how the beliefs and values espoused in this 13-page document had been circulating around the company in corridors, meeting rooms, and cafeterias for years, passed on from one generation to the next. These values are also articulated in the two pillars of organizational behavior at Toyota, "continuous improvement" and "respect for people." The underlying assumption is that every human being can make a contribution given the chance. The pillar of "respect for people" is reflected in Toyota human resources practices that aim to cultivate the following abilities in employees:

- To be able to think independently and from multiple perspectives, keeping an open mind and a long-term view

- To discover one's own capabilities through challenge
- To be able to take action to mobilize the organization

Toyota is cognizant of the benefits that accrue from cultivating the ability to think independently. It institutionalized this
approach as early as 1951 with a program to encourage workers on the production line to make suggestions about how to
improve the process. They were asked to use their heads as well
their hands on the production line by thinking about how they
could do things in a way that would lower costs, improve quality, and increase safety. At other companies, the responsibility
for thinking about such things was typically assigned to line
managers, but at Toyota it is the job of the line manager to
cultivate a working environment that stimulates line workers
to think creatively and make recommendations that the manager can translate into action. This philosophy is also applied
at the managerial level. Senior Managing Director in charge of
Human Resource Management, Akio Matsubara, recalls how
frequently he was told by his supervisors, "Don't leave important issues to others. Think them through by yourself." He
described how this "thinking culture" is encouraged:

> If you're in charge, you must be the best judge because
> others are less knowledgeable than you. However, you can't
> make sound judgments if you're ignorant [of the situation],
> so you have to survey the environment and [established]
> benchmarks and gather a broad range of information, and
> don't just swallow it whole. You have to use your head to
> think it all through and arrive at your own understand-
> ing. I like to instill this culture of thinking in every young
> employee when they are choosing a direction or making a
> big decision.[1]

Our interactions with Toyota people around the world over
a six-year period have convinced us that this practice is firmly
imprinted in its employees. After interviews with over 220
people, we have found the common characteristics at Toyota

to be an enthusiasm for making improvements, a readiness to listen and learn from others, to go to the source or genba to grasp the essence of a problem, an emphasis on teamwork, and the desire to take action quickly to solve a problem.

We have also found that the people at Toyota who have come up the ranks to reach senior executive positions are generally modest in character and humble about their capabilities, personifying the old Japanese adage that the head of an abundant rice plant hangs down. This unassuming behavior is also apparent in the members of the Toyoda family. For example, when Executive Vice President Akio Toyoda and three mid-level Toyota managers attended an author's MBA class session at Hitotsubashi University as guest speakers, the students were at first unable to point out Mr. Toyoda from his coworkers on their own.

Toyota executives are never satisfied with the status quo and are constantly in search of a better way. "At the very instant that we become satisfied, at the very moment we think that the status quo is good enough, that's when we start to decline," said the current President, Katsuaki Watanabe.[2] To enhance learning and keep improving, they have to stay humble and aware that there is always a better way, and it is up to them to discover it.

Toyota managers are not at all modest, however, in their praise of the Toyota work ethic. They say there is "honor and excitement" in the workplace, that it is "energizing and fun," and allows each member of the management team to "develop, grow, and flourish." Notably, most of these comments come from current and former Toyota managers and executives in the United States, such as Jing Tadeo, John Kramer, and Jim Press:

[Toyota Motor Sales, U.S.A.,] gets the most requests to share best practices and host visitors from other countries, and they [always] open their doors. . . . It is an honor for them to share their vast knowledge with [employees] in different countries; they are excited to meet people from overseas.

—Jing Tadeo, Toyota Motor Sales, U.S.A,
Manager, Global Knowledge Center[3]

I was earning less as general manager of the Toyota regional operation than the assistant general manager or other upper level managers at Chrysler or Ford. But we had different motivations, and we liked what we did. The company was very energizing. We were allowed a lot of freedom in how we practiced our craft. So, you leave your ego at the door sometimes and just go in and do the job and have fun and have a nice life with your family.

—John Kramer, Toyota Motor Sales, U.S.A.,
Vice President, Head of the Global Knowledge Center[4]

When Toyota started growing in the United States in the mid-1960s, the first group of employees had [previously] been with small import companies [like] Reno Land Rover and British Leyland. They got this thing started. Then, in the late 1960s and early 1970s Toyota began getting people from Ford and General Motors. . . . These people who were there then are still there, so there is consistency of people and continuity. When you're constantly improving and you're not in a political environment you can do things the right way. They [people] grow and develop; they flourish.

—Jim Press, former President of Toyota Motor
North America[5]

The up-and-in human resource management system is the enabling environment for this development and growth, and it is particularly applicable to industries like automobile manufacturing, where learning from experience is important. Toyota President Watanabe acknowledged the importance of experience-based tacit knowledge in the automobile industry:

Tacit knowledge is having a knack or an instinct for something based on experience . . . the things that make human beings who they are. We put in a lot of continuous effort to create our own expertise. It's important to convert that [human-based] tacit knowledge into [instruction] manuals, and into machines or information technology and robotics . . . in other words, into explicit knowledge. But at the moment that it becomes explicit knowledge, that's the end; growth stops. To grow, you have to grow tacit knowledge [in human beings]. I call it the "spiral up" of tacit and explicit knowledge.[6]

In this chapter, we elaborate on the five key aspects of an up-and-in human resource management system as practiced at Toyota. It is part of a system of knowledge-creation management that can be emulated by other companies in the new, knowledge-based business environment and has the following characteristics:

1. Stable, long-term employment
2. Emphasis on training, training, and more training
3. Power in teamwork
4. Action orientation
5. Learning-based evaluation

Stable, Long-Term Employment

A mutual long-term commitment between a company and its employee in the form of stable, long-term employment is an essential aspect of up-and-in human resource management and knowledge-creation management in general. Human Resources General Manager Teruo Suzuki emphasized the importance of taking time: "Our power base comes from allowing our workers to take their time to develop at Toyota. . . . For sure, long-term employment has its merits for a company like ours."[7] For one thing, it justifies the investment of resources needed to develop organizational capabilities that only show benefits over time. Acquiring experience in several job functions or aspects of business operations equips managers to make better systemwide decisions. It takes time to develop this competence and requires hands-on experience and multiple job rotations. For example, Aiko Matsubara spent his first 14 years at Toyota in the personnel division, then moved into domestic sales for seven years, then back to personnel for five years, then to the engineering department for almost nine years. After four years at engineering, he was appointed director in corporate planning and product planning, before he became Senior Managing Director of Human Resource Management in 2003. This broad experience spanning sales, corporate planning, product planning, and research and development has convinced him that human resources should be tightly integrated with overall management.[8]

Long-term employment allows employees both the time they need to learn from experience and grow as well as the freedom to stumble along the way. The company sees value in learning from both successful and failed initiatives. The key is to share this learning with others, so the process only works if those who have experienced failure stay on and share that experience with others. Pooling this experience also builds corporate memory that can be leveraged for competitive advantage. For example, when Toyota launched the Scion project in 2000 as a new brand aimed at the U.S. youth segment, the team included two former members of the Genesis project with experience in nontraditional, grassroots marketing that became a major factor in Scion's success. The Scion's Chief Engineer was formerly assistant to the chief engineer for the Toyota *bB*, predecessor of the Scion *xB*.

Long-term employment allows Toyota to make the necessary commitment to educating and indoctrinating employees in the Toyota Way. Toyota believes that a truly global company must be guided by a common corporate culture. *The Toyota Way 2001* articulates the elements of that culture and defines how Toyota people around the world are expected to behave. The concepts that are the basis of *The Toyota Way 2001* transcend language and nationality, resonating in countries with a wide variety of customs, traditions, and business practices. Educating close to 300,000 employees around the world to understand and share these concepts is no easy task, and seeing that they are manifested in behavior and action at the company increases the difficulty by an order of magnitude. It requires the mutual commitment of the company and employees over time to move from understanding the concepts to actualizing them in practice in daily routines and behavior.

The commitment to long-term employment is deeply rooted in Toyota's history. In the late 1940s, as Japan slid into the recession that followed World War II, demand for vehicles shifted from the military to civilian use, but the country had little cash, and its infrastructure lay in ruins. During this period, Toyota struggled with increasing worker anxiety and labor disputes. In 1950, Toyota was near bankruptcy. As a condition for refinancing its loans, the bank required that it lay off more than 1,500 employees, representing one-fourth of its entire workforce. There was no other way to save the company. In his autobiography, former President Eiji Toyoda recalled how his uncle Kiichiro felt at that time:

> Just before the labor dispute finally subsided in June, Kiichiro went before the assembled members of the union. "Much as I'm against it," he told them, "unless we make these cuts, the company doesn't stand a chance." Then, in a tearful voice, he announced, "I'm personally taking responsibility for this by quitting."[9]

Honorary Chairman Shoichiro Toyoda also remembered how his father Kiichiro felt during those times. "Kiichiro didn't think layoffs were necessary," recalled Shoichiro. "Our company was like a family, and employees and the company worked together as a team. But when he had to lay people off, it made him feel that he should go, too, and he resigned as president."[10] When the founder of the Japanese automobile industry stepped down from the company he had founded, Toyota managers vowed that employees would never again have to endure such hardship. This is part of the collective memory of the company passed down from generation to generation, forging its commitment to long-term employment even in tough times.

During the Asian Financial Crisis of 1997, Toyota Motor Thailand weathered four straight years of losses with no job cuts. The order had come down from then President Hiroshi Okuda to "cut all costs but don't touch any people."[11] In August 1998, Moody's downgraded Toyota's credit rating from AAA to AA1, citing the policy of lifetime employment as one of the reasons.[12] This would cost Toyota more than $220 million per year in additional interest payments, but then Executive Vice President Iwao Ohkijima told the rating agency that Toyota would not abandon its commitment to long-term employment.

The tough times of the 1950s were a lesson to Toyota. It learned how to function with as few people in the factory as possible by requiring workers to master multiple skills in a variety of job functions. This enabled the company to maximize its use of human resources, and a worker with multiple skills would be in a better position to weather production cuts in an economic downturn and keep his or her job. Some 40 years later, the term "multiskilling" had entered the vernacular in global management practice.

Emphasis on Training, Training, and More Training

To build a multiskilled workforce, Toyota institutionalized a number of training programs, both on and off the job, that teach problem-solving skills. During their first 10 years at the company, employees are thoroughly trained in the fundamentals of thinking their way out of problems. Akio Matsubara described the philosophy behind this approach:

> When an employee solves a problem, he or she makes a contribution to corporate policy, which ultimately is connected to user satisfaction. We inculcate our employees with the idea that learning to solve problems well is the absolute minimum requirement for success at Toyota. There is simply no way this can be learned in just a few days of training, which is why it is critical that we retain the OJT system.[13]

Another feature of OJT at Toyota is the principle that each employee must have the freedom to make decisions based on his or her own judgment. Rather than follow a strict set of rules, employees make decisions based on a rough set of guidelines that direct the organization. Employees are encouraged to always consider the broader perspective by thinking as though they were managing at two levels higher in the organization. "I learned how to think thoroughly in my training," said former Toyota Senior Managing Director Zenji Yasuda. His first assignment in Toyota was to procure springs, and he was asked to predict what the market for springs would be like three years, five years, and 10 years after the liberalization of capital markets and trade. He made the mistake of asking his superiors what he should do and was scolded with the remark: "What do you want to do?" He recalled the episode as follows:

> When I had not thought things through thoroughly enough I was told that I needed to suffer more. . . . Even when my proposals were accepted they were only given lukewarm consent. Despite this response, I was only rejected twice in my entire career, both times on small projects that involved ethical issues.[14]

Toyota's OJT is known in the industry for being longer in duration and more varied. There are five categories of training companywide: qualification-based training, supervisor-oriented training, improvement-based training, management training, and knowledge or skills-based training, such as foreign language acquisition or personal improvement. The programs differ in length and content depending on the level and job function. For example, qualification-based training is always OJT, but the tasks depend on the managerial level of the trainee. A program for newly appointed group managers (a group is the smallest organizational unit at Toyota) consists of a three-month e-learning program, followed by cross-functional group training sessions meant to provide mutual stimulation and inspiration. One year before an employee becomes a section chief or *kakaricho*, he receives a four-day training session and is then given six months to jointly develop with his mentor a five-year vision plan for presentation before a group of the relevant division managers. The training program for managers or *kacho* emphasizes soft skills such as mentoring, as well as prioritizing commitments and resource allocation, restructuring operations, reengineering of the business, and how to rethink systems, a task that often takes a back seat to daily operations. From the first day of managerial training, every kacho trainee is asked to identify issues and immediately formulate changes.

Another distinguishing feature of Toyota training is the role played by talented individuals from various parts of the business as teachers and mentors. As teachers, they aim to produce a cadre of excellent leaders who learn through continuous experimentation. As mentors, they share stories of personal experiences, an exchange that passes on Toyota values to successive generations. It is a modern-day apprenticeship system that utilizes the skills and achievements of exemplar employees. Matsubara recalled what was expected of him as a mentor in a company training program:

> You have been a Toyota manager for years. What has the work meant to you? How have you, personally, developed in the business? What personal stories can you share that illustrate your theory of life and your attitude toward work? These are the typical questions of trainees, and they listen intently, with the view that what is most real and authentic is the wisdom derived from experience, and this view is consistent with [the] corporate culture.[15]

Retired factory worker Kiyoshi Tsutsumi is another exemplar who mentored in a training program designed to promote the use of seatbelts before they were required by law. According to Tsutsumi, training alone would not spur employees to change old habits. Sometimes singling out certain individuals as "bad" examples to drive a message home was the only way to get them to change. He shared the following story:

> I handed out to young factory workers the statistics on fatal accidents in which drivers had not used seatbelts, but there will always be those who drive without seatbelts. Then I asked one of the supervisors to stand in the company parking lot and list the names of those who were still not wearing seatbelts, and I passed this around the company, which had some effect. Finally, I took the drastic step of picking up a driver who repeatedly appeared on the list and made him drive the car wearing a seatbelt. Following up the training with this kind of action had immediate impact.[16]

As Toyota expands globally, it also expands training opportunities for non-Japanese employees. Toyota President Watanabe called the Global Production Center at its Motomachi plant in Toyota City a *dojo*, the Japanese name for a physical and mental training facility because it polishes up tacit or embodied knowledge of Toyota processes in hundreds of assembly line tasks.[17] The first Global Production Center was built in Japan, followed by one in the United States, then the United Kingdom, and Thailand; and Watanabe says more will be built in the future. As the company grows and expands to so many, different countries, the biggest fear of top management is that they might lose the discipline of continuous improvement or kaizen, especially on the factory floor. As observed by *Fortune* magazine, the number of trainees and their varied origins at the Global Production Center in Japan make it unique in the industry:

> [A] class of about 1,500 workers—half from overseas facilities in China, Malaysia, and Indonesia—[are] being drilled at stations for parts pickup, welding, painting, and plastic

stamping. At Screw Grommet Insertion Station No. 2, a worker from China struggled to keep pace with a computer. Elsewhere workers from Indonesia, perfecting their body-painting techniques, practiced a series of deep knee bends holding spray guns filled with water. Trainees at the Cylinder Insertion Station were given one minute to fit a sequence of progressively larger metal cylinders into a row of corresponding holes. It looked easy, but no one succeeded on the first attempt. The trainer, who can complete the sequence in 24 seconds, showed novices how to position their feet, distribute their weight, and hold each cylinder to get it right.[18]

With continuing global expansion, Toyota will have to look more aggressively outside the company for human resources at the supervisory level. "Up to now, we have been carried forward by a certain Mikawa-centric purity of thought, but the world is becoming one size larger and I'm not sure this makes us resilient enough," said Matsubara. "What we really need to do is to bring in more outside blood." One such effort, documented in the *Harvard Business Review*, describes the experience of a talented young American called Bob Dallis hired away from a U.S. competitor to fill an upper-level position at one of Toyota's U.S. plants. After 12 intensive weeks of training at the U.S. engine plant with 10 days in Japan, he discovered, among other things, that managers at Toyota are expected to act as enablers and to coach. He learned this lesson by observing the behavior of his Japanese mentor, who worked one-on-one with him for the duration in the United States and Japan:

> He came out of his training realizing that improving actual operations was not *his* job—it was the job of workers themselves. His role was to help them understand that responsibility and enable them to carry it out. His training taught him how to construct work as experiments, which would yield continuous learning and improvements, and to teach others to do the same.[19]

Power in Teamwork

Individual self-actualization is emphasized at Toyota as a function of teamwork. The exemplar employees who serve as teachers and mentors are not seen as hotshots separate from the group but as a reflection of the group in which leadership is distributed. "Toyota is not the kind of company where a select few shine," said Human Resources General Manager Teruo Suzuki. "It is not considered appropriate to have a select few running the company. Instead, Toyota depends on all the workers in the company bringing their strengths into play to demonstrate their power as a team."[20]

A car is built through the efforts of a lot of different people with different expertise. "Every single person is the main actor on the stage," said Watanabe.[21] This mindset is central to up-and-in human resource management and based on one of the founders' philosophies described in Chapter 6 that everybody should win. Everybody wins, but only in so far as their contribution strengthens the whole team, assuming that strength arises from the interaction of the different perspectives. "Every single person takes a lead role on the stage, but as an organization you want to create a situation where one plus one equals three or even five, not two. That's what I call a team," said Watanabe, adding that creating the environment for this kind of teamwork is the most important task of managers.[22] Toyota's simultaneous promotion of self-realization of the individual with the team transcends the paradox of either/or, and this is the core idea of up-and-in human resource management philosophy.

In the end, the greater emphasis is on the whole team over the individual. "We don't really make a big deal about individual achievement," said Matsubara. "Ultimately, what counts most is what we are able to achieve as a team. I believe this kind of thinking is another of our distinguishing features."[23] To demonstrate the point, he noted that when employees at Toyota are promoted they are not congratulated in the usual way. "Instead, we deliver a message like this: 'Congratulations on your selection. Many others were within a hair's breadth of being selected.

Keep that in mind as you do your job.'" And care is taken to prevent demoralization among those not promoted or accepted on a project. "We have a fear that if employees become demoralized, Toyota could fall apart," said Matsubara. "When we talk to those who didn't make it, we tell them sincerely that it was not because of their character, but because we had to limit the number of people." He emphasized the importance of empathy in conveying bad news to employees and said they are frequently considered for other projects to make them feel they have other opportunities.[24]

This "team-over-individual" spirit is a reflection of the second pillar of *The Toyota Way 2001*, "respect for people," which is interpreted at Toyota as, "respect for the individual realizing that power is consolidated in a team."[25] The point is elaborated as follows: "We believe each individual has the creative power for the independent achievement of his or her personal goals. We respect the values, abilities, way of thinking, and motivation of all team members." Thus, if an individual is able to achieve his or her personal goals, everybody wins.

To actualize this sentiment, everyone above the management level of kacho or section chief submits a "mission statement" at the beginning of each fiscal year in April. Managers jot down their personal goals on a sheet of paper and conduct self-evaluations according to the 10 behavioral requirements of the job (described further later in this chapter). The evaluations are reviewed by supervisors who also serve as the managers' coaches in a one-hour session held three times a year. "Of course, we want our people to challenge themselves by setting high standards and difficult objectives," said Matsubara. "While the results are important, we pay a lot more attention to how much effort has been put into the process,"[26] he added emphasizing the priority of means over ends and action over results.

Action Orientation

The preference for action is a quintessential Toyota trait. *The Toyota Way 2001* describes this preference in the section on genchi genbutsu or going to the frontline to see reality as it is: "We take action decisively in order to produce results. We neither play games impetuously nor waste time on endless discussion of possibilities. We seek a measured, steady pace toward decision making that results in timely action without the needless risk of haste."[27] As head of the Motomachi factory from 1996 to 1999, Toyota President Katsuaki Watanabe started the "One Rank Up" movement based on the conviction that the entire factory would move forward to the next stage only if each and every worker pitched in to help. He emphasized the importance of individuals taking small steps for the benefit of the whole:

> I asked the factory workers to take one year to engage themselves in one thing that they could boast about at the front line, something that they could be proud of in the world. It could be something as simple as making sure everybody greets each other, or getting 4S (*Seiri, Seiton, Seiketsu, Seiso*, meaning organized, well-ordered, neat, and clean) to the next level. . . . In order to produce results, you absolutely must act with dogged determination, steadily, and repeatedly. I occasionally venture forth to the front line to see [the results] for myself.[28]

The value of taking action is passed on through generations in popular phrases such as: "If you're 60 percent sure, take action" or "It's better to fail doing something than doing nothing." What matters more than the results is the "process" of taking action to achieve results. "Otherwise, tradition tells us there can be no development of people and no fair evaluation,"[29] said Matsubara. This emphasis on the process of achieving personal goals articulated in one's mission statement is consistent with other process innovations at Toyota such as *kanban, andon, kaizen*, and others. It is also aimed at building the knowledge assets of the company for continuous innovation. Toyota is process-driven to improve the process of knowledge creation overall, in every aspect of the business. Hence, the *Prius* was a project to develop a new product as well as a new product development process. Similarly, the Scion was a project to develop a new product along with a new sales and marketing process.

Learning-Based Evaluation

Toyota has developed a unique set of criteria for evaluating managers. Remuneration below the level of kacho or section chief is based 50 percent on seniority and 50 percent on performance. For those at the kacho level and above, salary is based 100 percent on performance related to results as well as process. To evaluate process performance, the company looks at how goals are achieved; how issues are handled and resolved; how organizational skills are fostered; and how people are developed, motivated, and empowered. More specifically, they are evaluated in five categories on the following points:

1. *Creative handling of issues:*

   Innovative way of thinking not bound by custom.

   Development and presentation of plans based on a mid- to long-term perspective.

2. *Resolution of issues:*

   Appropriate situational judgment.

   Decision making.

   Persistence (resilience, tenacity).

3. *Organizational management skills:*

   Prioritized commitment of resources and reengineering of business.

   Establishment of a framework/system for completing work.

4. *Utilization of human resources:*

   Fair evaluation (of individuals) and feedback.

   Preplanned mentoring and nurturing (of subordinates).

5. *Personal magnetism:*

   Trust from and empowerment of (organizational) members.

Like the salary structure, evaluation criteria also differ according to the level of position. For general staff, more weight is given to creative handling and resolution of issues, with the emphasis on developing the tacit skills needed to identify and create challenges and build specialized knowledge. For managers, the last three categories of organizational management, utilization of human resources, and personal magnetism are more important. All employees evaluate themselves, grading their activities under each of the 10 points as very good (double circle), good (circle), or fair (triangle). They discuss their self-evaluations with superiors three times a year,[30] which helps them keep track of their progress and prevent organizational apathy from setting in.

What is striking about the specific evaluation criteria is their fuzziness. The last category of personal magnetism (*jinbo*) is meant to describe how much trust and respect the person has earned from others. *Jinbo* is a very vague term that is open to interpretation and extremely difficult to quantify. A superior can only evaluate a manager according to this criterion if he or she has the opportunity to share contexts and experiences with the manager. Realizing this, the human resources department came up with a more detailed breakdown of each of the 10 points. For example, under personal magnetism, the point concerning "trust from and empowerment of organizational members" is broken down as follows: (1) takes an open and fair attitude toward staff members and earns their trust, (2) empowers staff members by engaging in business with sincerity and passion and being a visible role model, and (3) endeavors constantly to maintain and improve workplace morale. Further, on the point of persistence under resolution of issues, the following two points are added: (1) stands forth and demonstrates the determination to persist till the very end, even under a difficult set of circumstances; and (2) is persistent in convincing and coordinating people around him or her and overcoming obstacles. However, these additional points are also rather fuzzy and open to interpretation.

One of the evaluation criteria that is quintessentially Toyota is persistence or resilience. This trait is seen as part of the corporate DNA and is described in Japanese *nebari tsuyosa*, which translates literally as "adhesive strength." The genesis of this trait can be found in the words of Sakichi Toyoda, founder of the Toyota Automatic Loom Works, which preceded the establishment of Toyota Motor Corporation: "Endure a hundred times, strengthen yourself a thousand times, and you will complete your tasks in short order." Toyoda's persistence was born of the region of Kosai-shi, where he grew up and is known for cultivating individuals of strong character, endurance, and resilience due to its simple yet rugged living conditions.

The current President, Watanabe, is fond of describing this persistence with his favorite saying, "Pick a friendly fight," which he used repeatedly in an interview.[31] "If your boss refuses you something that you really want to do, don't give up," he said. "Try pitching it two or three times. By the third time, the boss will realize, 'Hey, this guy is serious.' On the first try, the proposal was denied, on the second try, a small bud surfaced, and on the third try there were a number of times when the boss ended up telling me, 'If you're this adamant, you can do it.' In the end, I was able to do what I really wanted to do despite the opposition, so I must say that my bosses were really good." Watanabe also described his effort as a member of the public relations team to get the company to publicize technological innovations:

> I had argued that we should publicize the work of the Higashi Fuji Research Center. My repeated requests were turned down because there was no precedent for disclosing [research activities] to the community. I finally said to the director in charge of technological development, "Don't you resent the fact that in the media Toyota is portrayed as excelling in sales while Nissan is portrayed as excelling in technology?" Normally, I would have been berated for being such a big mouth, but he agreed to make public even our most sensitive [technological] secrets.[32]

The notion of picking a friendly fight at Toyota grows out of training its people to resolve contradictions by arguing things out to the last detail and without compromise. Matsubara described the process as cultivating a healthy anxiety in the workplace:

> There are always two sides to every story and maybe even three or four conflicting simultaneous realities we must grapple with. In these situations, we try to argue things out through-and-through, ideally without forcing any side to compromise on its responsibilities, and ultimately drawing out the pieces of wisdom that should be applied to the matter at hand. So, in a sense, we are always consciously bringing a certain level of anxiety with us, a good kind of anxiety, into the frontline.[33]

It is this kind of process that builds resilience in the organization.

Conclusion

In this chapter, we described Toyota's up-and-in approach to human resource management as the third integrative force that binds the global organization together. As we have shown in previous chapters, Toyota's penchant for experimentation in pursuit of impossible goals and its embrace of a diversity of perspectives in pursuit of local customization undoubtedly raises the level of anxiety in the organization. But these expansive forces produce a healthy anxiety that does not result in dysfunction because employees know that their individual livelihoods are not on the line. This provides a stable environment that allows them to think for the benefit of the company and over the long term, while also helping to preserve the corporate memory that is so essential to advancement and innovation.

The policy of up-and-in human resource management is supported by the core values of "continuous improvement" or kaizen and "respect for people." These values are articulated in *The Toyota Way 2001*, which is informed by the founders' philosophies. There are five characteristics of up-and-in human resource management: long-term employment; on-the-job training for continuous improvement; the notion that everybody should win through teamwork; a preference for action; and learning-based evaluation criteria. We would argue that the up-and-in approach to human resource management is more suitable to industrial production in the knowledge age because it puts the human being, rather than machines, at the center of production. Ikujiro Nonaka, author of the knowledge-creation theory of global business management, has emphasized the importance of viewing the human being as part of a whole and in relationships that can be characterized as "I-Thou" rather than self and other:

> The philosopher Martin Buber speaks of the "I-Thou" relationship.[34] This is the relationship that emerges when one speaks to the whole man, as distinct from the "I-It" relationship that objectifies the other as a thing. The process of speaking to an object is fundamentally different from that of speaking to another being. Are you really engaged in two-way dialogue? I believe the knowledge worker is the epitome of the emotional animal. He spends night and day obsessing over the differences between the ideal and reality, and is hurt by even the faintest slight. The question of whether or not one can share in those emotions is undoubtedly of critical importance in knowledge-based management.[35]

In the next chapter, we show that Toyota functions by constructively pitting expansive and integrative forces against each other because it has deep pockets, the commitment to develop organizational capability, and the people to pursue this time-consuming and expensive process.

CHAPTER 9

Toyota's Resource Base

By the time the Lexus *LS400* debuted in 1989, Toyota had sunk $1 billion in the project over six years—three times more and two years longer than what it normally invested to develop a new car at the time.[1] This prompted the LS400 Chief Engineer, Ichiro Suzuki, to remark, "Certainly, we spent a lot of money, but we believed that it was critical for our new luxury car franchise to succeed with this car. If this car failed, I thought Toyota would have to abandon entry into the U.S. luxury car market for some time."[2]

The Lexus was not just a new car, but a new brand for Toyota with a new franchise based on an entirely new business model. To give it a running start, Toyota developed a proprietary satellite communications system linking all the dealers in a network to exchange information on daily sales, car and parts inventories, and service requests. This innovation allowed the Lexus dealers to operate with car inventory levels that were about 3 times smaller than rival dealers of American or European cars, minimizing the impact of fluctuating sales to operate more profitably. The system was not cheap—Toyota spent $4 million to set it up and each dealer had to invest $170,000 to connect to it.[3]

Was launching the Lexus a risky proposition? Most certainly, it was. This was not a standard model upgrade where success depends on a fast response to market changes. It was the strategic launch of a completely new car into a new market segment—one of the riskiest endeavors any automaker can make to remain competitive in the industry. The two biggest risks—that the car will fail to sell or that defects will force its complete recall—are what automakers strive to avoid by developing cars outfitted with the latest technology based on designs that meet the needs of future customers identified in marketing research. These factors are also critical to make new cars stand out in the market.

However, one common element that can undermine a development effort is time, particularly a lack of time to make the investment needed to perfect the car design. A car that is rushed through development runs the risk of manufacturing defects and other problems of quality, lowering the standing of the automaker in the eyes of the consumer. Toyota understands this risk, which is why it spent six years developing the Lexus LS400. But an investment of time alone is insufficient. Toyota also spent large sums of money building capability to market the Lexus by developing the right dealer network, training employees, and designing a marketing campaign to kick off the brand.

The Lexus case shows how Toyota's resource base—money, organizational capability, and people—acts as an enabler and an amplifier, allowing the company to expand and integrate the two sets of contradictory forces that drive its growth. The system worked because Toyota made aggressive capital investments supporting organizational development and training of people to an extent that other companies cannot or are unwilling to match.

We find Toyota's approach to accumulating and deploying its capital and human resources to be a significant factor in the company's continued success as an automaker. This approach has three aspects:

1. Investing in efficiency to increase profits
2. Reinvesting profits to cultivate organizational capability and people required for growth
3. Making a long-term commitment to people, reinforcing their potential to create efficiency gains

In this chapter, we examine how Toyota builds, allocates, and improves its resources in accordance with these convictions, ensuring a positive outcome of the interaction of the six forces.

Investing in Efficiency

In the industrial age, one key driver for success was higher efficiency relative to competitors. That is, minimal production waste, manufacturing flexibility, cost and quality leadership, product reliability, and quick response to market changes. In that setting, the focus is on developing systems or innovations that drive the hard side of the company. In Toyota's case, that included the Toyota Production System (TPS), its logistics management, and fast product development. Toyota's hard-nosed approach to efficiency stems from its early experiences in the auto industry. We examine two aspects of its approach: running an efficient production system and investing in manufacturing and development capacity.

Running an Efficient and Profitable Production System

Toyota was a latecomer to the automobile industry. By the time it started producing cars in the 1930s, Ford had already sold more than 15 million Model T's and General Motors was the world's largest car manufacturer, with operations spanning the globe. As a small player, Toyota relied on bank loans to finance the expansion of its plants and pay for marketing and technology development. The labor dispute of 1950 that put Toyota on the verge of financial collapse and resulted in the lay-off of one-fourth of the workforce strongly influenced its current attitude to resource management.

From that point onward, every activity at Toyota City was approached with the continuous aim of eliminating *muda*, *mura*, and *muri* (waste, unevenness, and excess burden). This would lower production costs throughout the supply chain and prevent a recurrence of another financial crisis. This frugality meant shrinking idle inventory levels on every production line, a process that prompted just-in-time sourcing of parts and the birth of the Toyota Production System. From the late 1950s onward, it refined this system, introducing practices like stockless production or *kanban* and adopting industry best practices (referred to as world-class manufacturing). Toyota was slow to start production outside of Japan, preferring instead to concentrate know-how at its domestic plants. It was not until the 1980s that it started manufacturing outside of Japan and began exporting its manufacturing principles so all of its production lines produced high-quality cars at low cost regardless of location.

Toyota's frugality also affected product development. While Western automakers preferred to design and produce most vehicle parts in-house, Toyota used suppliers to both design and produce parts, which kept Toyota's costs under control by shifting responsibility for cost control to its suppliers. Parts were supplied through a bidding process that gave the winners the biggest share of the Toyota pie, but they had to share their innovations with the losers, who were each awarded a smaller share of the pie, allowing them to stay in the game and catch up. This way, Toyota sustained multiple, reliable sources for every key component and kept suppliers from slipping into bankruptcy.

The emphasis on eliminating muda, mura, and muri in operations allowed Toyota to reduce costs more than anyone in the industry in the production of vehicles like the *Corolla* and the IMV, both sold in over 140 countries. In 2006, Toyota's production plant in the United States led the market in total manufacturing productivity per vehicle (29.9 hours versus 32.4 at General Motors, 32.9 at DaimlerChrysler, and 35.1 at Ford) and capacity utilization (103 percent versus 93 percent at General Motors, 88 percent at DaimlerChrysler, and 77 percent at Ford).[4] Toyota cars take less time to make and prices being equal, generate more profit than those of its competitors. That profit is $125 more per unit compared to the restructured General Motors based on manufacturing productivity alone.[5]

Each car Toyota sold in fiscal year 2007 contributed an industry-leading average of $2,088 to its pretax bottom line (versus runners up Nissan, at $1,576, and Honda, at $1,390), a figure it strives to increase by continuously improving the efficiency of operations. With more than 9 million cars sold each year (including Daihatsu and Hino), Toyota's bottom line is now the new benchmark in the industry.

Investing in Manufacturing and Development Capacity

Toyota first became consistently profitable during the 1980s, increasing the amount of cash reserves at the company ninefold to more than $15 billion by 1990. It maintained this level of cash throughout the decade, hence the nickname "Toyota bank." From 2001 to 2007, Toyota's net income more than tripled to $14 billion, yet its dividend payout rose by only $2.2 billion (to $2.9 billion) while cash holdings increased by $3.6 billion (to $20 billion). In 2006 and 2007 alone, cost reduction efforts had decreased operating expenses by approximately $2 billion.[6] So where does Toyota's accumulating profit end up?

For starters, a substantial portion has been used for new production facilities and to upgrade existing infrastructure for expansion. From 2001 to 2007, spending in this area rose from $9.6 billion to $24 billion, a compounded annual growth rate of 16 percent, outpacing the industry average of 3 percent during the same period. In 2007, Toyota's capital spending ($24 billion) was higher than Honda ($5.1 billion), Ford ($6 billion), and General Motors ($7.5 billion) combined. Another big portion of profits from 2001 to 2007 went into rising research and development costs (from $3.8 billion to $7.5 billion) mainly for environmentally friendly technologies, cell battery technology, and advanced technologies related to collision safety and vehicle stability. In 2006, Toyota's investment in research and development ($6.9 billion) was slightly lower than Ford's ($7.2 billion) and DaimlerChrysler's ($7 billion), the two top spenders in the industry.[7] A third area where Toyota spent big was in training facilities for employees, dealers, and distributors.

From 1990 to 2006, the two key regions on the receiving end of Toyota's investments included the United States, with direct investment exceeding $14 billion,[8] and Europe, where it spent almost $8 billion establishing nine production centers, four logistics facilities, two centers for research and development, two training facilities, and several support centers.[9]

The magnitude of Toyota's investments seems unusual, considering that the mature auto industry has a low potential for return on long-term investment due to lesser prospects for growth. From 1999 to 2007, the compounded annual growth rate of the global auto industry was just 3.1 percent (number of vehicles sold), while revenue growth for the top 10 automakers averaged less than 5 percent. The wide gaps in operational efficiency that once separated Toyota from competitors have narrowed in recent years. For example, the difference in the number of labor hours per vehicle between the most productive and the least productive automakers in the United States has dropped from 17.2 hours in 1998 to 5.2 in 2006.[10]

In this efficiency-driven manufacturing environment, where advantages constantly shrink as competitors emulate each other's best practices, managing for the short-term becomes a trump card. Endeavors that yield long-term or uncertain results—such as developing an untested technology or localizing operations to improve market coverage—are put on the back burner in favor of projects that generate short-term gains, are less risky, and emphasize cost benefits or standardization. Yet, Toyota continues to invest heavily in this efficiency-driven mature industry. Why? Because it considers auto manufacturing a growth industry. The reason, according to the current President Katsuaki Watanabe, is that there are only 800 million cars in the world for a population of over six billion people:

> This is roughly one in eight. Three quarters of all cars are concentrated in areas with just one quarter of the [world's] population . . . places like the United States, Japan, and key countries in Europe. Only one quarter of all cars are in locations with three quarters of the population. In

China, there are over 1.3 billion people, but only a fraction of them own cars. The same could be said of India. So, if you think of the diffusion of cars, there's definitely a big growth potential. Globally speaking, [automobile manufacturing] is a growth industry.[11]

Looking back, it becomes apparent how Toyota has come to the conclusion that the auto industry is a growth industry. From 1980 to 2007, its revenue grew 13-fold to $203.8 billion, even as it was forced to adjust the price of exports as the yen appreciated from 220 to 114 yen per dollar. This translates into an annual growth rate of 10.1 percent since 1980. In such a high growth environment, Toyota's long-term investments generate bigger payoffs than a series of short-term profit-driven ones. This is analogous to creating a retirement fund early in your working career rather than waiting till you are closer to retirement age. The cumulative effect of compounding interest over time reaps larger returns, regardless of how much more you invest later in life. In a similar fashion, Toyota continues investing to expand manufacturing flexibility, to develop new technologies needed for future innovation, and to improve local operations to better respond to market changes, generating the long-term returns that increase efficiency and competitiveness and assure its lead over competitors.

Cultivating Organizational Capability and People Required for Growth

As manufacturing efficiency increases, employees become redundant. A 10-person production line producing X number of parts per hour at 70 percent efficiency could make the same number of parts in the same amount of time with fewer employees if efficiency increased to 80 percent. In an efficiency-driven manufacturing environment, redundancies from efficiency gains typically result in workforce reductions. Yet, from 1980 to 2006, as Toyota's average number of labor hours per car shrank from 39 to 22, its production capacity increased almost threefold to 9,017,000 units and headcount increased sixfold to 286,000.[12] Although manufacturing efficiency increased, workforce growth outpaced increases in production capacity. This seems to contradict the conventional view that higher efficiency leads to a smaller workforce.

One of the reasons for faster growth in the workforce relative to production capacity is obvious. Toyota expanded outside Japan and entered new market segments overseas during this period, increasing operational complexity and duplication in sales, marketing, administrative, and information technology (IT) functions. In the 11-year period between 1997 and 2007, Toyota opened 31 new plants around the world. The growth of small-scale overseas facilities countered the benefits of concentrated production in Toyota City, causing productivity to decline. In 1997, Toyota was making 33.1 vehicles per employee, but by 2002, this figure dropped to 25.6. However, by 2007, with the addition of 10 new plants, productivity improved to 31.7.

The other reason for the higher workforce growth is subtler. Toyota knew that the auto industry was a knowledge-driven industry, where growth depended not only on an efficiency-driven approach, but on organizational capability and people. Instead of shedding redundant workers, Toyota enhanced its practice of retraining and reassigning them, recognizing the potential of experienced employees to continue to contribute to the company. At the same time, the addition of new employees was carefully controlled and their performance closely monitored. This practice ensured that existing know-how could be passed on to others and retained in corporate memory. In a knowledge-driven industry, the investments Toyota makes to enhance organizational capability and people generate the biggest payoff in sustaining growth. The turnaround at Toyota in Puerto Rico demonstrates the basic principle of this approach.

Toyota started selling cars in Puerto Rico in the 1960s by partnering with a privately owned distributor. Its cars were well received due to their quality, reliability, and most importantly, affordability, and by the 1980s, the distributor operated about 50 Toyota sales outlets throughout the island. However, these dealerships operated independently and focused on pumping up sales, with little investment in facilities or service, resulting in consistently low customer satisfaction. Locally, the cars were nicknamed "Tojotas," a combination of the Spanish words *todo* (all), *jodido* (messed up), and Toyo*ta*, implying that if a car went in for service, it would remain in a state of disrepair. By the early 1990s, even though Toyota's cars were highly regarded for their quality, the brand image had suffered, and annual sales slumped to below 17,000 units.[13]

In 1994, Toyota bought out the distributor and with the help of sales and marketing specialists from Toyota Motor Sales, U.S.A., instituted a dealer improvement program focusing on three key areas: sales, service, and spare parts. Toyota de Puerto Rico, the local affiliate, started a Program of Excellence—a dealer development program based on kaizen and Plan-Do-Check-Act cycles in the three areas. The number of sales outlets was reduced to 25, and after years of neglect, dealers began investing to upgrade and expand facilities to handle spare parts and service calls.[14]

By 1998, Toyota sales were on the rise in Puerto Rico, but lingering issues concerning the brand remained. Although its quality was highly rated, customers dismissed Toyota cars as boring. To differentiate Toyota from competitors and expel the "boring" label, the pitch had to switch from a rational message to an emotional one. It took a risk by increasing its spending on radically new advertising that made people excited about the Toyota brand by associating it with values like "adventure," "energy," "irresistibility," and "fun."[15]

By 2004, the percentage of consumers who recalled seeing a Toyota advertisement jumped to 63 percent from 16 percent in 1997, and 40 percent of them mentioned Toyota first when asked to name any car brand. Annual sales increased to over

37,000 units from 20,000, outpacing market growth. Toyota became the market leader with a 25.9 percent market share, a full 15 percentage points higher than second-place Ford.[16]

The turnaround at Toyota de Puerto Rico demonstrates two areas where Toyota has persistently invested resources in order to cultivate organizational capability and people and grow in a knowledge-driven auto industry. These areas are: (a) building better dealerships and (b) building the brand.

Building Better Dealerships

Toyota limited the number of dealers selling its cars in Puerto Rico so it could make sufficient profit to reinvest in the dealerships. With fewer dealers, Toyota can increase the support it allocates to each one, with more face-to-face meetings, more time for reviewing dealer marketing strategies and getting feedback, and more targeted troubleshooting. Lexus, Scion, and Toyota rated highest in the 2006 North American Dealers Association dealer satisfaction survey (average rating of 90 versus the industry average of 71.2), based on factors such as the level of support dealers receive and how well the automaker responds to their feedback. The benefits of limiting the number of dealerships are huge. In the United States in 2006, for example, Toyota had just over 1,400 dealers compared to GM's 13,800 and Ford's 7,000. For one thing, Toyota dealers beat all rivals in terms of average units sold (1,760 versus the industry average of 705).[17] These numbers suggest that Toyota dealers, on average, earn higher profits than their rivals. What typically happens is that they reinvest their profits to expand or improve their facilities and hire more employees. This helps to keep the customer coming back. Toyota dealers create a virtuous circle of spending on improvements in customer service to increase sales and profits.

Even when a dealer is not performing well, Toyota will not dump them so long as they are willing to learn the Toyota Way of doing business to improve operations, as shown in the case of Toyota de Puerto Rico. Toyota faced a similar situation in Thailand during the 1990s, where its unit sales per dealer were lower than Honda and Isuzu, its two key rivals there. It conducted a study of the Thai market from 1994 to 1996 and found that 70 percent of new car purchasers were referred by existing customers.[18] It also found that dealerships suffered from low motivation among sales staff due to low pay and little opportunity for professional growth or promotion. The study revealed that dealership managers spent more time selling cars than running the business because their pay was mainly in sales commissions.

To improve its Thai dealerships, Toyota introduced dealer-training programs in 1997 at a local Toyota Education and Training Center. Dealers were granted access to the accumulated best practices and know-how sourced from Toyota dealers throughout the world. Toyota changed the sales approach to reduce the reliance on purchase incentives, which Thai dealers had often used to boost sales volume. The focus shifted toward explaining the product better to customers with events like test-driving campaigns. To improve coordination of activities, it introduced "control boards" at each dealership, displaying information on delivery schedules for the entire market. These types of changes did not have a direct impact on dealer profitability, but they shifted the focus away from margin-eroding incentives toward improving customer service.

In 2001, reform of the Thai dealerships expanded with the "Thai for Excellence" campaign designed to improve staff motivation by enhancing their role in the sales process. Under this campaign, Toyota expanded the scope of product training that had been dedicated to a select few local trainers and extended it to every sales employee in the country. They also encouraged dealers to join special events like prelaunch viewing of vehicles and promotional contests. With these reforms, Toyota's Thai dealers climbed to the number one ranking in the J.D. Power and Associates, Sales Satisfaction Index by the early 2000s, while increasing Toyota's share of the Thai passenger car market from 29 percent in 1995[19] to just over 48 percent in 2006.[20] The dealer-network grew to 88 centers with 238 showrooms throughout the country, and sales in Thailand rose to 1,600 units per dealer, rivaling the performance of Toyota's dealers in the United States.[21]

Building the Brand

When Toyota first started exporting cars to the United States in late 1950s, the car's novelty and mechanical simplicity were enough to attract the curious first customer. As sales expanded in 1960s, Toyota earned a reputation for affordable, reliable cars, and by the 1970s, the Toyota brand came to stand for quality, dependability, and fuel economy. But in the late 1980s, it had to play a new game when it entered the luxury segment with the Lexus brand.

For the first time in its history, Toyota had to build a new brand from scratch. The Lexus could not draw on the existing values of the Toyota brand—affordability, quality, dependability, and fuel economy—because the combination was unsuitable for a luxury-class car as refined as the LS400. Every element supporting the new brand, including the sales approach, the dealer network, and spare parts procurement, was designed to provide an unparalleled level of service in the industry. This inspired the theme of the first Lexus marketing campaign— the relentless pursuit of perfection. The Lexus brand had to embrace such emotional qualities as aspiration (pursuing perfection) and inspiration (perfection is elusive). As in the case of Toyota de Puerto Rico, these emotional qualities had to be sewn into the customers' mindset. In launching Lexus, Toyota learned to cultivate the organizational capability of using brand as a critical resource essential for growth.

Toyota extended this capability to build a brand in Europe over a short period of time. The 1999 launch of the first generation subcompact Yaris in Italy exemplified this approach to advertising. For the launch, Toyota flooded the Italian market with promotions and advertisements to maximize exposure. Some 400 demonstration models were made available for journalists, compared to the usual 30, and the vehicle was advertised in 37 national and sports daily newspapers, in 311 television spots, 600 radio spots, 4,300 billboards, and in web site banners.[22]

The Yaris marketing blitz paid off handsomely. In 1999, alone, Toyota booked over 45,000 orders and sold 25,000 units, almost doubling the company's revenue in the Italian market. More important, the marketing campaign successfully positioned the Yaris as the top-end vehicle in its class, allowing Toyota to sell them at a premium relative to similarly outfitted models from Fiat, Peugeot, and Renault. That same year, Toyota became the top selling Japanese brand in Italy, and its brand awareness and brand recognition[23] shot up from 9 percent to 15 percent and from 58 percent to 70 percent, respectively.[24]

Toyota's approach for the 2005 launch of the second generation Yaris in France was more emotionally based. It aimed to connect the Yaris with French consumers, who disdained foreign brands. The marketing campaign emphasized Yaris' French roots—a car built in France by French workers—to assuage doubts concerning the foreign heritage of the Toyota brand. This emotion-inspired approach was also used in the 2002 campaign that linked the Scion to popular music, art, and fashion as well as the 2006 campaign to promote the full-size Tundra as "the all-new, built-in-America Toyota truck," as described in Chapter 5.

Toyota's marketing budget for a new car typically ranges from $30 to $60 million, but it ultimately depends on the model, the market, and the strategic value of the launch. For example, the one-month price tag for the first generation Yaris campaign in Italy was small at $6.6 million, yet big for a market the size of Italy.[25] The 2002 prelaunch marketing campaign for the Scion brand in the United States consumed an estimated $50 million, with 60 percent of that on grassroots marketing, which is typically outside the usual, high-priced advertising channels in print and television media.[26] The strategic importance of the U.S. pickup truck market is reflected in the large sums of money automakers spent on advertising for that segment. Toyota's advertising budget for the launch of its new Tundra in

2006 was slightly north of $100 million, a modest sum compared to the $292 million General Motors spent promoting its 2007 *Silverado*.[27]

Abundant financial resources are required to advertise and market brands in the auto industry, especially in the United States. In 2006, Toyota spent almost $3.4 billion[28] advertising globally, 58.9 percent of this amount in the United States alone.[29] This translates to an average advertising expense of $713 per unit sold in the United States compared to $697 per unit sold for General Motors and $774 for Ford. Although Toyota's average advertising expense per unit sold is more or less on par with its rivals, its marketing campaigns span a limited number of marques (three versus eight at General Motors and eight at Ford),[30] which means Toyota spends more per marque in the United States. However, outside of the United States, Toyota enjoys a significant advantage. In 2006, it spent just $231 in advertising per unit sold outside of the United States, with General Motors and Ford spending $482 and $772, respectively.[31]

Making a Long-Term Commitment to People

In the auto industry, long-term projects are riskier than short-term ones, which is why Toyota persistently invests to cultivate the organizational capability of developing people willing to take risks. The company's view that it is investing in a high-growth industry rather than a mature one changes how it perceives risk. The often-repeated phrase in the organization "if you're 60 percent sure, take action" symbolizes Toyota's tolerance toward risk and speaks volumes about the company's willingness to spend big and try new things in the pursuit of growth—even if the benefits are not immediately obvious or directly measurable. When Toyota de Puerto Rico first launched its emotion-inspired advertising campaign, it could not predict if it would work or if customers would become confused and stop buying. It was a gamble. "Don't play it safe, everybody plays it safe," said Mario Davíla, President of Toyota de Puerto Rico. "Take a risk, . . .

when you live on the edge you see more things."[32] Employees will take risks if they feel confident, safe, and supported as they venture into uncharted territory. This requires a deep understanding of the Toyota Way, where learning stems from the successes as well as the failures experienced, and training plays a key part to get employees comfortable with this process.

Training and developing employees is a long-term investment, even lifelong, with the need for continuous upgrading of skills. Companies that want to keep their employees up to date and motivated need excellent educational programs. Toyota training programs play a vital role in strengthening the integrative effect of the "founders' philosophies" by disseminating Toyota Way values throughout the global workforce via a fortified "nerve system" that connects all employees.

When Toyota expanded throughout Asia from the 1970s onward, it focused on market penetration and growth, but poor service and low customer satisfaction levels forced it to focus on customer service at its dealerships in the region. It exported methods used by its Japan-based dealers experienced in customer-first practices, recognizing the critical role of after-sales service to increasing revenues and improving customer satisfaction.[33] Satisfied customers were likely to call for service more frequently and also more likely to make future car purchases from a dealer that had provided outstanding service. The practice promoted repetition of the sales cycle, reinforcing the dealer's future revenue stream. Implementing this concept outside Japan required a comprehensive training regime that expounded Toyota Way values at every level of the organization, from the local offices and distributors to the dealerships.

During the 1980s and 1990s, Toyota's Indonesian sales subsidiary, Toyota Astra Motor (a joint venture with PT Astra International), built a comprehensive training program. It consisted of core courses for Toyota employees, outsourced courses for specific departmental needs, fee-based courses for dealers covering topics like sales, customer service, and spare parts, and technical courses for factory workers. Toyota Astra Motor also offered a one-year executive training program for future managers.[34] The

Toyota Astra Motor program covered two key areas: hard or technical skills and the soft skills in human relations, services, problem solving, and effective decision making based on the Toyota Way.

The value of this training became evident during the 1997 Asian Financial Crisis. The rupiah lost 85 percent of its value (falling from 2,400 per dollar to a low of 16,000 per dollar), causing new car prices to shoot through the roof. To cope with the anticipated drop in vehicle sales, Toyota Astra Motor introduced "five-day vacation weeks" and offered early retirement benefits to 1,100 employees, pioneering such initiatives in the region.[35]

However, it resisted a plan by Toyota headquarters in Japan to close one of its two local production plants, arguing that it would "miss the boat" once the Indonesian market recovered. This decision gave Toyota Astra Motor time to prepare its facilities to produce the *Soluna,* a passenger car for the Asian market first introduced in Thailand in 1997. By 2000, the Indonesian market recovered, and Toyota Astra Motor successfully marketed and launched the Soluna, increasing its share of passenger car sales in Indonesia to 27.5 percent, from 9.1 percent in 1998.[36] Mikio Nomura, former Executive Vice President of Toyota Astra Motor, credited his coworkers' deep understanding of the Toyota Way values in supporting his decision not to scale back production. They stuck their necks out by discarding the less risky plan proposed by headquarters and choosing the riskier route of preparing for production of the Soluna.

Developing people's soft skills and ingraining them in the Toyota Way values is an arduous and time-consuming task. Because people and their tastes are different from one market to the next, there are no shortcuts to the acquisition of soft skills. The endeavor is critical to increasing the potential of people to contribute to the company over the long term.

Global and Local Training

Training people on hard skill topics—like auto transmission and suspension maintenance, electrical systems, and body repair—is easy to do in a classroom and workshop setting. How does Toyota train employees in soft skills like effective decision making, mentoring, problem solving, optimizing team performance, or the ability to be creative and innovative? How does it instill Toyota values like kaizen, genchi genbutsu, respect for people, everybody should win, and customer first, dealers second, and manufacturer last into its people? Teaching soft skills is more difficult and requires a setting that cultivates social interaction and understanding, as well as introspection and self-discovery among students and instructors alike. To impart such learning to employees, dealers, and distributors in places like Thailand and Indonesia and to support local training in the United States, Toyota has recently accelerated investments in education by establishing four dedicated facilities: the Toyota Institute, the Global Knowledge Center, the Global Production Center, and the University of Toyota.

Toyota Institute

The first of Toyota's key training facilities is the Toyota Institute, established in January 2002 at Toyota's headquarters. With a staff of 43 full-time employees in charge of global education and headquarters training, it runs two programs—one for developing global leaders and the other for developing global trainers capable of instructing other associates in Toyota Way basics such as problem solving, on-the-job training, and policy deployment.

In the leadership development programs, Toyota employees, who will eventually become global leaders, are groomed in skills of leadership and business management based on the Toyota Way and become part of a network of other Toyota global leaders. There are three programs—the executive development program, the junior executive development program, and the leadership development program.[37]

The nine-month executive development program, with an enrollment of 40 of Toyota's most senior managers from its headquarters and overseas centers, sees trainees learn the basics of the Toyota Way, exchange best practice experiences and hone their leadership and strategic-thinking skills during a three-day session at the Wharton Business School. The capstone project requires trainees to develop plans addressing their division's managerial issues and present them to Toyota senior management, including the president, over a two-day session, before receiving individual leadership assessments and revised action plans that are implemented on their return to their respective divisions.

The junior executive development program, with an enrollment of 60 Toyota mid-level managers, also sees trainees learn the basics of the Toyota Way before developing plans designed to enhance the competitiveness of Toyota's affiliated companies and presenting them to Toyota managing directors.

In the leadership development program, 40 mid-level managers from Toyota's overseas centers also learn about the Toyota Way, but the emphasis is on developing solutions for managerial issues expected to emerge at their local companies within five years due to Toyota's global operations and future strategy.

Global Knowledge Center

The second key training facility is the Global Knowledge Center, established in July 2002 in the same building as the University of Toyota. Its purpose is to unify the knowledge, expertise, and best practices of Toyota distributors around the world. The Global Knowledge Center and its sister facility, the European Knowledge Center, educate distributors in the Toyota Way using several "hands-on" programs that encourage knowledge exchange. These include: the Toyota Way in Sales and Marketing Discovery Program, an 8-day course emphasizing genchi genbutsu; the Train the Trainer (T3) program, a 4-day workshop to prepare distributor and dealer employees to become trainers in the Toyota Way in Sales and Marketing values in their home markets; the Kaizen Experience and Exchange Network (KEEN) program, a series of workshops in best practices in sales and marketing among Toyota distributors with advice on how to localize such practices. The Global Knowledge Center also dispatches trainers to educate employees at Toyota distributors worldwide to help infuse the Toyota Way into daily operations.[38]

To supplement its programs, the Global Knowledge Center began publishing *Best-Practice Bulletins* in 2002. They consist of case studies describing innovative approaches at various Toyota distributors around the world. Topics range from customer service and dealer network management to human resource management and marketing. They might include examples such as changing the layout of the service area to increase visual access for the customer of the repair work being done or how to create a warm and friendly show-room atmosphere that enhances the purchaser's experience. The Global Knowledge Center also produces *Team TOYOTA* magazine to promote global understanding of the Toyota Way in Sales and Marketing. And in 2003, the Global Knowledge Center established the Knowledge Bank, a web site where distributors can download Global Knowledge Center training materials and best-practice bulletins, product information, and online teaching aids such as the University of Toyota's training and development courses. The Knowledge Bank also hosts interactive forums where distributors can link up with Toyota experts worldwide and get advice on implementation of global best practices.[39]

As of 2006, more than 20,000 people had experienced Global Knowledge Center training in the Toyota Way in Sales and Marketing Discovery or T3 programs or under the tutelage of a T3 trainer, and in 2007 the center recovered more than 50 percent of its expenses through fees charged to trainees. With 24 staff based mainly in the United States, the Global Knowledge Center aims to become a self-financed training center by 2012, with a product mix that is 50 percent on-site program offerings and 50 percent consulting in Toyota Way in Sales and Marketing best practices. According to Toyota Motor Sales, U.S.A., Vice President and head of the Global Knowledge Center, John Kramer, the biggest challenge going forward is designing new training programs that cope effectively with Toyota's continuing global growth.[40]

Global Production Center

The third key training facility is Toyota's Global Production Center, with sister facilities in Europe (England), Asia (Thailand), and North America (United States). This is where production staff are taught hard and soft skills including the Toyota Production System and kaizen in a simulated work environment (as described in Chapter 8). These facilities are expensive—the North American Production Support Center, a refurbished training facility in Kentucky, was established in 2006 at a cost of $12 million with 29 employees including seven full-time trainers with over 15 years of field experience.[41] That same year, the European center was established for $18.5 million with 20 full-time employees and 11 training facilities.[42]

According to Toyota President Watanabe, these facilities will serve as centers of knowledge exchange where instructors and trainees exchange know-how through rigorous activities that promote face-to-face interaction, a process he described as a "spiral up" as trainees learn and improve. "We will use Japan as the base, but will extend this process to other parts of the world," said Watanabe. "In America, spiral up at America's level, in Europe, at Europe's level, in Asia, at Asia's level, in China, at China's level." He emphasized that employees have to recognize their own limits and invest the time needed to reach their own new level. According to Watanabe, this climbing up process must continue for Toyota to progress.[43]

University of Toyota

The fourth key training facility is the University of Toyota, established in April 1998 in Torrance, California, as a central repository of Toyota educational programs for employees and dealers in the Toyota, Lexus, and Scion divisions in the United States. As a corporate university, the University of Toyota is designed to achieve four principal goals: to inculcate Toyota culture and corporate values in the workforce, to develop leadership and managerial talent, to standardize know-how and organizational processes, and to promote communication among employees with few opportunities to interact with each other outside this environment.

Other automakers have similar institutions. GM University at General Motors' global headquarters in Detroit provides classroom instruction to GM employees and dealers supplemented by web-based interactive distance learning in a comprehensive program involving more than 3,200 courses.[44] By comparison, the University of Toyota has a more limited curriculum of about 200 courses on topics like product knowledge, sales process, financial services, and managerial development.[45] Courses are taught by 83 full-time instructors experienced in the field, supported by 65 staff and business partners.[46] Instruction is focused on developing Toyota-specific soft skills, and courses are structured to allow employees to apply their learning in daily routines. The skills include the practice of root-cause analysis by asking the question "why" five times; the practice of visualization using A3 paper; and the practice of incremental improvement or kaizen to solve problems using Plan-Do-Check-Act cycles. Giving employees opportunities to practice what they are taught and get immediate feedback emphasizes on-the-job and hands-on training.

For example, we observed the production simulation workshop at the University of Toyota in which employees assembled plastic toy cars to learn the principles of just-in-time manufacturing. In the first phase of the exercise, employees worked together in a line, each performing a specific task, like attaching the wheels. The aim was to produce a specified number of cars within a certain period of time in the classic *push* system perfected by Ford to build the Model T. But as the assembly work proceeded and time ran out, employees found that they still had *work-in-process* in the form of unused parts piling up all along the line, resulting in excess inventory, including mismatched colors with respect to order requests, and a number of defects in the finished cars.

In the second phase, employees were organized into *island* groupings with each island specializing in the assembly of several parts and expected to maintain the quality of their output.

Each car was assembled based on demand, and anyone could stop production if there was a quality problem, demonstrating the *pull* system of production instituted by Toyota. Progress was slow at first, but over time, employees adjusted and learned from each other, eventually surpassing their production speed under the push system while reducing the amount of work-in-process, excess inventory, and the number of defects in each car, thereby, minimizing lost sales opportunities.

This kind of structured, hands-on training program requires a large pool of dedicated and experienced frontline managers who can also instruct effectively in intangible concepts like the company's mission, vision, and values. These managers must be able to coach with a firm, but hands-off approach. They must also be good listeners and able to provide encouragement and guidance regardless of the setting or cultural differences among employees.

In 2003, the University of Toyota was recognized as a model corporate university by the International Society for Performance Improvement[47] and the International Quality and Productivity Center.[48] In 2006, over 1,837,000 Toyota and dealer employees took just-in-time electronic courses at the University of Toyota, while another 80,000 completed the production simulation workshop.[49]

Conclusion

In today's shareholder-driven business environment, companies are expected to focus resources on productive activities and divest or close underperforming business ventures. In a mature industry, where growth is low or stagnant, companies can grow by reallocating underutilized capital and personnel resources into areas where there is higher growth potential. Earnings are used to diversify for future growth and are paid out as dividends to shareholders. The process of diversification and improvements in efficiency creates redundancies in the form of employees whose skills no longer match current or future needs or facilities that are no longer useful, and these are released back into the market. Employees are retired or laid off, and assets are sold to other companies that need those resources. The aim is to run as efficiently as possible.

At Toyota, this process is reversed. Toyota plows most of its profit back into existing operations. It does not diversify much, nor does it pay a substantial dividend to shareholders, and redundant employees are trained and reassigned, not laid off. Toyota Chairman Fujio Cho explained why Toyota is a breed apart from its peers:

> Every top executive at Toyota has experienced many failures. If someone fails, they are expected to fix it by themselves, and they are not supposed to repeat the same mistakes. If employees fail, they will be scolded but their careers will not be negatively affected. We have to waste resources by trying many things when we are unsure which are best. This idea comes from our predecessors in the company. Toyota does not skimp on R&D expenditures by betting everything on one technology. Everybody at the top seems to agree on this. However, the biggest difference between Toyota and the other companies is the way Toyota spends money. Toyota focuses on the long-term potential. Other companies might not want to do this because their priority is to keep their shareholders happy.[50]

Toyota aims to expand the soft side of the company and complement its already efficient hard side. This is a practical approach resulting from its view that the auto industry is a high-growth knowledge-driven industry, and efficiency alone does not guarantee continued success. In the era of the knowledge worker, growth comes from long-term investments in organizational capability and people, not from a series of short-term investments for short-term gains. Toyota has recognized that cultivating ideas from anywhere—the factory floor, the office, or the field—is critical in the knowledge-driven industry, and this requires learning how to initiate ideas, innovate, and take a different approach. This is why Toyota spends so much to build better dealers, market its brands, and train its employees in the Toyota Way. According to Toyota Senior Advisor Hiroshi Okuda, striking the right balance is key:

> As more companies raise capital from the stock market, they start paying more attention to shareholders and to the return on equity. However, if we restrain needed investments or divest businesses without trying to fix them in order to secure short-term profits, then the priorities are completely wrong. Top management's role is to balance between investments for long-term growth and short-term profitability.[51]

Table 9.1 compares the two ways of handling resources to achieve growth in the auto industry—the earnings-driven approach versus Toyota's knowledge-driven approach.

The earnings-driven approach emphasizes short-term moves that generate quick results, but degrades capability in the long run as redundant resources are released and know-how is lost. Growth is primarily achieved through strategic acquisitions

TABLE 9.1 Earnings-Driven and Knowledge-Driven Approaches to Growth in the Auto Industry

	Earnings-Driven Approach	Knowledge-Driven Approach	Force
Improve market coverage by . . .	Increasing number of dealers	Building better dealers	Up and in
Grow through . . .	Diversification and acquisitions	Organic growth	Impossible goals
Expand efficiency by . . .	Concentrating activities	Localizing operations	Local customization
Achieve innovation by . . .	Acquiring technology	Trial and error	Experimentation
Improve speed with . . .	Strict organizational rules	Communication	Nerve system
Handle redundancies by . . .	Releasing resources (up or out)	Retraining and reassigning resources	Up and in

of other companies, stifling the incentive to develop technology in-house. Growth is also achieved by quickly adapting to changes in the market, usually by accelerating the pace of diversification through acquisitions, requiring strict organizational rules that promote speed and control the flow of information. Over time, this approach leads a company to focus on efficiency metrics, with little consideration for making investment in cultivating organizational capability and people.

The knowledge-driven approach takes a long-term view to achieve growth. Instead of releasing redundant human resources, employees are retrained and reassigned. Growth is organic, not acquisitive, driven by trial-and-error, in-house development of key technologies, and the localization of operations to develop know-how and capability. Communication is multilayered, allowing information and know-how to diffuse throughout the organization. This approach seeks to cultivate organizational capability and people and make risky investments that take time to develop. Humans are at the center of this approach.

Toyota has been a quintessential exemplar of the knowledge-driven approach to growth thus far. Looking to the future, what dangers does it face? In Chapter 10, we look at the risks that could send the company into a downward spiral of decline.

CHAPTER 10

A Company Always in Danger

As Toyota forges a new era in the automobile industry, we find the company well positioned to continue leading the pack with a business management innovation that nurtures the soft side of industrial production in the knowledge era. In the post-Ford era of globalization, a mature industry becomes a knowledge-driven industry when companies operate according to knowledge-based management, thereby expanding their potential to innovate and grow. At Toyota, this approach is guided by six forces that interact to keep it moving forward while driving it to extremes. Based on an understanding of how knowledge is created by human beings, Toyota operates successfully in a culture of radical contradiction that continuously yanks the organization out of its comfort zone just long enough to allow it to regroup and move in leaps and bounds. This is the way it makes sense of the increasingly complex global environment in which it operates, finding new solutions beyond contradiction, not in compromise or balance, but in higher levels of performance.

However, Toyota's unorthodox distributed leadership combined with the lack of strategic focus and lackluster financial incentives for employees and investors comes with risks. In addition to the common risk factors associated with unionization, political backlash, quality control, and increasing material costs faced by all manufacturers in today's global economy, the following issues specific to Toyota risk derailing the operation of the six forces, sending the company into a downward spiral of decline:

1. Organizational growth pains
2. Employee complacency
3. Cultural rigidity
4. Workforce diversity
5. Insular approach to the capital markets
6. Rise of new competitors

Organizational Growth Pains

In its early days, Toyota followed a Japan-centric approach to international management where key functions and decision making were centralized at headquarters. This was in stark contrast to General Motors, which had established autonomous regional subsidiaries. Instead, Toyota put priority on pushing a full line of its products into every market. Only from the mid-1980s onward did it begin to delegate manufacturing and sales authority to regional headquarters. As they learned from the IMV project, delegation is a pressing issue. The complexity of a global approach increases exponentially with every plant Toyota adds to its global network, with new employees, new supply lines and distribution centers, and new transportation networks requiring more and better communication, coordination, and training.

Toyota's regional units now participate in decisions made about their operations. So far, this has worked because employees share and practice the Toyota Way, but it becomes increasingly difficult with the rapid addition of new plants across the globe. Cracks are already appearing, most prominently in the form of increasing vehicle recalls due to defective components common to many models. From 2003 to 2004, Toyota recalls almost doubled from 975,902 to 1,887,471 vehicles worldwide, dropping by 29 percent to 1,339,219 cars in 2006. In 2007, Toyota recalled nearly 700,000 vehicles worldwide.[1] These recalls affected every product line, including Lexus and Scion, and in 2007, *Consumer*

Reports dropped Toyota from first place to third in its ranking of predicted vehicle reliability based on a 10-year history.[2]

The swelling rank of new employees at Toyota also taxes their process of upgrading skills on the job, which is labor intensive and time consuming. The Toyota Way espouses on-the-job training to master new skills that can be applied immediately in daily tasks in keeping with the philosophy of continuous improvement. But trainers become scarce as the demand for them increases, and the size of Toyota is making it increasingly difficult to diffuse and implement all the practice-based improvements created daily. One way of dealing with this is to expand participation at facilities like the Global Production Center in Japan and its European and Asia-Pacific branches, as well as at the North American Production Support Center, the Toyota Institute, and the Global Knowledge Center. Another effort is the "Back-to-Basics" program in which every factory worker in North America is retrained in the basic steps they learned since joining the company. This program is scheduled for completion by the end of 2009.[3] The program was expanded in November 2007 to include the entire global workforce.[4]

Toyota is currently teaching the basics of the Toyota Production System (TPS) to foreign managers in a rigorous 13-week training program that pairs each trainee with an experienced TPS mentor. The first part of the program, usually six weeks in length, has trainees undergo a series of exercises where they observe a team of workers, make process changes to improve their performance, evaluate the results, and repeat the sequence to establish a predefined improvement target. The next six weeks of the program mirrors the first, but the target for improvement is the machines on the production line rather than employees. This entails patient observation of the frequency of machine faults and development of a studied understanding of how they work so trainees can recommend design changes to effect improvements. The final week of the program takes place at one of Toyota's assembly plants in Japan and accelerates the pace of implementation of improvements from one or two improvements per day to two or three per hour.[5] This is meant to enhance a trainee's ability to see and resolve problems, giving them ample opportunity to experiment with solutions and get feedback from employees on the line.

By the end of their TPS training, Toyota managers advance from being effective problem solvers themselves to becoming mentors capable of creating the environment for effective problem solving as a fundamental practice of continuous improvement (kaizen), based on participation at the front line (genchi genbutsu). They learn to listen, empower, and trust other employees to arrive at solutions both independently and in cooperation with others. These are the critical leadership qualities required of managers in a knowledge-creating company.

It remains to be seen whether Toyota's communication, coordination, and training systems will catch up with its continuing expansion.

Employee Complacency

On several occasions during the course of our interviews, we encountered employees who spoke of the Toyota Way as reality written in stone rather than the evolving system of values it is meant to be. These individuals tended to sideline or even ignore new ideas that did not fit their dogmatic viewpoint. The delusion that outsiders do not understand Toyota and will always be proved wrong when they disagree with the Toyota Way is evidence of a mindset of complacency developing in the ranks since the mid-1990s that is clearly harmful to continued growth. While there is no harm in showing pride in past accomplishments, when the staff at the head office start to believe their own press, business planning becomes routine, stale, and ineffective.

"The two things I fear most are arrogance and contentment," said President Katsuaki Watanabe.[6] He said that he has continuously reminded his managers during 2007 that contentment always precedes decline, that even the strongest fortress can collapse from a tiny crack made by a single ant, and that they should plug any leaks to ensure management is watertight.

To combat complacency, Watanabe initiated the "80,000 People Communication" program in 2007, requesting that all Japan-based employees communicate with coworkers across organizational boundaries to quickly identify and solve any problems affecting daily operations. If the problem could not be permanently fixed in short order, they had to designate a leader and create a follow-up plan with targets for resolving the outstanding issues. Watanabe acknowledged that asking all employees to identify, communicate, and fix problems takes time away from their normal tasks, making them less efficient in the short term, but he said, "doing nothing now and letting problems grow unchecked costs much more in the future."[7]

Vice President for Scion, Mark Templin, exemplifies this resolve. The fact that 50 percent of Scion owners in the market for a new car choose another Toyota would be viewed by most as a success.[8] Templin's view, however, is that half of all Scion customers are being lost to competitors. He said Toyota has to address this exodus, and he notes that the "graduation" of Scion customers to other Toyota vehicles will create a demand for Scion-like options, including accessories and haggle-free purchasing from Toyota dealers. These customers also aspire to own luxury vehicles by the time they are in their 30s, a full 10 years younger than the baby-boom generation, which means the Lexus also will have to include options that match these tastes. Some changes have already taken place, including accessories developed for the Lexus *IS-F* and interactive Web-based online customer service, a standard offering for Scion owners, which now includes the Toyota *FJ Cruiser* and the entire line of Lexus vehicles.

In 2007, Toyota Motor Sales, U.S.A., executives initiated a program called Everything Matters Exponentially (em^2), to address customer sales satisfaction and service issues. Toyota dealerships had ranked below the industry standard in the 2007 J.D. Powers and Associates survey.[9] The program evaluates each step in the supply chain and improves customer service throughout. This requires more genchi genbutsu—going to the front lines and seeing things firsthand. For example, to improve product development, Toyota designers spend more time with customers where they live, either in crowded cities or in the countryside, to garner clues that will help them make products that target lifestyle needs. To improve sales and service, Toyota has taken the unusual step of monitoring the way its dealerships treat customers while offering tailor-made recommendations for change.[10]

Can Toyota reverse the encroaching complacency in the corporate culture with these initiatives? Perhaps it's time to revise *The Toyota Way 2001*.

Cultural Rigidity

Industry observers have suggested that Toyota employees are prone to groupthink, characterized as a preference for consensus building and an aversion to new ideas or concepts from outside the organization. One reason is Toyota's up-and-in human resource management, which favors recruiting fresh talent over mid-level managers. The other is Toyota's strong focus on the auto industry, which dampened demand to hire expertise from other industries. One look at Toyota's all-male, all-Japanese executive board would support this observation. Toyota's up-and-in policy also applied to its suppliers where it preferred to strengthen existing relationships and took a conservative approach when dealing with new suppliers. And Toyota's nerve system, while very efficient at monitoring the needs of customers, dealers, and distributors, tended to ignore the situation of suppliers. Cultural rigidity is becoming a pressing issue as the demand for environmentally friendly cars in the auto industry increases, requiring Toyota to forge stronger relationships with outside partners to successfully co-develop new technologies (e.g., integrated circuitry from NEC, voltage converters for hybrid propulsion systems from Mitsubishi Electric, battery technology from Panasonic, biodiesel technology with ENEOS, and alternative fuels with Showa Shell).

Toyota tries to tackle cultural rigidity by rotating employees between divisions and across markets to increase opportunities for knowledge exchange. For example, Toyota Motor Sales, U.S.A., Vice President of Customer Services Nancy Fein spent 25 years at the Toyota division before joining the Lexus division. Likewise, Mark Templin was Vice President of Marketing at Lexus before joining the Scion group in 2005. Lexus hires Scion "champions" or best-practice experts to import knowledge of and experience with innovative marketing techniques, like the Scion's use of concert and sports venues and the popular virtual world Second Life to advertise new models.

Toyota also tries to breakdown aversion to new ideas by encouraging employees to look at other industries for new ideas and inspiration. This method is being employed with Lexus, to try to redefine luxury customer service. What defined luxury service in the U.S. market of the 1990s, such as a complimentary stay in a hotel if a vehicle quits working in a remote location, free gasoline, and a same class loaner vehicle during repairs, is no longer adequate for the luxury consumer. Nancy Fein said they identified the next level of luxury experience for the Lexus consumer by looking outside the company and the auto industry to the hospitality, consumer electronics, retail, and aviation industries—at companies such as Four Seasons Hotels and Resorts, Apple, Dean & Deluca, and Virgin Atlantic.[11] One enterprising Lexus dealer even paired with Neiman Marcus to put a boutique inside the dealership for customers waiting for servicing.

The concept of "crunch teams" was adopted from the Four Seasons where employees team up to handle service backlogs. Typically, customers are served on a first-come first-serve basis. This system breaks down when there is a surge in service calls. Overwhelmed service personnel begin to rush, reducing attention to detail and the level of service as well. The crunch teams, composed of dealership personnel from sales associates to managers, kick into action during demand spikes to handle a service backlog without compromising on quality.

Another borrowed concept is the Lexus "genius bar," an innovation from Apple Stores, where customers get personalized training in use of the equipment. Today's luxury cars consist of a dizzying array of high-tech functions that are often confusing and intimidating. The Lexus genius bar tutors customers one-on-one in the use of the satellite navigation system, wireless systems, climate control, and the audio system. Better understanding of their vehicles makes customers more confident in their purchase and gives dealers the feedback they need on customer preferences. These innovations in sales process are credited with moving Lexus up four ranks to first place in the 2007 J.D. Powers and Associates survey on sales satisfaction.[12]

Learning and adopting service-oriented best-practices from other industries is a relatively easy step. The more difficult task is to create new practices internally. Can Toyota increase the diversity of its executive board by adding non-Toyota, non-Japanese, and non-automotive expertise? In a knowledge-driven industry, where technical capability and insights into market demand and societal needs are critical to success, will Toyota be able to form the critical long-standing alliances with companies from diverse industries whose practices, expertise, and technologies it must adopt to get and stay ahead of its competitors?

Workforce Diversity

Another criticism of Toyota in Japan is that it tends to recruit employees of a similar character—hard working, motivated by a learning-based work environment, attracted to an unrestricted corporate culture, and mostly Japanese, which, accounts for the language barrier that exists between the mostly Japanese workforce at Toyota and their global operations. Of Toyota's 299,394 employees in 2007, only 38 percent were based outside of Japan,[13] while half of high-level management positions overseas were staffed by employees transferred from Japan. The rise of new competitors in key markets, like China and India, will be a significant challenge for Toyota's largely homogeneous operation.

Toyota has learned that diversifying the workforce is a double-edged sword because the values and needs of employees of different backgrounds sometimes clash with the demands of a strong corporate culture, leading to disagreement and conflict. According to Executive Vice President Tokuichi Uranishi, increasing the number of non-Japanese managers in the organization will increase demand for performance-based evaluation and incentive systems, which is not a standard practice in Toyota, especially in Japan.[14] Former Senior Managing Director Zenji Yasuda agreed that diversifying the workforce was necessary, but was concerned this would increase red tape across the organization and restrict management flexibility to make judgments based on intuition about a person and his or her capabilities.[15]

As Toyota expanded in the United States, turnover in its middle-management ranks ranged from 5 percent to 10 percent during 2005 and 2006, representing a significant loss of investment in training. Many employees cited excessive overtime and poor communication in the organization as reasons for their departure.[16] Each resignation also represents a loss to collective corporate memory. These turnover rates are considerably lower than the industry average of 16 percent,[17] but Toyota is now planning to decentralize project management away from the U.S. manufacturing subsidiary at Erlanger, Kentucky, into two new regional centers opening in California and Texas in 2010, cutting down travel time for the managers.

Toyota's practice of hiring employees on short-term contracts, which affords it a significant cost advantage—roughly $800 per vehicle compared to the restructured General Motors[18]— is also under pressure, mostly from Japan's shrinking workforce. In 2007, in an effort to keep employees in-house, Toyota converted 1,200 of its 10,000 part-time employees into full-time contracts at its assembly plants in Japan, an increase of 30 percent from the previous year.[19] Toyota is also developing a program called the "global career path" for promising managers hired outside of

Japan, which includes training at the Toyota Institute and a series
of internal job rotations.

Toyota President Katsuaki Watanabe, Executive Vice
President Tokuichi Uranishi, and Toyota Motor Sales, U.S.A.
Vice President Tony Fujita all acknowledged that internation-
alizing Toyota headquarters is a growing concern with the
challenges of workforce diversity. Toyota faces the difficulty of
attracting good people in growing markets with its lower remuneration levels and the slow pace of promotion characteristic of
up-and-in human resource management. Will they be forced to
resort to performance-based incentives that cause employees
to focus on results rather than process?

Insular Approach to the Capital Markets

Many Japanese companies attribute their success to their long-
term view of investment to continually expand market share for
future growth, sometimes at the expense of short-term profit.
They say that this is how many of them became dominant players in industries such as consumer electronics during the 1970s
and 1980s. However, during the same period, profitability at
these companies slowly declined relative to their non-Japanese
competitors, with return on assets (ROA) only half that of their
U.S. counterparts.[20] The long-term focus of Japanese companies is based on expectations that projects generating big
returns over the long term override the need to be profitable
today. This approach works as long as markets are expanding,
but when Japan's bubble economy burst in the early 1990s,
many Japanese companies continued expanding capacity while
revenues stagnated, resulting in severe financial losses.

Toyota followed this pattern of continuing to invest in
capacity but also monitored short-term financial health, and it
accumulated capital by paying out a low dividend—practices
learned during the early days of financial hardship in the 1950s.
This helped it to weather the storm of the post-bubble years in
Japan and continue to grow throughout the 1990s. However,

Toyota's low dividend and lower level of return on investment capital (ROIC) relative to competitors also depressed its share price to below the inherent value based on company earnings and growth rates. In the five years prior to 2001, Toyota's annual dividend payout averaged less than $700 million with ROIC just 4.3 percent. This low market capitalization could invite unwelcome interest from activist shareholders or in the form of a hostile takeover bid, although this in unlikely in the near future.

To mitigate the threat of external influence, Toyota is trying to boost its stock price by increasing the dividend to make its stock more attractive to investors. From 2001 to 2007, the dividend payout rose fourfold to $2.9 billion.[21] In addition, Toyota has narrowed its profitability gap with Nissan and Honda. In the five years prior to 2007, Toyota's ROIC reached 7 percent compared with Nissan and Honda at around 8.5 percent.[22] The discrepancy with Nissan can be attributed to its profit-driven approach under Chairman Carlos Ghosn, but the gap with Honda, which also takes a long-term approach to investment and project development, is a concern of shareholders.

Can Toyota continue to realign and use its resources as effectively as its rivals do now? Adhering to strict financial targets is one way of improving financial discipline, but tracking short-term financial metrics, like return on equity or return on sales, conflicts with the long-term approach of investing in future growth. The jury is still out on whether Toyota can continue to achieve both short-term efficiency improvements and long-term discipline for growth.

Rise of New Competitors

Japanese carmakers suffered from the post-bubble era of deflation but they did not face any real threat from a competitor that might be benefiting from lower labor costs or a protected market. This has changed dramatically with the surge in growth in Korea, China, and India in the past decade. In 2006, new auto companies emerged with global ambitions and growth rates exceeding 20 percent,[23] such as China's Dongfeng Motor Corporation, Shanghai Auto Industry Corporation, and Chery Automobile, or India's Tata Motor. They are selling affordable vehicles of increasing quality as they scale up production capacity. Since the 1970s, Toyota has grown by selling affordable and fuel-efficient vehicles like the *Camry, Corolla, Corona,* and *Hilux,* into the volume segment of every key market. The new rivals in the auto industry are trying to gain a foothold in the market segment with the greatest potential for future growth—new customers for low-priced four-wheeled vehicles in emerging markets. They represent a formidable challenge to Toyota.

In 2008, Tata Motor launched the *Nano* in India, a small car priced just $2,500. Chery Automobile is already exporting cars to Russia for an average unit price of $5,000. In response, Nissan is co-developing a $3,000 car with an Indian motorcycle manufacturer for launch in 2010, while Renault, a major stakeholder in Nissan, is producing the $5,000 *Logan* for emerging markets. Nissan and Renault are also co-developing a shared-platform $7,000 car scheduled for release in 2009.[24] Meanwhile, California-based Tesla Motors is set to establish a strong presence in the high-end alternative-fuel car market with the 2008 launch of its high-performance *Tesla Roadster,* an all-electric vehicle with a base price of $98,950.[25] Toyota plans to stake its claim in the low-priced car market by producing a $7,000 car in India starting in 2010. It is also trying to move ahead in alternative-fuel technologies by increasing spending on research and development of environmentally friendly technologies, including hybrid, fuel cell, and battery technologies.

Of all the risks facing Toyota, the rise of new competitors poses the single biggest threat. These new rivals are likely to emphasize short-term results with top-down management enabling quick decision making to move quickly to provide a targeted product in a focused strategic approach that is completely opposite to Toyota's. Although this scenario is reminiscent of Toyota's early years as the new player in the market, the new rivals have leaped across the learning curve by acquiring technology through joint ventures and cooperative alliances, while sourcing parts from established suppliers in the United States, Japan, and Europe. What took Toyota four decades to develop, the new rivals have learned in under ten years, and many of them also have the financial backing to rival the Toyota bank.

Can Toyota address the immediate demands of new customers in emerging markets and keep its commitment to make a positive contribution to society? Can Toyota's long-term investment policy withstand the pressures of a potential decline in output due to loss of market share? Can it remain true to the founders' philosophies and the Toyota Way, even with a larger and more diverse workforce?

Conclusion

The five risks presented in this chapter pose a clear danger that imperils Toyota's position as the industry's top carmaker and present a true test of the company's extreme performance model of business management. If Toyota tries to overcome these risks by emphasizing expansion at the expense of integration, it will undermine the cohesiveness of its cultural integrity and dilute the values binding the organization together. Likewise, if it opts to reinforce existing operational and cultural norms that increase organizational inertia, it will constrain its ability to innovate and self-renew towards higher levels of achievement.

However, if Toyota persists to test new solutions that mitigate the risks it faces and foster healthy instability and tension among the six forces, it will strengthen its ability to cope with risk and tackle ever-greater challenges as it reaches new levels of extreme performance. Doing so requires recasting each risk not as an obstacle to be stamped out, but as a challenge to be overcome. This may lead to new contradictions and paradoxes, which when embraced will serve as catalysts for further change and growth. Only then will Toyota solidify its reputation as the top carmaker, and bear the standard of organizational and operational excellence as the world's greatest manufacturer for years to come.

CHAPTER 11

What Your Organization Can Learn from Toyota: Ten Powerful Contradictions

To an outsider, Toyota's extreme performance model of business management is hard to understand. As we mentioned in Chapter 1, the company moves forward gradually while also advancing in big leaps. It is frugal with its resources while spending extravagantly on people and projects. It is both efficient and redundant. It cultivates an environment of stability as well as paranoia. It is hierarchical and bureaucratic, but encourages dissent. It demands that communication be simplified while building complex communication networks.

As we dug deeper into unearthing why Toyota's extreme performance model might be considered a role model of contemporary business practice, we found the company steeped in contradictions, opposites, and paradoxes. Unearthing Toyota was like peeling an onion and never reaching the center. After peeling a number of layers, we came to realize that the company actively embraces and cultivates contradictions, rather than passively coping with them. In fact, we realized that Toyota thrives on paradoxes, harnessing opposing propositions to energize itself.

Making sense of all the contradictions, opposites, and paradoxes became central to our investigation as a larger pattern of expansion and integration began to emerge. We tracked this pattern through six case studies over 220 interviews with Toyota employees, distributors, and car dealers and identified three expansive forces and three integrative forces. The three expansive forces consist of impossible goals, experimentation, and local customization, while the three integrative forces consist of the founders' philosophies, nerve system, and up-and-in human resource management system, as shown in Figure 11.1. As we mentioned in Chapter 2, the three expansive forces lead Toyota toward new challenges and greater diversity and complexity, while the three integrative forces allow the company to weave together and internalize these experiences and perspectives and make sense of the more complex environment in which it operates.

FIGURE 11.1   The Six Forces in Toyota.

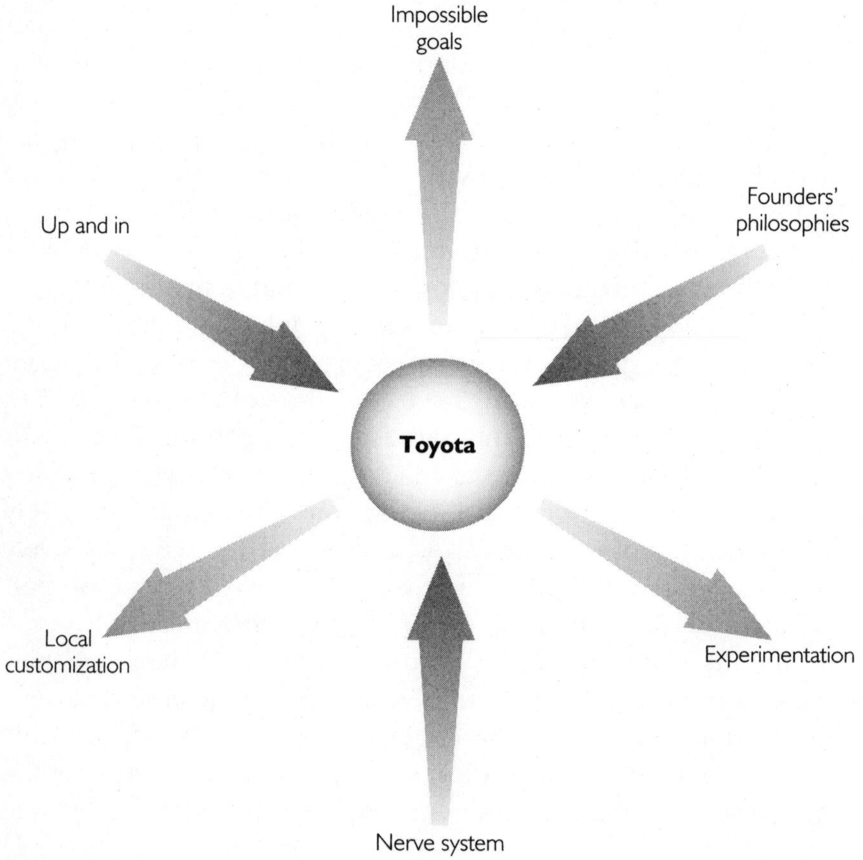

The six forces complement each other in opposition and create complex dependencies that drive Toyota to an extreme state of disequilibrium. Any change in one of the forces disrupts this state, creating a tension that serves as a catalyst to send the company off to a new trajectory. Since Toyota instigates continuous change through kaizen, it is in a state of continuous instability. As shown in Figure 11.2, the predominance of the forces at one point in time (i.e., arrows pointing inside or outside the sphere differ in strength from one state to the other) changes. As a result, the trajectory, which is marked with periodical leaps and bounds, changes over time. The trajectory spirals up to a higher level as the company continuously pursues innovation and self-renewal in the resolution of opposites.

How can other companies emulate Toyota, one of the world's best-run, most successful companies? The following request we often receive from outsiders misses the point: "Tell me the one thing I should learn from Toyota." One thing is clear: emulating Toyota is not easy. It takes time. It also requires abundant resources. For starters, however, we suggest three steps to companies wanting to emulate Toyota's extreme performance model of business management:

1. **Embrace contradictions as a way of life.** Most companies stop growing because they stick to processes and practices that generated past successes, leading to organizational rigidities. Reaching new customers, new segments, and new geographic areas and tackling the challenges posed by competitors, new ideas, and new practices trigger the changes and improvements needed to break down existing rigidities. Companies must embrace these challenges and create their own contradictions to achieve higher levels of performance.

2. **Develop routines necessary to resolve those contradictions.** In Toyota's case, they included genchi genbutsu, the PDCA model, the eight-step process, A3 reporting, mieruka approach, obeya system, ask "why" five times routine, to name a few. Unless companies teach employees how to tackle problems rigorously, they will not be able to harness the power of contradictions.

FIGURE 11.2 Evolution at Toyota, induced by the interaction of expansive and integrative forces that result in a state of perpetual change.

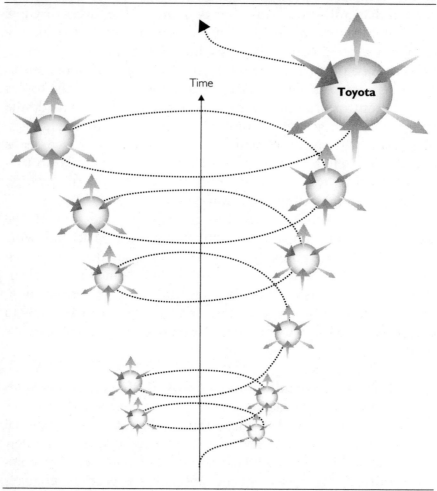

Note: The progress of this evolution, which is typically incremental, is also characterized by big leaps and bounds as the company evolves into a larger and more complicated entity over time.

3. **Let all the employees and outside constituents come up with solutions.** Executives and managers alike must be open to criticism and contradiction if they want to source new ideas from any point in their organization's ecosystem. This requires time, patience, and frequent face-to-face interaction.

We focus this entire chapter on analyzing how Toyota went about embracing contradictions.

Embrace Contradictions

The more turbulent the times, the more contradictions there are. As a result, corporate success has never been more fragile. Only a few companies have proven themselves capable of changing as fast as the environment around them and dealing with complexities surrounding them. One of the main reasons why companies fail today is their tendency to kill contradictions, opposites, and paradoxes by sticking to old routines created by their past success.

In contrast, the image that describes Toyota's expanding and integrating organizational dynamics resulting from the six forces is one of constant renewal—akin to the moment the butterfly is about to emerge from its cocoon, or the green tomato with the potential to ripen. This image mirrors the nature of human creativity—a process of change where knowledge acquisition occurs at many levels, both tacit and explicit. This is a powerful concept Toyota embraced when it shifted to a capability-driven approach in the knowledge-driven industry during its rise to become the top car manufacturer in the world. President Katsuaki Watanabe explains this concept as follows:

> We need to create a routine in which tacit knowledge and explicit knowledge can spiral up effectively. That requires human effort. We humans should go all out to create a solid educational routine that enables the knowledge level to spiral up . . . and do it globally.[1]

As Watanabe pointed out in Chapter 8, explicit knowledge becomes obsolete the moment it is created. Growth stops once tacit knowledge is converted into explicit knowledge in the form of a manual, a standard, a machine, information technology (IT), a computer, or a robot. So, for any organization to grow in a knowledge-driven industry, it must enlarge and polish tacit knowledge. Only by learning new things through experience and action will knowledge grow. As such, new knowledge is created through the spiral-up interaction of two dichotomous and opposing types of knowledge—tacit and explicit. New knowledge is also created by connecting our unique perspective with that of others, which are often contradictory. Only through such dichotomy and contradiction is new knowledge created.

Besides the tacit/explicit dichotomy, we have made references to a number of dichotomies throughout the book, including:

- Industrial and knowledge society
- Manufacturing and knowledge-driven industry
- Hard side and soft side of management
- Short-term efficiency and long-term capability
- Before and after the IMV
- Moving gradually and taking a big leap
- Cultivating frugality and spending huge sums
- Operational efficiency and redundancy
- Cultivating stability and mindset of paranoia
- Bureaucratic hierarchy and freedom to dissent
- Simplified and complex communication
- Expansive and integrative forces
- Global standardization and local customization
- Digital and analog communication web
- Formal and informal organization
- Up-or-out and up-and-in system
- Earnings-driven and knowledge-driven approach

In addition, we touched on the opposing demands placed on the Toyota development team in developing a new car for a new market in various chapters. For example, in Chapter 3 we listed the technical contradictions Chief Engineer Ichiro Suzuki faced in developing the first Lexus. No compromise or tradeoffs were allowed. All of the contradictions listed next had to be resolved in order for Lexus to achieve success in the U.S. market:

- High-speed control/stability and excellent riding comfort
- Fast and smooth rides and outstanding fuel efficiency
- Superb noise reduction and lightweight
- Elegant styling and outstanding aerodynamic performance
- Warm ambience and functional cabin
- High-speed stability and excellent air resistance

The dichotomies and contradictions listed have been alluded to in one form or another in the previous chapters. What may not be so obvious is our contention that each of these six forces and the supporting resource base contains a paradox or two. In all, we identified 10 new contradictions. As we take a cursory look at each of them next, we hope this last mile of our journey will deepen your understanding of the six forces.

Contradiction 1—Impossible Goals: "Know Where Reality Stands to Take on Impossibly High Goals"

As we mentioned in Chapter 1, when Katsuaki Watanabe became President in 2005, he spoke of his dream of developing a car that can make the air cleaner as it runs; a car that will not hurt drivers or pedestrians and never gets into an accident; a car that can make drivers healthier the longer they drive it; a fuel-efficient car that can go from one coast of the United States to the other on one tank of gas and eventually around the world. He is still talking about these dreams today. At the same time, however, he emphasized the importance of knowing "where you stand at the ground level." He used this phrase to gauge the gap between reality and the ideal. He is a dreamer, but at the same time, he is quite down to earth, as the following quote indicates:

> Always set your objectives high. If it is only a 5 percent or 10 percent improvement, people will stop challenging. At

the same time, you need to know where reality stands. In a human being, you can measure reality in terms of your current height, weight, and how the heart or the lung is functioning. For an overseas operation, that could be the current level of productivity, the defect ratio on quality, or the depreciation rate. Knowing where reality lies and how high the target has been set, you can measure the gap and ask yourself how the gap is going to be filled and how long it may take to fill that gap.[2]

Contradiction 2—Experimentation: "Conduct Small, Interim Experiments to Realize the Occasional Big Jump"

One historically proven approach to experimentation within Toyota is to start small and take incremental steps. Toyota's development of the *Prius* reflected this thinking. Toyota was keenly aware of the future transition toward alternative power-train technologies, but started the experiment on a small scale initially, even though it knew that hybrid technology was a partial solution. If you recall, the first several prototypes got off to a bumpy start, but Toyota did not give up, increasing its commitment incrementally. Similarly, Toyota took an incremental approach in launching Scion. It was first launched in California, but the company waited eight months before launching it in the South and East Coast of the United States to find out what worked and what did not work, making many incremental improvements in the interval.

Although these experiments started out small and incremental, the company ended up investing a vast amount of resources, both money and time, by the time they were completed. These experiments eventually produced the periodical leaps and bounds in the organization, as depicted in Figure 11.2.

Contradiction 3—Local Customization: "Localize to Become Global"

Toyota has moved away from the traditional "export model" to a more "locally customized" model of international management in recent years. Under the local customization model, Toyota set up multiple production centers in key local markets, each one with a tailored set of activities that best addressed the specific conditions of the local markets in which it operated. Toyota incorporated local customer tastes and demands into the development and design process of the single-platform IMV in Asia, the subcompact Yaris in Europe, and the youth-targeted Scion as well as the full-size Tundra pickup truck in the United States. As we have seen, Toyota developed new products and new business models that addressed the needs of new customers in specific local markets in each of these cases.

At the same time, Toyota assembled local best practices from the IMV project in Asia, the Yaris in Europe, the Scion and Tundra projects in the United States at the Global Knowledge Center, which serves as the company depository and the training center for best practices in sales and marketing for the worldwide organization. In addition, Toyota established another training facility—the Global Production Center—to disseminate its best practices in manufacturing, where the production staff learns about the Toyota Production System and kaizen in a simulated work environment. As was pointed out earlier, the company invested a lot of time and money into establishing these global centers. Toyota is trying to establish a self-reinforcing cycle where know-how and capability developed to address specific local needs is shared globally, stimulating new innovation as other local operations adopt, evolve, and share new practices. This is not easy, and it requires persistent inquisitiveness, constant learning, and a challenging working environment. In the process of writing this book, we provided Toyota candid feedback regarding our concerns for the future, which are mentioned in the previous chapter. We are confident the company will recast the risks we pointed out as challenges to resolve.

Contradiction 4—Founders' Philosophies: "Cherish the Founders' Philosophies to Nurture Future Leaders"

The historic words of Sakichi Toyoda ("Open the window. It's a big world out there."), Kiichiro Toyoda ("Each person fulfilling his or her duties to the utmost can generate great power when

gathered together"), Shotaro Kamiya ("Customer first, dealers second, and manufacturer last"), Taiichi Ohno ("Ask 'why'
five times about every matter"), and other founders still live on
within Toyota today.

The founders' beliefs and values, which were organized under
the two pillar concepts of "continuous improvement" (kaizen) and
"respect for people" in *The Toyota Way 2001*, have been imprinted
on members of the worldwide Toyota organization through constant practices reinforcing these concepts. We found the Toyota
people we interviewed to be keen on making continuous improvements, listening and learning from others, working as a team,
going to the genba, grasping the essence of the problem, and taking quick actions. President Watanabe carries around in his wal-
let a small sheet of paper that has the "Five Main Principles of
Toyoda" espoused by Sakichi Toyoda printed on it. He believes
these still serve as the guiding beacon for Toyota today.

Contradiction 5—Founders' Philosophies: "Remain Incomplete in Order to Grow"

For any organization to grow in a knowledge-driven industry, it
must recognize that it is still incomplete, that it does not know
best, that there is room for improvement, and that tomorrow
will be better than today. Being incomplete is similar in spirit to
kaizen, which we said earlier is synonymous with "never be satisfied with the status quo." President Watanabe was quoted in
Chapter 8 as saying, "At the very instant we become satisfied, at
the very moment we think that the status quo is good enough,
that's when we start to decline." He continued on admitting:
"We are still incomplete, with lots of problems and issues at
hand. They cut across the fields of development, production,
sales, service, quality, cost, and technology development. We're
still not there. There are a lot of things we need to do."[3]

At the same time, President Watanabe sees the auto industry
as a growing knowledge-driven industry full of promise, where
growth can be achieved by enhancing organizational capability and people. "If you think of the diffusion of automobiles, the

possibility is absolutely great," he said. "Thinking globally, the auto industry is a growth industry."[4] Jim Press, former President of Toyota Motor North America, used a green tomato metaphor to convey the same message: "Green tomatoes know their futures are still ahead of them, while red tomatoes quit growing."[5] Even today, when many observers consider the auto industry to be a red tomato, Toyota reimagines it to be green, and full of potential.

Contradiction 6—Nerve System: "Creating an Interconnected World through an Analog Web in the Digital Age"

Operating on the assumption that "everybody knows everything," information within Toyota flows freely up and down the hierarchy and across functional and seniority levels, extending outside the organization to suppliers, customers, and dealers. What is noteworthy is that in this age of the digital web, Toyota has created this interconnected world through analog means. Toyota's nerve system is an analog communication web with people serving as its neurotransmitters. Company insiders believe that it outperforms even the most advanced computer.

At the same time, of course, Toyota has developed an advanced IT system linking the company with its customers, dealers, and suppliers. For example, Lexus customers in Japan can now access a dedicated Lexus call center 24 hours a day, where they can make both car-related inquiries and reservations for hotels and restaurants. In the United States, Scion customers can select the options to customize their car online and link up with other owners to exchange ideas about tuning online as well.

Contradiction 7—Nerve System: "Bad News First to Become a Good Corporate Citizen"

Toyota managers learn from their training and experience that suppressing coworker opinion stops the creation of new ideas. Withholding opinion also undermines the process of critical evaluation, diminishing the potential for innovation. This is why

Toyota encourages employees to speak their mind and voice contrary opinion. The problem-solving culture at Toyota encourages all its employees to admit that problems exist, to make them visible, to see them as opportunities for improvement, to identify their root cause, and to take concrete countermeasures to prevent a recurrence. That's how a good corporate citizen at Toyota should behave.

"I can sleep peacefully at night as long as problems are shared and made visible at the same time," said President Watanabe. He continued, "If problems are tucked away, that will keep me up at night. So I tell everyone not to hide anything. Please give me the bad news first." The give-me-the-bad-news culture at Toyota encourages employees to be honest about having made a mistake. Making mistakes is all right, since to err is human. But hiding it, or not making it open, goes against Toyota's culture, which is based on being honest.

Contradiction 8—Up-and-In Human Resource Management: "To Maximize Productivity, Don't Let Go of People"

The means of production shifted as nations shifted from the industrial society to the knowledge society. In the industrial society, the means of production were assembly lines, machinery, robots, and automation. In the knowledge society, the means of production became the head and hand of every employee, which are metaphors for explicit knowledge and tacit knowledge, respectively.

In the era of the knowledge worker, the investments that generate the most value are those that cultivate organizational capability and people, who one day will create new ideas and innovation. This is why Toyota goes to great lengths to retain its employees, to train them using an extensive array of training programs at its designated facilities, and to develop them over the long term. Cultivating capability and people takes time and effort. Letting go of people in a knowledge-driven industry drains the company of its means of production as well as the corporate memory accumulated over the years in the head and hand of the knowledge worker.

Contradiction 9—Up-and-In Human Resource Management: "Appeal to Human Compassion to Increase Industrial Production"

We postulated at the end of Chapter 8 that up-and-in is a new model of human resource management fit for industrial production in the knowledge era. It represents a much more human approach to industrial production because it positions humans, rather than machines, at the center of all things. Employees work hard at Toyota, not because of a high salary or a quick promotion, but for the satisfaction that comes from improving and achieving something new every day. The two pillars of the Toyota Way—"continuous improvement" (kaizen) and "respect for people"—are founded on a somewhat naïve and optimistic view of humans, that everyone can make a contribution if given the chance.

Since knowledge workers are the epitome of the emotional animal, they also get satisfaction working in a team-based environment, where they feel their efforts have contributed to the entire organization as well as society at large. In a knowledge-driven environment, President Watanabe feels that the levers that drive employee motivation are very sensitive to soft factors, such as the ability to contribute to the country, society, or region, as well as the team. Appealing to individual compassion is also important, he contends.[6] These are the incentives that motivate the workforce to be hard working, be loyal, openly express opinions, take risks, and put in the extra mile.

Contradiction 10—Resource Base: "Say No to Shortcuts for Long-Term Gains"

Cultivating the head and hand of every employee requires continuous training and development. It is a long-term investment, even lifelong, with the need for continuous upgrading. It also requires an atmosphere of mutual respect, where employees feel their opinions count, their contributions make a difference, and their efforts yield visible and constructive results. There are no shortcuts to cultivating capability and people. It takes persistent effort over a long time in order to achieve positive results.

As mentioned, Toyota goes to great lengths to train and develop its employees over the long term. Toyota's training programs play a vital role in strengthening the integrative effect of the founders' philosophies by disseminating the Toyota Way values throughout the global workforce via a fortified nerve system that connects all employees. "Toyota gives [employees] leeway to spend resources as they see fit," said former Senior Managing Director Zenji Yasuda. "The only rule is that spending money contributes to the business in the long term. What is never accepted is using money to achieve short-term goals, like cost reduction measures that damage the company over the long term," he added.[7]

Conclusion

The contradictions drive Toyota to a state of disequilibrium, propelling it away from its comfort zone and instilling healthy tension and instability within the organization. This tension becomes the catalyst for movement forward, finding new solutions beyond contradiction, not in compromise or balance, but in higher levels of performance, as we have emphasized repeatedly. The first step to emulate Toyota is to recognize that contradictions, opposites, and paradoxes are a way of life within the company. Toyota relentlessly pits opposing forces against each other to realize continuous innovation and constant renewal.

Should you emulate Toyota's extreme performance model? We think you should, because it is a very human model of business management where each employee forms a vital part of the organization whole. Being human, it is an incomplete model. Being incomplete, there is room for change and renewal. Toyota's extreme performance model is the closest business management model that mirrors human life. Charles Handy says the following about life, which applies equally well to the extreme model we postulated: "Life will never be easy, or perfectible, or completely predictable. . . . To make it livable at all levels, we have to learn to use the paradoxes—to balance contradictions and inconsistencies—as an invitation to find a better way."[8]

Be forewarned. Living with contradictions, opposites, and paradoxes is not easy. However, once you pass the threshold, you will realize the wisdom of your choice. As Charles Handy points out, the world will look different and less frightening:

> [Living with contradiction] can be like walking in a dark wood on a moonless night. It is an eerie and, at times, a frightening experience. All sense of direction is lost; trees and bushes crowd in on you; wherever you step, you bump into another obstacle; every noise and rustle is magnified; there is a whiff of danger; it seems safer to stand still than to move. Come the dawn, however, and your path is clear; the noises are now the songs of birds and the rustle in the undergrowth is only scuttling rabbits; trees define the path instead of blocking it. The wood is a different place. So will our world look different and less frightening if we can bring light to the paradoxes.[9]

Toyota has brought light to the contradictions, opposites, and paradoxes and has given birth to an extreme performance model of business management to light our way into the future. An extreme model, we believe, is universal.

Selected Auto Industry Figures and Comparisons

Chapter 1—Extreme Toyota

FIGURE A.1 Total revenues (1997 to 2006) of the five largest car manufacturers.

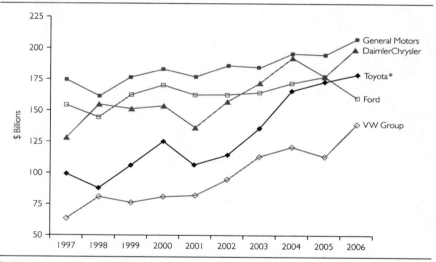

*Figures are for the fiscal years ending in March.
Source: Revenue figures for 1997 to 2006 from Thomson One Banker Analytics, May 6, 2007.

FIGURE A.2   Automotive segment revenues and regional distribution of the
10 largest car manufacturers in 2006.

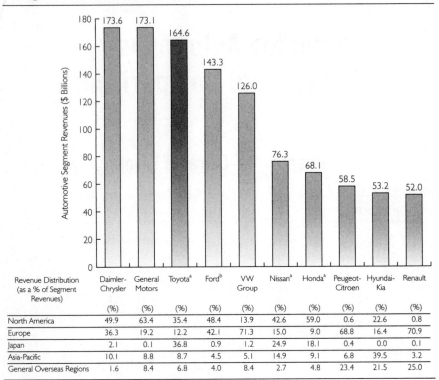

Revenue Distribution (as a % of Segment Revenues)	Daimler-Chrysler	General Motors	Toyota[a]	Ford[b]	VW Group	Nissan[a]	Honda[a]	Peugeot-Citroen	Hyundai-Kia	Renault
	(%)	(%)	(%)	(%)	(%)	(%)	(%)	(%)	(%)	(%)
North America	49.9	63.4	35.4	48.4	13.9	42.6	59.0	0.6	22.6	0.8
Europe	36.3	19.2	12.2	42.1	71.3	15.0	9.0	68.8	16.4	70.9
Japan	2.1	0.1	36.8	0.9	1.2	24.9	18.1	0.4	0.0	0.1
Asia-Pacific	10.1	8.8	8.7	4.5	5.1	14.9	9.1	6.8	39.5	3.2
General Overseas Regions	1.6	8.4	6.8	4.0	8.4	2.7	4.8	23.4	21.5	25.0

[a]Figures are for the fiscal year ending in March.
[b]Africa is included in Asia-Pacific.
Source: Author analysis of company annual reports and *2007 Global Market Data Book*
(New York: Automotive News, 2007).

FIGURE A.3   Toyota's net income (1997 to 2006) compared to its peer group average.

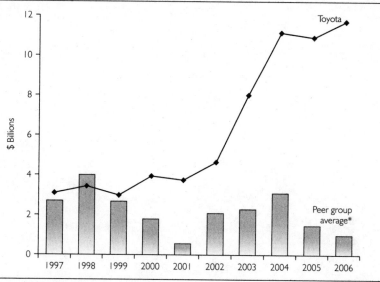

*Peer group includes DaimlerChrysler, Ford, General Motors, Honda, Hyundai-Kia, Nissan, Peugeot-Citroen, Renault, and VW Group.
Source: Net income figures for 1997 to 2006 from Thomson One Banker Analytics, May 6, 2007.

FIGURE A.4   Toyota's operating profit margin (1997 to 2006) compared to its peer group average.

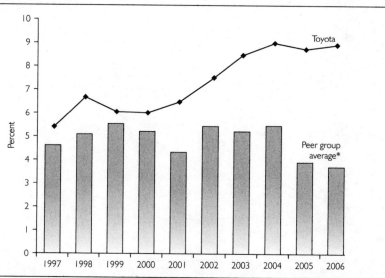

*Peer group includes DaimlerChrysler, Ford, General Motors, Honda, Hyundai-Kia, Nissan, Peugeot-Citroen, Renault, and VW Group.
Source: Operating profit margin figures for 1997 to 2006 from Thomson One Banker Analytics, April 14, 2007.

FIGURE A.5 Ten-year market capitalization of the 10 largest car manufacturers (1997 to 2006).

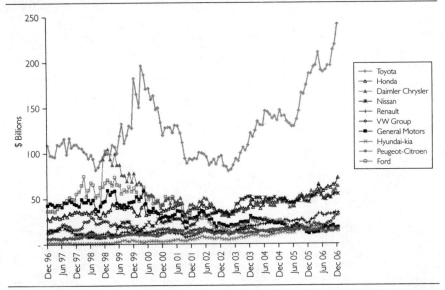

Source: Monthly market capitalization based on same day USD rates from Thomson One Banker Analytics, November 19, 2007.

FIGURE A.6 Vehicle production (1999 to 2006) of the five largest car manufacturers.

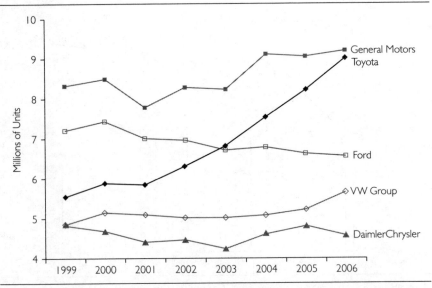

Source: Company annual reports, *Global Market Data Books* (New York: Automotive News, 2000–2007).

FIGURE A.7   Dividend payout ratio of the 10 largest car manufacturers in 2004.

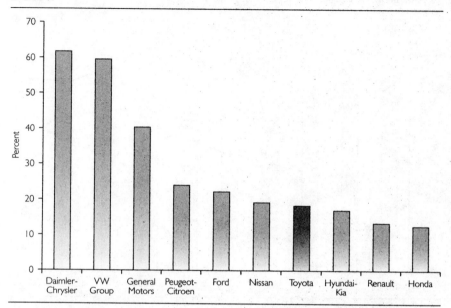

Note: The year 2004 was chosen as the comparison period because all 10 companies had a positive payout ratio that year.

Source: Payout ratio 2004 from Thomson One Banker Analytics, February 26, 2007. (Based on ratio of dividends per share to an adjusted EPS.)

FIGURE A.8   Toyota's return on invested capital (1997 to 2006) compared to its peer group average.

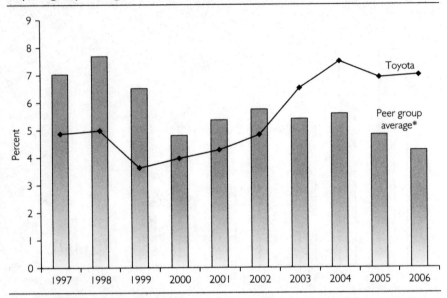

*Peer group includes DaimlerChrysler, Ford, General Motors, Honda, Hyundai-Kia, Nissan, Peugeot-Citroen, Renault, and VW Group.
Source: Return on invested capital figures for 1997 to 2006 from Thomson One Banker Analytics, April 14, 2007.

FIGURE A.9 Average remuneration for executive managers of the 10 largest car manufacturers in 2005.

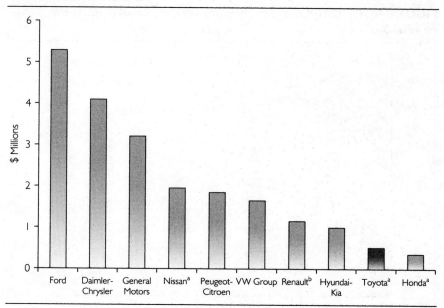

[a]Figures are for the fiscal year 2006.
[b]Figure based on 2004 estimates.
Source: Author estimates from company annual reports (Nissan, Peugeot-Citroen, Renault, and VW Group), proxy statements (Ford and General Motors), 20-F Forms (DaimlerChrysler, Honda, and Toyota), and a proxy paper (Hyundai; from http://glasslewisco.com/downloads/sampleresearch/proxypaper/hyundaimotors.pdf [accessed January 2007]).

Chapter 2—Six Forces

FIGURE A.10   Global sales market share (1999 to 2006) of the five largest car manufacturers.

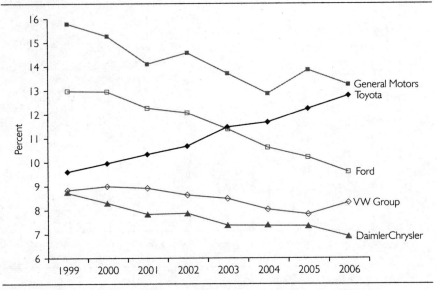

Note: In 1999, Toyota's market share was 9.6 percent. By 2006, this had grown to 12.8 percent, an increase of almost 0.5 percentage points per year.
Source: Company annual reports, *Global Market Data Books* (New York: Automotive News, 2000–2007).

FIGURE A.11   Total vehicle sales (1999 to 2006) of the five largest car manufacturers.

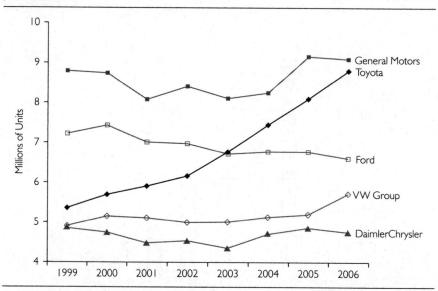

Note: In 2002, Toyota's sales amounted to almost 6.2 million units. By 2006, this had grown to 8.8 million units, an increase equivalent to 650,000 units per year.
Source: Company annual reports, *Global Market Data Books* (New York: Automotive News, 2000–2007).

FIGURE A.12 Vehicle sales and distribution of the 10 largest car manufacturers in 2006.

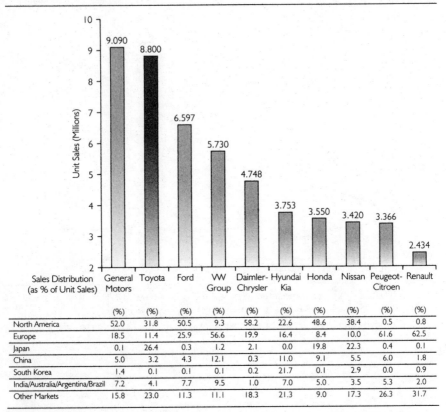

Sales Distribution (as % of Unit Sales)	General Motors	Toyota	Ford	VW Group	Daimler-Chrysler	Hyundai Kia	Honda	Nissan	Peugeot-Citroen	Renault
	(%)	(%)	(%)	(%)	(%)	(%)	(%)	(%)	(%)	(%)
North America	52.0	31.8	50.5	9.3	58.2	22.6	48.6	38.4	0.5	0.8
Europe	18.5	11.4	25.9	56.6	19.9	16.4	8.4	10.0	61.6	62.5
Japan	0.1	26.4	0.3	1.2	2.1	0.0	19.8	22.3	0.4	0.1
China	5.0	3.2	4.3	12.1	0.3	11.0	9.1	5.5	6.0	1.8
South Korea	1.4	0.1	0.1	0.1	0.2	21.7	0.1	2.9	0.0	0.9
India/Australia/Argentina/Brazil	7.2	4.1	7.7	9.5	1.0	7.0	5.0	3.5	5.3	2.0
Other Markets	15.8	23.0	11.3	11.1	18.3	21.3	9.0	17.3	26.3	31.7

Note: Toyota sold a total of 8.8 million units, of which 31.8 percent were sold in North America, 26.4 percent in Japan, 11.4 percent in Europe, 3.2 percent in China, 4.1 percent in India/Australia/Argentina/Brazil, and 23.1 percent in other markets (including South Korea).
Source: Author analysis of company annual reports and *2007 Global Market Data Book* (New York: Automotive News, 2007).

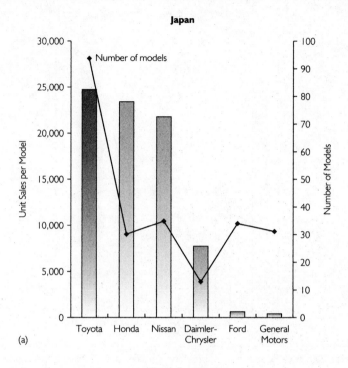

(a)

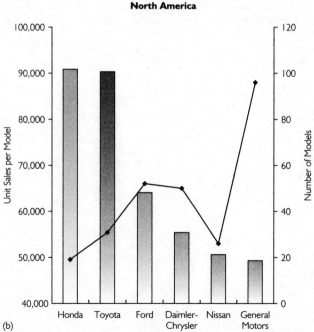

(b)

FIGURE A.13 (Continued)

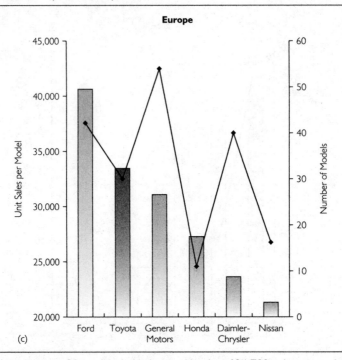

(c)

Note: Toyota, with over 90 models, led in Japan with sales of 24,700 units per model. Honda led North America with 90,800 units per model (19 models), followed by Toyota with 90,300 (31 models). In Europe, Toyota sold 33,400 units per model (30 models), the highest among the Japanese makes.

Source: Author analysis of 2007 Global Market Data Book (New York: Automotive News, 2007).

Chapter 3—Impossible Goals

FIGURE A.14   Number of models sold in Japan by the 10 largest car manufacturers in 2006.

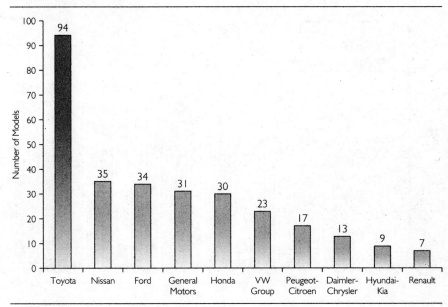

Source: Company annual reports, *2007 Global Market Data Book* (New York: Automotive News, 2007).

Chapter 9—Resources

FIGURE A.15   Toyota's cash holdings (including short term investments), net income, and dividend payout (1980 to 2006).

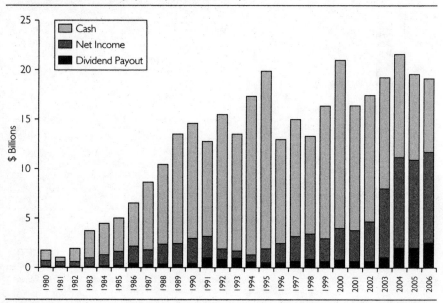

Note: Dividend payout calculated from net income times payout ratio.

Source: Figures for cash, net income, and payout ratio for 1980 to 2006 from Thomson One Banker Analytics, February 26, 2007.

FIGURE A.16   Unit sales per dealer and dealer satisfaction rating for the U.S. market in 2006.

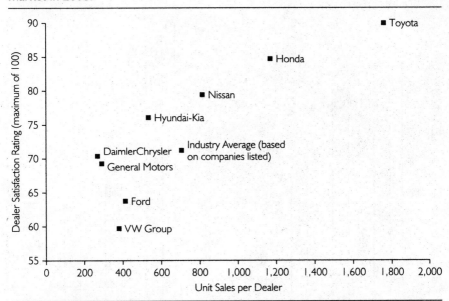

Note: Toyota's dealers led the field with sales averaging 1,760 units per dealer and a Dealer Satisfaction Rating of 90, ahead of Honda (1,173 units per dealer, rating of 84.7) and Nissan (815 units per dealer, rating of 79.4). The industry average was 705 units per dealer and a rating of 71.2. Dealer satisfaction ratings are based on the average of a carmaker's brands. For example, Toyota had 221 Lexus dealers with a dealer satisfaction rating of 96, 991 Scion dealers with a rating of 90.9, and 1,224 Toyota dealers with a rating of 88.1. The average dealer satisfaction is the sum of each brand's dealer rating times the number of dealers, divided by the overall number of dealers. The result for Toyota is an average dealer satisfaction rating of 90.
Source: Author analysis of *2006 Dealer Attitude Survey* (McLean, VA: North American Dealers Association, 2006), *2007 Market Data: North America Sales* (New York: Automotive News, 2007), *2007 Market Data: Dealer Data* (New York: Automotive News, 2007).

FIGURE A.17 Advertising expense per unit sold of the four largest car manufacturers in 2006.

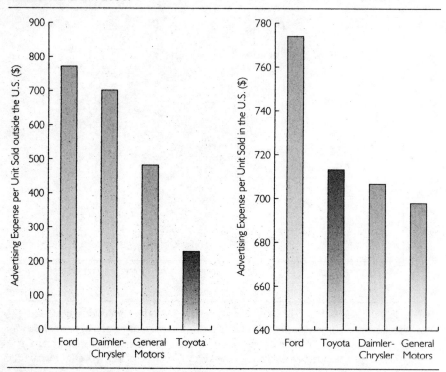

Note: The left graph depicts the advertisement expense per unit sold outside the United States, while the right graph shows the advertising expense per unit sold in the United States. *Source:* Author analysis of company annual reports, *AdvertisingAge Datacenter 2007 Marketer Profiles Yearbook* (New York: Crain Communications, Inc., 2007).

Literature Review

With the assistance of Monitor Group, our literature review of the publications about Toyota (1980 to 2007) identified a total of 48 English books and 382 Japanese books that were related to the central theme of this book—Toyota's management of both the "soft" side and the "hard" side of the company.

Of the 48 English books on Toyota, 12 were published during the 1980s, 17 during the 1990s, 9 from 2001 to 2005, and 10 from 2006 to 2007 (in Table B.1). Half of these focused on the Toyota Production System.

The Japanese books on Toyota covered a wider range of topics, including human resource management and innovation issues, and only 25.4 percent focused on the Toyota Production System. The rising number of publications in recent years

TABLE B.1   Number of Books in English and Japanese about Toyota (1980 to 2007)

Period	English Books	Japanese Books
1980–1985	3 (2)	44 (10)
1986–1990	9 (6)	50 (12)
1991–1995	5 (2)	35 (8)
1996–2000	12 (6)	44 (8)
2001–2005	9 (3)	125 (34)
2006–2007	10 (5)	84 (25)
Total	48 (24)	382 (97)

Note: Numbers in parenthesis reflect the number of books that focus on the Toyota Production System.

reflects an increasing interest on Toyota in Japan. From 2001 to 2007, a total of 209 books were published, more than the 173 published from 1980 to 2000.

Literature Review Methodology

The keyword "Toyota" was used to search for book titles registered in the Library of Congress (United States), the British Library (U.K.), and the libraries of five Japanese universities (Hitotsubashi University, Keio University, Kyoto University, Tokyo University, and Waseda University). The resulting list of titles was first screened to exclude entries on auto manuals, Toyota conferences, and books on topics including Toyota cars and Toyota City. The list was screened once more using the keywords "TPS," "Production," and "System" in the title and subject headings to identify those books focusing on the Toyota Production System. Each entry in this final list was reviewed to determine if it actually focused on the Toyota Production System or on some other topic. A similar method was used to compile the list of Japanese book titles.

For those interested in learning more about Toyota, we have compiled the following short list of the major books and articles published between 1980 and 2007 that are not a part of the References section.

Selected English Book Publications on Toyota (1980 to 2007)

Basu, S. *Corporate Purpose: Why It Matters More Than Strategy*. New York: Garland, 1999.

Besser, T. L. *Team Toyota: Transplanting the Toyota Culture to the Camry Plant in Kentucky*. Albany: State University of New York Press, 1996.

Coffey, D. *The Myth of Japanese Efficiency: The World Car Industry in a Globalizing Age*. New York: Edward Elgar, 2007.

Cusumano, M. A., and K. Nobeoka. *Thinking beyond Lean: How Multi-Project Management Is Transforming Product*

Development at Toyota and Other Companies. New York: Free Press, 1998.

Dyer, J. H. *Collaborative Advantage: Winning through Extended Enterprise Supplier Networks*. New York: Oxford University Press, 2003.

Fujimoto, T. *The Evolution of a Manufacturing System at Toyota*. New York: Oxford University Press, 1999.

Hino, S. *Inside the Mind of Toyota: Management Principles for Enduring Growth*. Translated by Andrew Dillon. New York: Productivity Press, 2006.

Japan Management Association, ed. *Kanban Just-in-Time at Toyota: Management Begins at the Workplace*. Translated by David J. Lu. Cambridge, MA: Productivity Press, 1989.

Johnson, H. T., and A. Broms. *Profit beyond Measure*. New York: Free Press, 2000.

Liker, J. K. *Toyota Culture: The Heart and Soul of the Toyota Way*. New York: McGraw-Hill, 2007.

Liker, J. K. *The Toyota Way: 14 Management Principles from the World's Greatest Manufacturer*. New York: McGraw-Hill, 2004.

Liker, J. K., and D. Meier. *Toyota Talent: Developing Your People the Toyota Way*. New York: McGraw-Hill, 2007.

Magee, D. *How Toyota Became #1: Leadership Lessons from the World's Greatest Car Company*. New York: Portfolio Hardcover, 2007.

May, M. E. *The Elegant Solution: Toyota's Formula for Mastering Innovation*. New York: Free Press, 2007.

Monden, Y. *The Toyota Management System: Linking the Seven Key Functional Areas*. Translated by Bruce Talbot. Cambridge, MA: Productivity Press, 1993.

Morgan, J. M., and J. K. Liker. *The Toyota Product Development System: Integrating People, Process, and Technology*. New York: Productivity Press, 2006.

Nemoto, M. *Total Quality Control for Management: Strategies and Techniques from Toyota and Toyoda Gosei*. Translated by D. Lu. New Jersey: Prentice-Hall, 1987.

Ohno, T. *Toyota Production System: Beyond Large-Scale Production*. Portland, OR: Productivity, 1988.

Ohno, T. *Workplace Management*. Translated by Andrew P. Dillon. Cambridge, MA: Productivity Press, 1988.

Osono, E. "Learning and Self-Renewing, Network Organization: Toyota and Lexus Dealers." In *Japan Moving Toward a More Advanced Knowledge Economy*, vol 2. Edited by H. Takeuchi and T. Shibata. Washington, DC: World Bank, 2006.

Reingold, E. M. *Toyota: People, Ideas, and the Challenge of the New*. London: Penguin Books, 1999.

Togo, Y., and W. Wartman. *Against All Odds: The Story of the Toyota Motor Corporation and the Family that Created It*. New York: St. Martin's Press, 1993.

Womack, J. P., D. T. Jones, D. Roos, and D. S. Carpenter. *The Machine that Changed the World*. New York: Rawson Associates Scribner, 1990.

Yasuda, Y. *40 Years, 20 Million Ideas: The Toyota Suggestion System*. Translated by Fredrich Czupryna. Cambridge, MA: Productivity Press, 1991.

Selected English Articles on Toyota (1980 to 2007)

Adler, P. S., and R. E. Cole. "Designed for Learning: A Tale of Two Auto Plants." *MIT Sloan Management Review 34* (Spring 1993): 85–94.

Ahmadjian, C. L., and J. R. Lincoln. "Keiretsu, Governance, and Learning: Case Studies in Change from the Japanese Automotive Industry." *Organization Science 12* (November 2001): 683–701.

Bremner, B., C. Dawson, K. Kerwin, C. Palmeri, and P. Magnusson. "Can Anything Stop Toyota? An Inside Look at How It's Reinventing the Auto Industry." *BusinessWeek*, November 17, 2003.

Dyer, J. H., and W. Chu. "The Determinants of Trust in Supplier-Automaker Relationships in the U.S., Japan, and Korea." *Journal of International Business Studies 31* (June 2000): 259–285.

Dyer, J. H., and N. W. Hatch. "Relation-Specific Capabilities and Barriers to Knowledge Transfers: Creating Advantage through Network Relationships." *Strategic Management Journal 27* (August 2006): 701–720.

Dyer, J. H., and N. W. Hatch. "Using Supplier Networks to Learn Faster."*MIT Sloan Management Review 45* (Spring 2004): 57–63.

Dyer, J. H., and K. Nobeoka. "Creating and Managing a High-Performance Knowledge-Sharing Network: The Toyota Case." *Strategic Management Journal 21* (March 2000): 345–367.

Evans, P., and B. Wolf. "Collaboration Rules." *Harvard Business Review* (July–August 2005): 96–104.

Ghemawat, P. "Regional Strategies for Global Leadership." *Harvard Business Review* (December–January 2005): 98–109.

Kogut, B. "The Network as Knowledge: Generative Rules and the Emergence of Structure." *Strategic Management Journal 21* (March 2000): 405–425.

Lieberman, M. B., and R. Dhawan. "Assessing the Resource Base of Japanese and U.S. Auto Producers: A Stochastic Frontier Production Function Approach." *Management Science 51* (July 2005): 1060–1075.

Lieberman, M. B., L. J. Lau, and M. D. Williams. "Firm-Level Productivity and Management Influence: A Comparison of U.S. and Japanese Automobile Producers." *Management Science 36* (October 1990): 1193–1215.

Liker, J. K., and T. Y. Choi. "Building Deep Supplier Relationships." *Harvard Business Review* (December 2004): 104–113.

Nishiguchi, T., and A. Beaudet. "The Toyota Group and the Aisin Fire." *MIT Sloan Management Review 40* (Fall 1998): 49–59.

Rao, R. D., and L. Argote. "Organizational Learning and Forgetting: The Effects of Turnover and Structure." *European Management Review 3* (January 2006): 77–85.

Reinhardt, F. L. "Opinion: Place Your Bets on the Future You Want." *Harvard Business Review* (October 2007): 42–43.

Sobek, D. K., II, J. K. Liker, and A. Ward. "Another Look at How Toyota Integrates Product Development." *Harvard Business Review* (July–August 1998): 36–49.

Spear, S. J., and H. K. Bowen. "Decoding the DNA of the Toyota Production System."*Harvard Business Review* (September 1999): 97–106.

Stewart, T. A., and A. P. Raman. "Lessons from Toyota's Long Drive."*Harvard Business Review* (July–August 2007): 74–83.

Ward, A., J. K. Liker, J. J. Cristiano, and D. K. Sobek II. "The Second Toyota Paradox: How Delaying Decisions Can Make Better Cars Faster."*MIT Sloan Management Review 36* (Spring 1995): 43–61.

Watanabe, K., T. A. Stewart, and A. P. Raman. "Inculcating Culture: The Toyota Way."*Economist*, January 19, 2006.

Watanabe, K., T. A. Stewart, and A. P. Raman. "Lessons from Toyota's Long Drive." *Harvard Business Review* (July–August 2007): 74–83.

Watanabe, K., T. A. Stewart, and A. P. Raman. "Toyota: The Car Company in Front."*Economist*, January 27, 2005.

Chapter 1 Extreme Toyota: An Organization Powered by Creative Contradictions

1. See Appendix A "Chapter 1—Extreme Toyota," for additional figures comparing the largest auto manufacturers, including total revenues (Figure A.1), geographical distribution of automotive revenues (Figure A.2), net income (Figure A.3), operating profit margin (Figure A.4), market capitalization (Figure A.5), and vehicle production (Figure A.6).

2. J.D. Power and Associates, "J.D. Power and Associates Reports: Buick and Lexus Brands Tie for Highest Rank in Vehicle Dependability, (press release, Westlake Village, CA, August 9, 2007), J.D. Power and Associates web site, http://www.jdpower.com/corporate/news/releases/pressrelease.aspx?ID=2007130 (accessed March 2008).

3. The term "deep smarts," as coined by Dorothy Leonard and Walter Swap in *Deep Smarts* (Boston: Harvard Business School Press, 2005), is considered a type of tacit knowledge by Ikujiro Nonaka and Hirotaka Takeuchi in their book *The Knowledge-Creating Company* (New York: Oxford University Press, 1995), 152.

4. From company annual reports. For a past comparison, see note 1, dividend payout ratio of the 10 largest car manufacturers in 2004 (Figure A.7).

5. Return on invested capital (ROIC) is a measure of the effective utilization of capital (owned or borrowed in the form of equity or debt) in a company's operations. It is calculated by dividing net income (after taxes) by total assets (minus cash and non-interest-bearing liabilities). See note 1, return on invested capital (Figure A.8).

6. See note 1, remuneration for executive employees of the 10 largest car manufacturers in 2005 (Figure A.9).

7. Toyota Motor Corporation 2007, June 25, 2007 20-F (Tokyo: Toyota Motor Corporation, 2007), 70, http://www.sec.gov/Archives/edgar/data/1094517/000119312507141459/d20f.htm#rom32719_23 (accessed March 10, 2008).

8. Akio Matsubara, "Special Committee for Management Innovation—Japanese Management" (presentation made during the conference hosted by the Japan Productivity Center for Socio-Economic Development, Tokyo, October 11, 2004).

9. Ever since Collins and Porras coined the term "the genius of the AND" in *Built to Last*, which was published in 1994 (New York: HarperCollins), the need to embrace contradictions has been hurled to the center stage of management thinking. They argued that successful companies figure out a way to have both A AND B, instead of choosing A OR B. Thus, successful companies do well both in the short term AND in the long run. They seek to be both highly idealistic AND highly profitable. They preserve both tightly held core ideology AND stimulate vigorous change and movement. Other management writers followed suit, pointing out the need to pursue both continuous improvement AND disruptive technology; both product and process innovation AND business concept innovation; both economies of scale and scope AND economies of speed; both order AND chaos; both efficiency AND creativity; both global AND local; both personal humility AND professional will, and the list goes on.

10. Excerpt from the Lexus Covenant, which is presented in its entirety in Chapter 6.

11. OJT Solutions, *Toyota no Kuchiguse* [Favorite Phrases within Toyota] (Tokyo: Chukei Shuppan, 2006), 169.

12. David Welch, "Why Toyota Is Afraid of Being Number One," *BusinessWeek*, March 5, 2007, www.businessweek.com/agazine/content/07_10/b4024071.htm (accessed March 2007).

13. Chunichi Shimbun-sh, ed., *Toyota no Sekai* [The World of Toyota] (Nagoya, Japan: Chunichi Shimbun-sha, 2007), 214.

14. Based on an exchange rate of 117 yen per dollar.

15. *Toyota Up Close*, 2, from Toyota company web site, www
.toyota.co.jp/en/pdf/2006/toyota_up_close0611.pdf (accessed
January 2008).

16. Yoshimi Inaba, interview by authors, sourced from case:
Emi Osono, "The Global Knowledge Center: Sharing the
Toyota Way in Sales and Marketing" (ICS case no. A050003E,
Hitotsubashi University, Tokyo, 2005), 4. All titles of execu-
tives and employees are from the time of interview.

17. Alex Taylor III, "Toyota's Secret Weapon,"*Fortune*, August 23,
2004, http://money.cnn.com/magazines/fortune/fortune_arch
ive/2004/08/23/379403/index.htm (accessed February 2007).

18. "Toyota Sekai Saikyo eno Kakuto" [Toyota's struggle to be the
World's Strongest], *Nikkei Business*, February 26, 2007, 67.

19. "Toyota-Shiki Shigoto no Kyokasho" [Textbook on Toyota-
style Work], *President,* September 12, 2005, 27.

20. Katsuaki Watanabe, interview by authors, Tokyo, October
10, 2007.

21. Osamu Katayama, "Bumon wa Nakayoku Kenka Seyo"
[Departments Should Pick a Friendly Fight], *Voice,* November
2005, 139.

22. Ian Rowley, "Fighting to Stay Humble," *BusinessWeek*, March 5,
2007, www.businessweek.com/magazine/content/07_10/
b4024073.htm (accessed March 2007).

23. Toyota refers to its employees as "associates."

24. See note 8.

25. Deborah Ancona, Thomas W. Malone, Wanda J. Orlikowski,
and Peter M. Senge, "In Praise of the Incomplete Leader,"
Harvard Business Review, February 2007, 92–100.

26. Ikujiro Nonaka, "The Knowledge Creating Company," *Harvard
Business Review,* November–December 1991, 96–104.

27. *Aufheben,* a German word, in this context, means, "to sublate." In Hegelian philosophy, "to sublate" means to achieve
(or reach) a higher level of coexistence (or unity) through
contradiction.

28. In the language of dialectic thinking, a form of thought that goes back to ancient Greece and is closely associated with the German philosopher Hegel, a higher-order solution is reached by transcending *thesis* and *antithesis* through a process of *synthesis*, or *aufheben*.

Chapter 2   Six Opposing Forces That Drive the Company's Expansion—and Keep It from Breaking Apart

1. See Appendix A"Chapter 2—Six Forces," for figures comparing the five largest auto manufacturers, including global market shares (Figure A.10) and total vehicle sales (Figure A.11).
2. See note 1, vehicle sales and distribution of the 10 largest car manufacturers in 2006 (Figure A.12).
3. See note 1, units sold per model in Japan, North America, and Europe in 2006 for the three largest American and Japanese car manufacturers (Figure A.13).
4. Jim Press, interview by the authors, August 1, 2006, Tokyo.

Chapter 3   The Force of Impossible Goals

1. *The Toyota Way 2001* (internal Toyota Motor Corporation publication, Tokyo), April 2001, 11.
2. According to Toyota, the aim of "harmonious growth" is "to develop and establish new technologies to enable the environment and economy to coexist harmoniously." From the Toyota company web site, www.toyota.co.jp/en/environ ment/vision/policies/index.html (accessed June 2007).
3. Yoshio Ishizaka, interview by authors, July 25, 2006, Tokyo.
4. See note 1, p. 6.
5. Yoshimi Inaba, interview by authors, from Emi Osono, "The Birth of Scion: Can Toyota Attract Young Customers?" (ICS case no. A040010E, Hitotsubashi University, Tokyo, 2004), 7.
6. Yoshimi Inaba, interview by authors, August 21, 2006, Tokyo.

7. *Toyota Value* (internal Toyota Motor Corporation publication, Tokyo, October 2003), 38.

8. "Always optimizing" is an essential Toyota value that aims "to harmonize multiple elements simultaneously at the highest possible level of performance." See note 7, p. 3.

9. See note 7, p. 43.

10. Michael E. Porter, *On Competition* (Boston: Harvard Business School Press, 1998), 59.

11. James Collins and Jerry Porras, *Built to Last* (New York: HarperCollins, 1997), 52.

12. Ford Motor Company, "Ford in Europe: The First Hundred Years," Ford Motor Company web site, http://media.ford.com/article_display.cfm?article_id=14707 (accessed June 2007).

13. "Rensai: Sakinzu beshi; Toyota 'Sekai Saikyo' he no Kakuto" [Serialization: Stay Ahead of the Times; Toyota Fighting to Be the Strongest Manufacturer in the World], *Nikkei Business*, May 7, 2007, 8.

14. Katsuaki Watanabe, interview by authors, October 10, 2007, Tokyo.

15. See note 14.

16. Emi Osono, "The Birth of Scion: Can Toyota Attract Young Customers?" ICS case no. A040010E, Hitotsubashi University, Tokyo, 2004), 4.

17. Jon Gertner, "From 0 to 60 World Domination," *New York Times*, February 18, 2007. Copyright © 2007 The New York Times. All Rights Reserved. Used by permission and protected by the Copyright Laws of the United States. The printing, copying, redistribution, or retransmission of the material without express written permission is prohibited.

18. See Appendix A "Chapter 3—Impossible Goals," for the number of models sold in Japan by the 10 largest car manufacturers in 2006 (Figure A.14).

19. Toyota Motor Philippines, "'06 Top 3 Best Selling Vehicles: Toyota Innova, Vios and Fortuner," Toyota company web site, www.toyota.com.ph/news_and_events/ne7.asp (accessed February 2007).

20. Toyota Motor Vietnam, "Toyota Vietnam Continues Growth in 2006," Toyota company web site, www.toyotavn.com.vn/asp/view/vn/cate_details.asp?code=10&id=1252&version=en (accessed February 2007).

21. Yoshio Ishizaka, interview by authors, from Emi Osono, "Lexus: The Challenge of the U.S. Luxury Car Market" (ICS case no. I0610E, Hitotsubashi University, Tokyo, 2006), 7.

22. Other originators of the IMV concept were Hiroyuki Watanabe, Director of Product Planning, and Kazuo Okamoto, Director of Engineering.

23. Zenji Yasuda, interview by authors, from Emi Osono, "Toyota's IMV Project: The Innovative International Multi-Purpose Vehicle" (ICS case no. I0702E, Hitotsubashi University, Tokyo, 2007), 8.

24. Akio Toyoda, interview by authors, from Osono, ICS case no. I0702E, 12.

25. See note 24, p. 9.

26. Hiroshi Nakagawa, interview by authors, from Osono ICS case no. I0702E, 9.

27. See note 26, p. 11.

28. See note 23, p. 11.

29. See note 24, p. 11.

Chapter 4   Eagerness to Experiment

1. *Team Toyota 10* (internal Toyota Motor Corporation publication, Tokyo) January–February 2004, 24.

2. See note 1.

3. Katsuaki Watanabe, interview by authors, October 10, 2007, Tokyo.

4. Zenji Yasuda, interview by authors, August 29, 2007, Shizuoka, Japan.

5. *Team Toyota 8* (internal Toyota Motor Corporation publication, Tokyo), September–October 2003, 26.

6. See note 5.

7. See note 5.

8. Akio Matsubara (presentation made during the "Special Committee for Management Innovation: Japanese Management" conference hosted by the Japan Productivity Center for Socio-Economic Development, October 11, 2004, Tokyo).

9. *The Toyota Business Practices* (internal Toyota Motor Corporation document, Tokyo), April 2005.

10. Akio Toyoda, interview by authors, from Emi Osono, "Toyota's IMV Project: The Innovative International Multi-Purpose Vehicle" (ICS case no. I0702E, Hitotsubashi University, Tokyo, 2007), 13.

11. Zenji Yasuda, interview by authors, from Osono, ICS case no. I0702E, 6–7.

12. See note 11, p. 7.

13. Emi Osono, "The Birth of Scion: Can Toyota Attract Young Customers?" (ICS case no. A040010E, Hitotsubashi University, Tokyo, 2004), 30.

14. The *Echo* was a new model, and the comparison was made with its predecessor, the *Tercel*. The newer *Celica* was the ninth model and was compared with the previous model.

15. "Redefining the Customer Experience (Scion),"*Best Practice Bulletin 26* (internal Toyota Motor Corporation publication, Tokyo), April 2005, 11.

16. Naomi Ishii, interview by authors, November 1, 2006, Tokyo.

17. *Team Toyota 24* (internal Toyota Motor Corporation publication, Tokyo), May–June 2006, 18.

18. *The Toyota Way 2001* (internal Toyota Motor Corporation publication, Tokyo), April 2001, 9.

19. See note 18.

20. See note 18, p. 7.

21. See note 10, p. 11.

22. Zenji Yasuda, interview by authors, August 29, 2007, Shizuoka, Japan.

23. See note 8.

24. Yoshio Ishizaka, interview by authors, July 25, 2006, Tokyo.

25. *Team Toyota 11* (internal Toyota Motor Corporation publication, Tokyo), March–April 2004, 16.

26. *Toyota Value* (internal Toyota Motor Corporation publication, Tokyo), October 2003, 33.

27. Adopted from original text, *Team Toyota 10* (internal Toyota Motor Corporation publication, Tokyo), January–February 2004, 16.

28. Reprinted by permission of *Nikkei Business*. From "Rensai: Sakinzu beshi; Toyota 'Sekai Saikyo' he no Kakuto" [Serialization: Stay Ahead of the Times; Toyota Fighting to Be the Strongest Manufacturer in the World], *Nikkei Business*, May 7, 2007, 9. Copyright © 2007 by Nikkei Business Publications Inc.; all rights reserved.

29. Scion's business model, with its emphasis on accessory sales, had the potential to improve a dealer's margin per unit sold compared to the standard Toyota dealer contract.

30. Yoshimi Inaba, interview by authors, August 21, 2006, Tokyo.

31. See note 11, p. 7.

32. See note 11, p. 13.

33. See note 30.

Chapter 5   Local Customization

1. Toyota City is located in Mikawa, a region in Aichi Prefecture, central Japan.

2. New United Motor Manufacturing, Inc.

3. Akio Matsubara (presentation made during the "Special Committee for Management Innovation: Japanese Management," conference hosted by the Japan Productivity Center for Socio-Economic Development, October 11, 2004, Tokyo).

4. Tokuichi Uranishi, interview by authors, September 26, 2007, Nagoya, Japan.

5. "Toyota Traditions,"*Team Toyota 5* (internal Toyota Motor Corporation publication, Tokyo) March–April 2003, 17.

6. See note 5.

7. Toyota Motor Corporation, *Toyota: A History of the First 50 Years* (Toyota City, Japan: Toyota Motor Corporation, 1988), 300.

8. See note 3.

9. See note 7, p. 287.

10. Gail Edmondson and Adeline Bonnet, "Toyota's New Traction in Europe," *BusinessWeek*, June 7, 2004, www.business week.com/magazine/content/04_23/b3886177.htm (accessed February 2007).

11. In Italy, from September 2002, the Antilock Braking System (ABS) had become a standard option.

12. Emi Osono, Norihiko Shimizu, and K. Yonten, "Toyota's Commitment to Europe: Italy and Germany" (ICS case no. A040008E, Hitotsubashi University, Tokyo, 2004), 6.

13. Norio Kitamura, interview by authors, from Osono, Shimizu, and Yonten, case no. A040008E, 6.

14. See note 12, p. 11.

15. "The New Yaris Launch in France," *Best Practice Bulletin 35* (internal Toyota Motor Corporation publication, Tokyo), August 2006, 2.

16. See note 15, p. 9.

17. See note 12, p. 16.

18. Emi Osono, "The Birth of Scion: Can Toyota Attract Young Customers?" (ICS case no. A040010E, Hitotsubashi University, Tokyo, 2004), 3.

19. See note 18.

20. See note 18, pp. 8–9.

21. Tetsuya Tada, interview by authors, November 18, 2003, Toyota City, Japan.

22. See note 18, p. 10.

23. Ford had aggressively offered optional accessories and shared the car design specifications with the accessory manufacturers. Before Scion, Toyota avoided this out of concern of the potential for an increase in quality problems.

24. See note 18, p. 15.

25. See note 18.

26. See note 18.

27. "Remixing Youth and Toyota," *Team Toyota 5* (internal Toyota Motor Corporation publication, Tokyo), March–April 2003, 11.

28. "Redefining the Customer Experience (Scion),"*Best Practice Bulletin 26* (internal Toyota Motor Corporation publication, Tokyo), April 2005, 8.

29. "Tundra: The Truck That's Changing It All," *Team Toyota 30* (internal Toyota Motor Corporation publication, Tokyo), May–June 2007, 8.

30. See note 29, p. 11.

31. See note 29, p. 10.

32. David Welch, "Why Toyota Is Afraid of Being Number One," *BusinessWeek,* March 5, 2007, www.businessweek.com/mag azine/content/07_10/b4024071.htm (accessed March 2007).

33. Thomas L. Friedman, *The World Is Flat* (New York: Farrar, Straus and Giroux, 2005).

34. Yoshimi Inaba, interview by authors, from Emi Osono, "The Global Knowledge Center: Sharing the Toyota Way in Sales and Marketing" (ICS case no. A050003E, Hitotsubashi University, Tokyo, 2005), 14.

Chapter 6   The Founders' Philosophies

1. Akio Matsubara (presentation made during the "Special Committee for Management Innovation: Japanese Management" conference hosted by the Japan Productivity Center for Socio-Economic Development, October 11, 2004, Tokyo).

2. Emi Osono, Norihiko Shimizu, and K. Yonten, "Toyota's Commitment to Europe: Italy and Germany" (ICS case no. A040008E, Hitotsubashi University, Tokyo, 2004), 2–3.

3. See note 2, pp. 13–14.

4. Tokuichi Uranishi, interview by authors, September 26, 2007, Nagoya, Japan.

5. See note 1.

6. *The Toyota Way 2001* (internal Toyota Motor Corporation publication, Tokyo), April 2001, 6.

7. John Kramer, interview by authors, August 9, 2006, Tokyo.

8. Tony Fujita, interview by authors, August 2, 2006, Nagoya, Japan.

9. See note 4.

10. Kiichiro Toyoda purchased about 2 million square meters of land in Koromo-cho, some 30 km east of Nagoya, in December 1935. At that time, the site was barren property covered with trees. Toyoda bought this piece of land with the idea of building a full-scale automobile plant, which was completed three years after buying the property. Soon after, Toyoda recommended its suppliers move to Koromo-cho, which was in line with plans drawn up by the municipal authorities to have Koromo become an automotive industrial city centered around the Toyota Motor Corporation. In line with these developments, Koromo was renamed Toyota City.

11. See note 6, p. 11.

12. See note 6, p. 10.

13. Akio Toyoda, interview by authors, from Emi Osono, "Toyota's IMV Project: The Innovative International Multi-Purpose Vehicle" (ICS case no. I0702E, Hitotsubashi University, Tokyo, 2007), 12.

14. In fact, Toyota views the automobile industry as a knowledge industry, not just a manufacturing industry.

15. See note 1.

16. Fujio Cho, interview by authors, June 6, 2007, St. Petersburg, Russia.

17. Katsuyoshi Tabata, interview by authors, July 24, 2006, Tokyo.

18. See note 7.

19. See note 7.

20. Yukitoshi Funo, interview by authors, July 28, 2006, Tokyo.

21. *Team Toyota 6* (internal Toyota Motor Corporation publication, Tokyo), May–June 2002, 17.

22. Emi Osono, "The Global Knowledge Center: Sharing the Toyota Way in Sales and Marketing" (ICS case no. A050003E, Hitotsubashi University, Tokyo, 2005), 3.

23. Michael A. Cusumano, *The Japanese Automotive Industry: Technology and Management at Nissan and Toyota* (Cambridge: Harvard University Press, 1985).

24. Adapted from original quote, *The Toyota Way 2001*, 13.

25. Hiroshi Nakagawa, interview by authors, from Osono, case no. I0702E, 11.

26. Adapted from original quote, *The Toyota Way 2001*, 12.

27. *The Toyota Way in Sales and Marketing* (internal Toyota Motor Corporation publication, Tokyo), October 2001, 23.

28. See note 7.

29. OJT Solutions, *Toyota no Kuchiguse* [Favorite Phrases within Toyota] (Tokyo: Chukei Shuppan, 2006), 57.

30. "Covenant": A term deriving from the Jewish faith, meaning "a contract between God and Man."

31. Emi Osono, "Lexus: The Challenge of the U.S. Luxury Car Market" (ICS case no. I0610E, Hitotsubashi University, Tokyo, 2006), 13.

32. See note 31.

33. Joseph Bohn, "Dealer: Incredibly Efficient Recall," *Automotive News,* December 11, 1989, 43.

34. See note 31, pp. 10–11.

35. See note 6, p. 8.

36. See note 6, p. 9.

37. See note 6, p. 8.

38. See note 6, p. 8.

39. *Team Toyota 23* (internal Toyota Motor Corporation publication, Tokyo), March–April 2006, 16.

40. See note 17.

41. See note 20.

Chapter 7   Toyota's Nerve System—A Human Version of the World Wide Web

1. *Toyota in the World 2006*, 23–24, from Toyota company web site, www.toyota.co.jp/en/pdf/toyota_world/2006/toyota.pdf (accessed February 2007).

2. Toyota Motor Corporation, FY2007 *Annual Report* (Toyota City, Japan: Toyota Motor Corporation, 2007), 136, www.toyota .co.jp/en/ir/library/annual/pdf/2007/ar07_e.pdf (accessed January 2008).

3. Takahiro Fujioka, interview by authors, October 27, 2007, Nagoya, Japan.

4. Yoshimi Inaba, interview by authors, August 21, 2006, Tokyo.

5. See note 4.

6. OJT Solutions, *Toyota no Kuchiguse* [Favorite Phrases within Toyota] (Tokyo: Chukei Shuppan, 2006), 101–102.

7. John Kramer, interview by authors, August 9, 2006, Tokyo.

8. "Sales Satisfaction: Obeya Solution,"*Best Practice Bulletin 42* (internal Toyota Motor Corporation publication, Tokyo), July 2007, 6.

9. Hiroshi Nakagawa, interview by authors, from Emi Osono, "Toyota's IMV Project: The Innovative International

Multi-Purpose Vehicle" (ICS case no. I0702E, Hitotsubashi University, Tokyo, 2007), 9–10.

10. Yasuhiro Mishima, interview by authors, from Osono, ICS case no. I0702E, 10–11.

11. Naomi Ishii, interview by authors, November 1, 2006, Tokyo.

12. Osamu Katayama, "Bumon wa Nakayoku Kenka seyo" [Departments Should Pick a Friendly Fight], *Voice*, November 2005, 138.

13. Katsuaki Watanabe, interview by authors, October 10, 2007, Tokyo.

14. See note 11.

15. Yukitoshi Funo, interview by authors, July 28, 2006, Tokyo.

16. Mikio Nomura, interview by authors, from Emi Osono, "Toyota Motor Corporation Asia: An Historical Challenge" (ICS case no. A030008E, Hitotsubashi University, Tokyo, 2002), 15.

17. Koshiro Fukuda, interview by authors, from Osono, ICS case no. A030008E, 20.

18. Yasuhiro Mishima, interview by authors, sourced from case: Osono, ICS case no. I0702E, 10.

19. Akio Toyoda, interview by authors, sourced from case: Osono, ICS case no. I0702E, 11.

20. See note 15.

21. See note 7.

22. See note 15.

23. See note 4.

24. Tony Fujita, interview by authors, August 2, 2006, Nagoya, Japan.

25. See note 4.

26. See note 24.

27. The term Fireside Chat meeting stems from U.S. President Franklin D. Roosevelt's "Fireside Chats" broadcasted by radio to the nation during the Great Depression in the 1930s.

28. Emi Osono, "Lexus: The Challenge of the U.S. Luxury Car Market" (ICS case no. I0610E, Hitotsubashi University, Tokyo, 2006), 12.

29. See note 28, p. 11.

30. Jim Press, interview by authors, August 1, 2006, Tokyo.

31. See note 7.

32. See note 15.

33. Akio Matsubara (presentation made during the "Special Committee for Management Innovation: Japanese Management," conference hosted by the Japan Productivity Center for Socio-Economic Development, October 11, 2004, Tokyo).

34. Yoshio Ishizaka, interview by authors, from Emi Osono, "The Global Knowledge Center: Sharing the Toyota Way in Sales and Marketing" (ICS case no. A050003E, Hitotsubashi University, Tokyo, 2005), 2–3.

35. Katsuyoshi Tabata, interview by authors, July 24, 2006, Tokyo.

36. See note 33.

37. Takis Athanasopoulos, interview by authors, from Emi Osono, Norihiko Shimizu, and K. Yonten, "Toyota's Commitment to Europe: Italy and Germany" (ICS case no. A040008E, Hitotsubashi University, Tokyo, 2004), 24.

38. The University of Toyota was established in April 1998 to continuously improve TMS associate and dealer training through lifelong learning. Please refer to Chapter 9 for more information about this and other training institutions.

39. See note 34, p. 8.

40. See note 34, p. 9.

41. Erin Ilgen, interview by authors, from Osono, ICS case no. A050003E, 9.

42. See note 6, pp. 125–126.

Chapter 8   Up-and-In Human Resource Management

1. Akio Matsubara (presentation made during the "Special Committee for Management Innovation: Japanese Management," conference hosted by the Japan Productivity Center for Socio-Economic Development, October 11, 2004, Tokyo).

2. Katsuaki Watanabe, interview by authors, October 10, 2007, Tokyo.

3. Jing Tadeo, interview by authors, from Emi Osono, "The Global Knowledge Center: Sharing the Toyota Way in Sales and Marketing" (ICS case no. A050003E, Hitotsubashi University, Tokyo, 2005), 12.

4. John Kramer, interview by authors, August 9, 2006, Tokyo.

5. Jim Press, interview by authors, August 1, 2006, Tokyo.

6. See note 2.

7. Norifumi Mizoue, "Zenin sokoage 'sanju-go sai made sawo tsukenai' jinjino shikumi" [Everybody Should Grow. Personnel Structure That Makes No Difference Until 35 Years Old], *President*, September 12, 2005, 71.

8. See note 1.

9. Eiji Toyoda, *Toyota Fifty Years in Motion: An Autobiography by the Chairman Eiji Toyoda.* (New York: Kodansha International, 1987), 103.

10. Osamu Katayama, *Toyota ha ikanishite 'saikyo no shain' wo tukuttaka* [How Toyota Created the 'Strongest Employees'] (Tokyo: Shodensha, 2005), 182.

11. Emi Osono, "Toyota Motor Corporation Asia: An Historical Challenge" (ICS case no. A030008E, Hitotsubashi University, Tokyo, 2002), 7.

12. Moody's did note that lifetime employment was not a direct reason for the downgrade, but most managers at Japanese companies understood it to be so. In 2003, Moody's upgraded Toyota's credit rating to AAA.

13. See note 1.

14. Zenji Yasuda, interview by authors, August 29, 2007, Shizuoka, Japan.

15. See note 1.

16. OJT Solutions, *Toyota no Kuchiguse* [Favorite Phrases within Toyota] (Tokyo: Chukei Shuppan, 2006), 44–45.

17. See note 2.

18. Clay Chandler, "Full Speed Ahead," *Fortune*, February 7, 2005, http://money.cnn.com/magazines/fortune/fortune_arch ive/2005/02/07/8250430/index.htm (accessed February 2007). Copyright © 2005 Time Inc.; all rights reserved.

19. Reprinted by permission of the *Harvard Business Review*. From "Learning to Lead at Toyota" by Steven J. Spear, May 2004, 2. Copyright © 2004 by the Harvard Business School Publishing Corporation; all rights reserved.

20. See note 7, p. 69.

21. See note 2.

22. See note 2.

23. See note 1.

24. See note 1.

25. *The Toyota Way 2001* (internal Toyota Motor Corporation publication, Tokyo) April 2001, 13.

26. See note 1.

27. See note 25, p. 9.

28. "Toyota-shiki Shigoto no Kyokasho [Handbook of Toyota-Style Work],"*President*, September 12, 2005, 35.

29. See note 1.

30. Haru Miyadai, General Manager, Professional Development and Recruiting Department, Global Human Resource Division, Project General Manager, Toyota Institute. See note 1.

31. See note 2.

32. See note 28, p. 37.

33. See note 1.

34. Martin Buber, *I and Thou* (New York: Charles Scribner's Sons, 1958).

35. Ikujiro Nonaka commenting on Akio Matsubara's presentation on October 11, 2004.

Chapter 9   Toyota's Resource Base

1. S. C. Gwynne, "New Kid on the Dock," *Time,* September 17, 1990, 62.

2. Ichiro Suzuki, interview by authors, from Emi Osono, "Lexus: The Challenge of the U.S. Luxury Car Market" (ICS case no. I0610E, Hitotsubashi University, Tokyo, 2006), 10.

3. Osono, ICS case no. I0610E, 10.

4. Greg Gardner et al., Harbour Consulting, "2007 North America Press Release," *Harbour Report,* May 2007, www .harbourinc.com/resources/files/media/2007PressRelease.pdf (accessed November 2007).

5. Assuming a labor rate of $50 per hour, including bonuses and benefits, for both companies.

6. Cost reduction figures for 2006 and 2007 from Toyota Motor Corporation 20-F forms, as filed with the Securities and Exchange Commission on June 26, 2006 and June 25, 2007. See Appendix A "Chapter 9—Resources," for details on Toyota's cash holdings, net income, and dividend payout from 1980 to 2006 (Figure A.15).

7. Figures for capital expenses and research and development costs for 2001 to 2007 from Thomson One Banker Analytics, March 10, 2008, http://banker.thomsonib.com/.

8. Toyota Motor Corporation, "Direct North America Investment," Toyota company web site, www.toyota.com/about/ our_business/at_a_glance/our_numbers/direct_investment .html (accessed March 2008).

9. *Toyota in Europe* (Toyota Motor Europe brochure: Brussels, Belgium), March 2007, 22–28.

10. See note 4.

11. Katsuaki Watanabe, interview by authors, October 10, 2007, Tokyo.

12. Toyota's labor hours per car in 1980 from William J. Abernathy and Kim Clark, *The Competitive Status of the U.S. Auto Industry: A study of the Influences of Technology in Determining International Competitive Advantage* (Washington, DC: National Academy Press, 1982), 178. For Toyota's labor hours per car in 2006, see note 4.

13. "Driving with Confidence: Toyota de Puerto Rico," *Best Practice Bulletin 24*, (internal Toyota Motor Corporation publication, Tokyo), February 2005, 6.

14. See note 13, pp. 10–12.

15. See note 13, p. 7.

16. See note 13, pp. 5–6, 12.

17. See Appendix A "Chapter 9—Resources," for unit sales per dealer and dealer satisfaction rating for the U.S. market in 2006 (Figure A.16).

18. Emi Osono, "Toyota Motor Corporation Asia: An Historical Challenge" (ICS case no. A030008E, Hitotsubashi University, Tokyo, 2002), 9.

19. See note 18, pp. 25–26.

20. Toyota Motor Thailand, "Sales Summary," Toyota company web site, www.toyota.co.th/red/en/sales_summary.asp (accessed July 2007).

21. Toyota Motor Thailand, "History in Thailand," Toyota company web site, www.toyota.co.th/red/en/history.asp (accessed July 2007).

22. Emi Osono, Norihiko Shimizu, and K. Yonten, "Toyota's Commitment to Europe: Italy and Germany" (ICS case no. A040008E, Hitotsubashi University, Tokyo, 2004), 11.

23. *Brand awareness*, or brand recall, measures the percentage of people who remember a certain brand when a product category (e.g., "Automobile") is provided. *Brand recognition* measures the percentage of people who can identify a certain brand when a hint, such as a photograph, is provided.

24. See note 23.

25. See note 22.

26. Emi Osono, "The Birth of Scion: Can Toyota Attract Young Customers?" (ICS case no. A040010E, Hitotsubashi University, Tokyo, 2004), 16.

27. Jamie Lareau, "Big Trucks, Big Bucks," *Automotive News*, www .autoweek.com/apps/pbcs.dll/article?AID=/20060911/ FREE/60911001/1041/TOC01ARCHIVE (accessed July 2007).

28. Toyota Motor Corporation: *FY2006 Annual Report* (Toyota City, Japan: Toyota Motor Corporation, 2006), 91, www.toyota .co.jp/en/ir/library/annual/pdf/2006/ar06_e.pdf (accessed February 2007).

29. Bradley Johnson et al., "100 Leading National Advertisers," in *Advertising Age Datacenter 2007 Marketer Profiles Yearbook* (New York: Crain Communications Inc., 2007), http://adage .com/images/random/lna2007.pdf (accessed July 2007).

30. In 2006, General Motors' U.S. marques included Buick, Chevrolet, Cadillac, GMC, Hummer, Pontiac, Saab, and Saturn (GM Daewoo, Holden, Opel, and Vauxhall outside of the United States); Ford's United States marques included Aston Martin, Ford, Jaguar, Land Rover, Lincoln, Mazda (part-owned), Mercury, and Volvo; Toyota's marques included Lexus, Scion, and Toyota (Hino and Daihatsu outside of the United States).

31. See note 17, advertising expense per unit sold of the four largest car manufacturers in 2006 (Figure A.17).

32. See note 13, p. 9.

33. See note 18, p. 5.

34. See note 18, p. 14.

35. See note 18, p. 15.

36. See note 18, p. 23.

37. Toyota Motor Corporation, "Human Resources Development," Toyota company web site, www.toyota.co.jp/en/environmen tal_rep/03/jyugyoin03.html (accessed July 2007).

38. John Kramer, interview by authors, May 9, 2007, Tokyo.

39. Emi Osono, "The Global Knowledge Center: Sharing the Toyota Way in Sales and Marketing" (ICS case no. A050003E, Hitotsubashi University, Tokyo, 2005), 13.

40. See note 38.

41. Toyota Motor Corporation, "Toyota Celebrates the Opening of North American Production Support Center," Toyota company web site, www.toyota.com/about/news/manufac turing/2006/02/10–1-tmmna.html (accessed July 2007).

42. See note 9, p. 22.

43. See note 11.

44. General Motors Corporation, "GM University," General Motors company web site, www.gm.com/corporate/careers/life_at_ gm.jsp?p=gmu (accessed February 2008).

45. See note 39, p. 7.

46. Toyota Motor Corporation, Global Marketing Division, com- munication to authors, July 20, 2007.

47. International Society for Performance Improvement, "ISPI Recognizes Excellence in the Field of HPT," ISPI com- pany web site, www.ispi.org/awards/2003/awdwin2003.htm (accessed February 2007).

48. International Quality and Productivity Center, "2003 CUBIC Award Winners," IQPC company web site, www.iqpc.com/ cgi-bin/templates/0/document.html?topic=232&document= 42091&slauID=16& (accessed February 2007).

49. See note 46.

50. Reprinted by permission of *Shuukan Toyo Keizai*. From "Kii pahson intabyu" [Key Person Interview], February 22, 2003, 52–55. Copyright © 2003 by Toyo Keizai Inc.; all rights reserved.

51. "Nikkei Forum Global Top Management Meeting," *Nikkei Sangyo Shimbun*, October 8, 1999, 1.

Chapter 10   A Company Always in Danger

1. Toyota Motor Corporation, Global Marketing Division, com- munication to authors, May 22, 2007.

2. Consumer Reports, "Reliability Trends," ConsumerReports. org web site, www.consumerreports.org/cro/cars/pricing/best -worst-in-car-reliability-1005/overview/index.htm (accessed October 2007).

3. Lindsay Chappell, "Toyota to Send 30,000 Workers Back to Boot Camp," *Automotive News,* May 7, 2007, www.autonews .com/apps/pbcs.dll/article?AID=/20070507/MANUFACTURING /70504014 (accessed May 2007).

4. Katsuaki Watanabe, interview by authors, October 10, 2007, Tokyo.

5. Steven J. Spear, "Learning to Lead at Toyota,"*Harvard Business Review,* May 2004, 4.

6. See note 4.

7. See note 4.

8. Mark Templin, interview by authors, April 18, 2007, Tokyo.

9. "J.D. Power and Associates Reports: Lexus Ranks Highest in Sales Satisfaction as Industry Achieves Record High Results for a Second Consecutive Year," J.D. Power and Associates (press release, Westlake Village, CA, November 14, 2007), J.D. Power and Associates web site, www.jdpower. com/corporate/news/releases/pressrelease.aspx?ID=2007270 (accessed November 2007).

10. David Welch, "Staying Paranoid at Toyota," *BusinessWeek,* July 2, 2007, 80–82, www.businessweek.com/magazine/con tent/07_10/b4024071.htm (accessed March 2007).

11. Nancy Fein, interview by authors, April 19, 2007, Tokyo.

12. See note 9.

13. Based on *Toyota Motor Corporation Sustainability Report 2006,* from Toyota company web site, www.toyota.co.jp/ en/environmental_rep/06/download/pdf/e_report06.pdf, 79 (accessed April 2007).

14. Tokuichi Uranishi, interview by authors, September 26, 2007, Nagoya, Japan.

15. Zenji Yasuda, interview by authors, August 29, 2007, Shizuoka, Japan.

16. Lindsay Chappell, "Toyota Expands: And Tends to Growing Pains," *Automotive News*, April 23, 2007, www.autonews. com/apps/pbcs.dll/article?AID=/20070423/MANUFACTU RING/70420092/1128/BREAKING&refsect=BREAKING (accessed April 2007).

17. "Job Openings and Labor Turnover: January 2007," U.S. Department of Labor, Bureau of Labor Statistics (press release, Washington, DC, March 13, 2007), Bureau of Labor Statistics web site, ftp://ftp.bls.gov/pub/news.release/History/ jolts.03132007.news (accessed May 2007).

18. David Barkholz and Jamie Lareau, "UAW Deal Puts GM on Toyota's Heels," *Automotive News*, October 1, 2007, www.autonews.com/apps/pbcs.dll/article?AID=/20071001/ SUB/70930002 (accessed November 13, 2007).

19. "Hiring Policies Get Second Look,"*Nikkei Weekly*, April 23, 2007, 21.

20. Michael E. Porter, Hirotaka Takeuchi, and Mariko Sakakibara, *Can Japan Compete?* (Cambridge, MA: Perseus Press, 2000), 5.

21. Dividend payout figures for 1997 to 2007 from Thomson One Banker Analytics, March 10, 2008, http://banker .thomsonib.com/.

22. ROIC figures for 1997 to 2007 from Thomson One Banker Analytics, March 10, 2008, http://banker.thomsonib.com/.

23. Anne Wright Curtis, ed., "2006 Global Market Data Book," *Automotive News*, June 2006, 4, www.autonews.com/assets/ PDF/CA7170616.pdf (accessed May 2007).

24. "'Sanjyumanen' Sha: Raibaru ha Nirin" [300,000 Yen Car: Rival Is Two Wheels], *Nihon Keizai Shimbun*, November 26, 2007.

25. Tesla Motors, Inc., www.teslamotors.com/buy/buyPage1.php (accessed November 2007).

Chapter 11 What Your Organization Can Learn from Toyota: Ten Powerful Contradictions

1. Katsuaki Watanabe, interview by authors, October 10, 2007, Tokyo.

2. See note 1.

3. See note 1.

4. See note 1.

5. Michelle Krebs, "Toyota's Goal: Be a Green Tomato," *Edmunds.com*, May 18, 2006, www.edmunds.com/inside line/do/Features/articleld=115417 (accessed April 2007).

6. See note 1.

7. Zenji Yasuda, interview by authors, August 29, 2007, Shizuoka, Japan.

8. Reprinted by permission of the Harvard Business School Press. From *The Age of Paradox* by Charles Handy. Boston MA, 1994, 13. Copyright © 1994 by the Harvard Business School Publishing Corporation; all rights reserved.

9. See note 8, p. 14.

Abernathy, William J., and Kim Clark. *The Competitive Status of the U.S. Auto Industry: A study of the Influences of Technology in Determining International Competitive Advantage.* Washington, DC: National Academy Press, 1982.

Ancona, Deborah, Thomas W. Malone, Wanda J. Orlikowski, and Peter M. Senge. "In Praise of the Incomplete Leader." *Harvard Business Review*, February 2007, 92–100.

Barkholz, David, and Jamie Lareau. "UAW Deal Puts GM on Toyota's Heels." *Automotive News*, October 1, 2007, www.auto news.com/apps/pbcs.dll/article?AID=/20071001/ SUB/70930002 (accessed November 13, 2007).

Bohn, Joseph. "Dealer: Incredibly Efficient Recall." *Automotive News*, December 11, 1989, 43.

Buber, Martin. *I and Thou*. New York: Charles Scribner's Sons, 1958.

Chandler, Clay. "Full Speed Ahead." *Fortune*, February 7, 2005, http://money.cnn.com/magazines/fortune/fortune_archive/ 2005/02/07/8250430/index.htm (accessed February 2007).

Chappell, Lindsay. "Toyota Expands: And Tends to Growing Pains." *Automotive News*, April 23, 2007, www.autonews .com/apps/pbcs.dll/article?AID=/20070423/MANUFACTU RING/70420092/1128/BREAKING&refsect=BREAKING (accessed April 2007).

Chappell, Lindsay. "Toyota to Send 30,000 Workers Back to Boot Camp." *Automotive News*, May 7, 2007, www.autonews .com/apps/pbcs.dll/article?AID=/20070507/MANU FACTURING/70504014 (accessed May 2007).

Chunichi Shimbun-sha, ed. *Toyota no Sekai* [The World of Toyota]. Nagoya, Japan: Chunichi Shimbun-sha, 2007.

Collins, James, and Jerry Porras. *Built to Last*. New York: HarperCollins, 1997.

Consumer Reports. "Reliability Trends." ConsumerReports .org web site. www.consumerreports.org/cro/cars/pricing/

best-worst-in-car-reliability-1005/overview/index.htm (accessed October 2007).

Curtis, Anne Wright, ed. "2006 Global Market Data Book." *Automotive News*, June 2006, www.autonews.com/assets/PDF/CA7170616.pdf (accessed May 2007).

Curtis, Anne Wright, ed. "2007 Global Market Data Book." *Automotive News*, June 2007, www.autonews.com/assets/PDF/CA21401619.pdf (accessed June 2007).

Cusumano, Michael A. *The Japanese Automotive Industry: Technology and Management at Nissan and Toyota.* Cambridge, MA: Harvard University Press, 1985.

DaimlerChrysler AG. *2006 Annual Report.* Stuttgart, Germany: DaimlerChrysler AG, 2006. www.daimler.com/Projects/c2c/channel/documents/1003905_DCX_2006_Annual_Report.pdf (accessed May 2007).

DaimlerChrysler AG. *Form 20-F as filed with the Securities and Exchange Commission on March 6, 2006.* Stuttgart, Germany: DaimlerChrysler AG, 2006. www.daimlerchrysler.com/Projects/c2c/channel/documents/830126_dcx_form20f_fy_2005.pdf (accessed March 12, 2007).

"Driving with Confidence: Toyota de Puerto Rico." *Best Practice Bulletin 24.* Internal Toyota Motor Corporation publication, Tokyo, February 2005.

Edmondson, Gail, and Adeline Bonnet. "Toyota's New Traction in Europe." *BusinessWeek*, June 7, 2004, www.businessweek.com/magazine/content/04_23/b3886177.htm (accessed February 2007).

Ford Motor Company. *2006 Annual Report.* Dearborn, Michigan: Ford Motor Company, 2006. www.ford.com/doc/2006_AR.pdf (accessed May 2007).

Ford Motor Company. "Ford in Europe: The First Hundred Years." Ford Motor Company web site. http://media.ford.com/article_display.cfm?article_id=14707 (accessed June 2007).

Ford Motor Company. *Proxy Statement*, April 7, 2006, Dearborn, Michigan: Ford Motor Corporation, 2006. www.ford.com/doc/2006_proxy.pdf (accessed February 2007).

Friedman, Thomas L. *The World Is Flat.* New York: Farrar, Straus and Giroux, 2005.

Gardner, Greg, et al. "2007 North America Press Release." *The Harbour Report*, May 2007. Harbour Consulting, Inc. www .harbourinc.com/resources/files/media/2007PressRelease .pdf (accessed November 2007).

General Motors Corporation. *2006 Annual Report*. Detroit, Michigan: General Motors Corporation, 2006. www.gm.com/ corporate/investor_information/docs/fin_data/gm06ar/ download/gm06ar.pdf (accessed May 2007).

General Motors Corporation. "GM University." General Motors company web site. www.gm.com/corporate/careers/life_at _gm.jsp?p=gmu (accessed February 2008).

General Motors Corporation. *Proxy Statement*, April 28, 2006. Detroit, Michigan: Ford Motor Corporation, 2006. www .gm.com/company/investor_information/docs/stockholder _info/gmpxy/pxy06/Gm06ps.pdf (accessed February 2007).

Gertner, Jon. "From 0 to 60 to World Domination." *New York Times*, February 18, 2007, www.nytimes.com/2007/02/18/ magazone/18Toyota.t.html?pagewanted=4&ei=5088&en= 27f821c931ad585b&ex=1329454800&partner=rssnyt&emc =rss (accessed April 2007).

Gwynne, S. C. "New Kid on the Dock." *Time*, September 17, 1990, 62.

Handy, Charles. *The Age of Paradox*. Boston: Harvard Business School Press, 1994.

"Hiring Policies Get Second Look." *Nikkei Weekly*, April 23, 2007, 21.

Honda Motor Co., Ltd. *Form 20-F as filed with the Securities and Exchange Commission on June 30, 2006*. Tokyo: Honda Motor Co., Ltd., 2006. www.sec.gov/Archives/edgar/data/71 5153/000119312506140213/0001193125-06-140213-index .htm (accessed July 14, 2007).

Honda Motor Co., Ltd. *FY 2005 Annual Report*. Tokyo: Honda Motor Co., Ltd., 2006. http://world.honda.com/investors/ annualreport/2006/pdf/ar2006.pdf (accessed May 2007).

Hyundai Motor Company. *2006 Annual Report*. Seoul, Korea: Hyundai Motor Company, 2006. http://ir.hyundai-motor .com/eng/common/dataPDF/financial/business_ report/2006 percent20Annual percent20Report.pdf (accessed June 2007).

International Quality and Productivity Center. "2003 CUBIC Award Winners." IQPC company web site. www.iqpc.com/cgi-bin/templates/0/document.html?topic=232&document=42091&slauID=16& (accessed February 2007).

International Society for Performance Improvement. "ISPI Recognizes Excellence in the Field of HPT." ISPI company web site. www.ispi.org/awards/2003/awdwin2003.htm (accessed February 2007).

J.D. Power and Associates. "J.D. Power and Associates Reports: Buick and Lexus Brands Tie for Highest Rank in Vehicle Dependability." Press release, Westlake Village, CA, August 9, 2007, J.D. Power and Associates web site (http://www.jdpower.com/corporate/news/releases/pressrelease.aspx?ID=2007130; accessed March 2008).

J.D. Power and Associates. "J.D. Power and Associates Reports: Lexus Ranks Highest in Sales Satisfaction as Industry Achieves Record High Results For a Second Consecutive Year." Press release, Westlake Village, CA, November 14, 2007, J.D. Power and Associates web site (www.jdpower.com/corporate/news/releases/pressrelease.aspx?ID=2007270; accessed November 2007).

J.D. Power and Associates. "J.D. Power and Associates Reports: Redesigned Initial Quality Study Shows That Vehicle Design Plays as Critical a Role in Consumer Perceptions of Quality as Defects and Malfunctions." Press release, Westlake Village, CA, June 7, 2006, J.D. Power and Associates web site (www.jdpower.com/corporate/news/releases/pressrelease.asp?ID=2006082; accessed May 2007).

Johnson, Bradley, et al. *"100 Leading National Advertisers."* In *Advertising Age Datacenter 2007 Marketer Profiles Yearbook.* New York: Crain Communications, Inc., 2007. http://adage.com/images/random/lna2007.pdf (accessed July 2007).

Katayama, Osamu. "Bumon wa Nakayoku Kenka Seyo" [Departments Should Pick a Friendly Fight]. *Voice,* November 2005, 139.

Katayama, Osamu. *Toyota ha ikanishite 'saikyo no shain' wo tukuttaka* [How Toyota Created the 'Strongest Employee's]. Tokyo: Shodensha, 2005.

"Kii pahson intabyu" [Key Person Interview]. *Shuukan Toyo Keizai,* February 22, 2003, 52–55.

Krebs Michelle. "Toyota's Goal: Be a Green Tomato." *Edmunds .com*, May 18, 2006, (www.edmunds.com/insideline/do/ Features/articleId=115417; accessed April 2007).

Lareau, Jamie. "Big Trucks, Big Bucks."*Automotive News*, n.d., www.autoweek.com/apps/pbcs.dll/article?AID= /20060911/FREE/60911001/1041/TOC01ARCHIVE (accessed July 2007).

Lexus, a Division of Toyota Motor Sales, U. S. A. *"The Lexus Covenant."* Lexus web site (www.lexus.com/about/orporate/ lexus_covenant.html; accessed February 2007).

Liker, Jeffrey, and David Meier. *The Toyota Way Fieldbook: A Practical Guide for Implementing Toyota's 4Ps*. New York: McGraw-Hill, 2006.

Mizoue, Norifumi. "Zenin sokoage 'sanju-go sai made sawo tsukenai' jinjino shikumi" [Everybody Should Grow. Personnel Structure That Makes No Difference Until 35 Years Old]. *President*, September 12, 2005, 68–71.

NADA Industry Relations Support Systems. *2006 Dealer Attitude Survey*. McLean, VA: North American Dealers Association, July 2006.

"The New Yaris Launch in France." *Best Practice Bulletin 35*. Internal Toyota Motor Corporation publication, Tokyo, August 2006.

"Nikkei Forum Global Top Management Meeting." *Nikkei Sangyo Shimbun*, October 8, 1999, 1.

Nissan Motor Company. *FY 2005 Annual Report*. Tokyo: Nissan Motor Company, 2006. www.nissan-global.com/EN/ DOCUMENT/PDF/AR/2005/AR05_e_all.pdf (accessed February 2007).

Nonaka, Ikujiro. Comments during the Special Committee for Management Innovation—Japanese Management, hosted by the Japan Productivity Center for Socio-Economic Development, October 11, 2004, Tokyo.

Nonaka, Ikujiro. "The Knowledge-Creating Company." *Harvard Business Review* (November–December 1991): 96–104.

Nonaka, Ikujiro, and Hirotaka Takeuchi. *The Knowledge-Creating Company*. New York: Oxford University Press, 1995.

OJT Solutions. *Toyota no Kuchiguse* [Favorite Phrases within Toyota]. Tokyo: Chukei Shuppan, 2006.

Osono, Emi. "The Birth of Scion: Can Toyota Attract Young Customers?" Tokyo: Hitotsubashi University ICS Case No. A040010E, 2004.

Osono, Emi. "The Global Knowledge Center: Sharing the Toyota Way in Sales and Marketing." Tokyo: Hitotsubashi University ICS Case No. A050003E, 2005.

Osono, Emi. "Lexus: The Challenge of the U.S. Luxury Car Market." Tokyo: Hitotsubashi University ICS Case No. I0610E, 2006.

Osono, Emi. "Toyota Motor Corporation Asia: An Historical Challenge." Tokyo: Hitotsubashi University ICS Case No. A030008E, 2002.

Osono, Emi. "Toyota's IMV Project: The Innovative International Multi-Purpose Vehicle." Tokyo: Hitotsubashi University ICS Case No. I0702E, 2007.

Osono, Emi, Norihiko Shimizu, and K. Yonten, "Toyota's Commitment to Europe: Italy and Germany." Tokyo: Hitotsubashi University ICS Case No. A040008E, 2004.

Porter, Michael E. *On Competition*. Boston: Harvard Business School Press, 1998.

Porter, Michael E. Hirotaka Takeuchi, and Mariko Sakakibara. *Can Japan Compete?* Cambridge, MA: Perseus Press, 2000.

PSA Peugeot Citroen. *2006 Annual Report*. Paris, France: PSA Peugeot Citroen, 2006. www.psa-peugeot-citroen.com/document/publication/PSA_RA2006_GB_04-071183564927.pdf (accessed May 2007).

"Redefining the Customer Experience (Scion)." *Best Practice Bulletin 26*. Internal Toyota Motor Corporation publication, Tokyo, April 2005.

Renault. *2006 Annual Report*. Cedex, France: Renault, 2006. www.renault.com/renault_com/en/images/Rapport %20annuel %20-2006UK % 20%20OK %20230307_tcm1120-591464.pdf (accessed June 2007).

"Rensai: Sakinzu beshi; Toyota 'Sekai Saikyo' he no Kakuto" [Serialization: Stay ahead of the Times; Toyota Fighting to Be the Strongest Manufacturer in the World]. *Nikkei Business*, May 7, 2007, 8–9.

Rowley, Ian. "Fighting to Stay Humble." *BusinessWeek*, March 5, 2007, www.businessweek.com/magazine/content/07_10/b4024073.htm (accessed March 2007).

"Sales Satisfaction: Obeya Solution." *Best Practice Bulletin 42*. Internal Toyota Motor Corporation publication, Tokyo, July 2007.

"'Sanjyumanen' Sha, Raibaru ha Nirin" [300,000 Yen Car, Rival Is Two Wheels]. *Nihon Keizai Shimbun*, November 26, 2007.

Simon, Herbert A. *Administrative Behavior*. New York: Macmillan, 1947.

Spear, Steven J. "Learning to Lead at Toyota." *Harvard Business Review*, (May 2004): 1–9.

Taylor III, Alex. "Toyota's Secret Weapon." *Fortune*, August 23, 2004, http://money.cnn.com/magazines/fortune/fortune_archive/2004/08/23/379403/index.htm (accessed February 2007).

Team Toyota 5. Internal Toyota Motor Corporation publication, Tokyo, March–April 2003.

Team Toyota 6. Internal Toyota Motor Corporation publication, Tokyo, May–June 2002.

Team Toyota 8. Internal Toyota Motor Corporation publication, Tokyo, September–October 2003.

Team Toyota 10. Internal Toyota Motor Corporation publication, Tokyo, January–February 2004.

Team Toyota 11. Internal Toyota Motor Corporation publication, Tokyo, March–April 2004.

Team Toyota 16. Internal Toyota Motor Corporation publication, Tokyo, January–February 2005.

Team Toyota 23. Internal Toyota Motor Corporation publication, Tokyo, March–April 2006.

Team Toyota 24. Internal Toyota Motor Corporation publication, Tokyo, May–June 2006.

Team Toyota 30. Internal Toyota Motor Corporation publication, Tokyo, May–June 2007.

Tesla Motors, Inc. www.teslamotors.com/buy/buyPage1.php (accessed November 2007).

"2007 Market Data: Dealer Data." *Automotive News*, May 2007, www.autonews.com/assets/PDF/CA1862859.pdf (accessed June 2007).

"2007 Market Data: North America Sales." *Automotive News*, February 2007, www.autonews.com/assets/PDF/CA12984226.pdf (accessed May 2007).

Toyoda, Eiji. *Toyota Fifty Years in Motion: An Autobiography by the Chairman Eiji Toyoda*. New York: Kodansha International, 1987.

The Toyota Business Practices, Internal Toyota Motor Corporation document, Tokyo, April 2005.

Toyota in Europe. Toyota Motor Europe brochure. Brussels, Belgium, March 2007.

Toyota in the World 2006. From Toyota company web site. www .toyota.co.jp/en/pdf/toyota_world/2006/toyota.pdf (accessed February 2007).

Toyota Motor Corporation. "Direct North America Investment." Toyota company web site. www.toyota.com/about/our_ business/at_a_glance/our_numbers/direct_investment .html (accessed March 2008).

Toyota Motor Corporation. *Form 20-F as filed with the Securities and Exchange Commission on June 25, 2007*. Tokyo: Toyota Motor Corporation, 2007. http://www.sec .gov/Archives/edgar/data/1094517/000119312507141459/ d20f.htm (accessed March 10, 2008).

Toyota Motor Corporation. *FY 2006 Annual Report*. Toyota City, Japan: Toyota Motor Corporation, 2006. www.toyota .co.jp/en/ir/library/annual/pdf/2006/ar06_e.pdf   (accessed February 2007).

Toyota Motor Corporation. *FY 2007 Annual Report*. Toyota City, Japan: Toyota Motor Corporation, 2007. www.toyota.co.jp/ en/ir/library/annual/pdf/2007/ar07_e.pdf (accessed January 2008).

Toyota Motor Corporation, Global Marketing Division. E-mails to authors. May 22, 2007, and July 20, 2007.

Toyota Motor Corporation. "Human Resources Development." Toyota company web site. www.toyota.co.jp/en/environmen tal_rep/03/jyugyoin03.html (accessed July 2007).

Toyota Motor Corporation. *Toyota Motor Corporation Sustainability Report 2006*. From Toyota company web site. www.toyota .co.jp/en/environmental_rep/06/download/pdf/e_report06.pdf (accessed April 2007).

Toyota Motor Corporation. "Toyota Celebrates the Opening of North American Production Support Center." Toyota company web site. www.toyota.com/about/news/manufacturing/ 2006/02/10-1-tmmna.html (accessed July 2007).

Toyota Motor Corporation. *Toyota: A History of the First 50 Years*. Toyota City, Japan: Toyota Motor Corporation, 1988.

Toyota Motor Philippines. " '06 Top 3 Best Selling Vehicles: Toyota Innova, Vios and Fortuner." Toyota company web site. www.toyota.com.ph/news_and_events/ne7.asp (accessed February 2007).

Toyota Motor Thailand. *"History in Thailand."* Toyota company web site. www.toyota.co.th/red/en/history.asp (accessed July 2007).

Toyota Motor Thailand."Sales Summary." Toyota company web site. www.toyota.co.th/red/en/sales_summary.asp (accessed July 2007).

Toyota Motor Vietnam."Toyota Vietnam Continues Growth in 2006." Toyota company web site. www.toyotavn.com.vn/asp/view/vn/cate_details.asp?code=10&id=1252&version=en (accessed February 2007).

"Toyota Sekai Saikyo eno Kakuto" [Toyota's Struggle to be the World's Strongest]. *Nikkei Business*, February 26, 2007.

"Toyota-Shiki Shigoto no Kyokasho" [Textbook on Toyota-Style Work]. *President*, September 12, 2005, 27–35.

Toyota Up Close. From Toyota company web site. www.toyota.co.jp/en/pdf/2006/toyota_up_close0611.pdf (accessed January 2008).

Toyota Motor Corporation. *Toyota Value*. Internal Toyota Motor Corporation publication, Tokyo, October 2003.

Toyota Motor Corporation. *The Toyota Way 2001*. Internal Toyota Motor Corporation publication, Tokyo, April 2001.

Toyota Motor Corporation. *The Toyota Way in Sales and Marketing*. Internal Toyota Motor Corporation publication, Tokyo, October 2001.

"UAW Losing Pay Edge: Foreign Automakers' Bonuses Boost Wages in U.S. Plants as Detroit Car Companies Struggle." *Detroit Free Press*, February 1, 2007, www.aftermarketnews.com/default.aspx?type=art&id=80833& (accessed April 2007).

U.S. Department of Labor. *"2007 International Labor Comparisons,"* www.dol.gov/asp/media/reports/chartbook/chartbook_jan07.pdf (accessed February 2007).

U.S. Department of Labor, Bureau of Labor Statistics. "Job Openings and Labor Turnover: January 2007." Press release, Washington, DC, March 13, 2007, Bureau of Labor

Statistics web site. ftp://ftp.bls.gov/pub/news.release/History/
jolts.03132007.news (accessed May 2007).

Volkswagen AG. *2006 Annual Report*. Wolfsburg, Germany:
Volkswagen AG, 2006. www.volkswagen-media-services.
com/medias_publish/ms/content/en/broschueren/2007/03/
09/annual_report_2006_of_volkswagen_ag.standard
.gidoeffentlichkeit.html (accessed May 2007).

Welch, David. "Staying Paranoid At Toyota." *BusinessWeek*, July
2, 2007. www.businessweek.com/magazine/content/07_27/
b4041060.htm?chan=top+news_top+news+index_autos
(accessed July 2007).

Welch, David. "Why Toyota Is Afraid of Being Number One."
BusinessWeek, March 5, 2007. www.businessweek.com/mag
azine/content/07_10/b4024071.htm (accessed March 2007).